He called himself T
the title first give

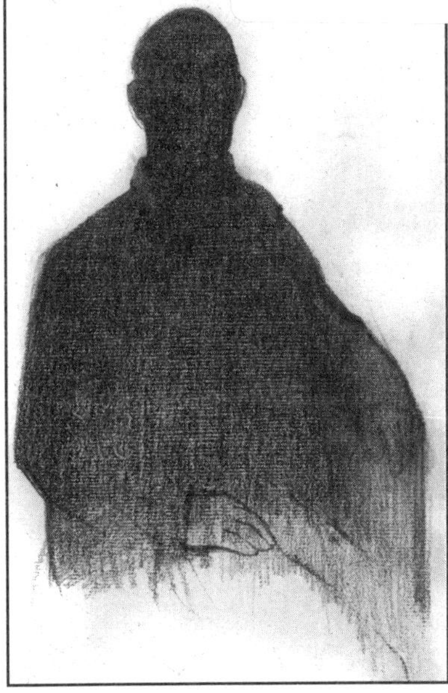

He was *powerful, iron-fisted, fiercely independent,* and
in all ways quite different from today.
So is his story.

In Joseph E. Garland's powerful representation, Capt. James William Pattillo emerges as the epitome of the Gloucester fisherman of the heroic period just before the Civil War. Before our eyes we see take shape a man who is a force of nature, born to drive and to command. Indeed, in him and his works we come to feel the thrust of maritime New England at its greatest, iron-fisted and iron-willed in all ways quite different from today.

By the time he was 20, Pattillo had his own small vessel and had tried his hand at the coasting trade, even at a bit of smuggling, as well as fishing on the banks. A fiercely independent spirit, he early became known from Cape North to Yarmouth. It was a serious brush with the authorities in Halifax that brought him to Gloucester in 1834, whence fleets of pinkies sailed in all seasons in search of finny wealth. . . .

The beauty of this book lies in Mr. Garland's complete union with his subject. For one not born and brought up on the New England shore, it is hard to appreciate the intimate feeling for the living past in this seaward-looking region. We have never come across anyone in its literature who has this feeling more strongly than Mr. Garland.

—*New York Times Book Review,* July 10, 1966

SEVEN ISLANDS BAY
ST. LAWRENCE RIVER
Madeleine River
Anticosti I.
GASPE PENINSULA
Gaspe
Cape des Rosiers
MALBAIE
Perce
Bonaventure I.
ORPHAN BANK
Paspébiac
CHALEUR BAY
Miscou Island
Gulf of St. Lawrence (North Bay)
PORT AU PORT BAY
Port au Port Pen.
EAST B
Port au
ST. GEORGE'S BAY
NEWFOUN LAND
BRADELLE BANK
Magdalen Islands
Cabot Strait
Pt. Escuminac
North Point
Cape Kildare
CASCUMPEQUE BAY
The Bight
MALPEQUE BAY
The Bend of the Island
ST. PETERS BAY
PRINCE EDWARD ISLAND
East Point
Cape North
Cheticamp
Margaree I.
Broad Cove
Cape Breton Island
Sydney
NEW BRUNSWICK
Northumberland Strait
Charlottetown
Cape George
Port Hood
Gut of Canso
Bras d'Or Lake
Louisburg
George Bay
CHIGNECTO BAY
Joggins
Pictou
Steep Creek
Arichat
Big Canso
Canso (Little Canso)
MISAINE BANK
Minas Basin
Guysborough
Whitehead
CANSO BANK
Bay of Fundy
NOVA SCOTIA
Sherbrooke
Wine Harbor
St. Marys River
Nine-Mile Lake
Windsor
Annapolis Royal
Digby
Chester
Prospect
Dartmouth
Halifax
Salmon River
ATLANTIC OCEAN
MAHONE BAY
Ketch Harbor
Lunenburg
BANQUEREAU BANK
Liverpool
Yarmouth
Port Joli
Shelburne
Sable Island
SABLE ISLAND (WESTERN) BANK
Cape Sable
0 25 50 100
Miles
Saml H. Bryant
N NNE NE ENE E ESE SE SSE S SSW SW WSW W WNW NW NNW

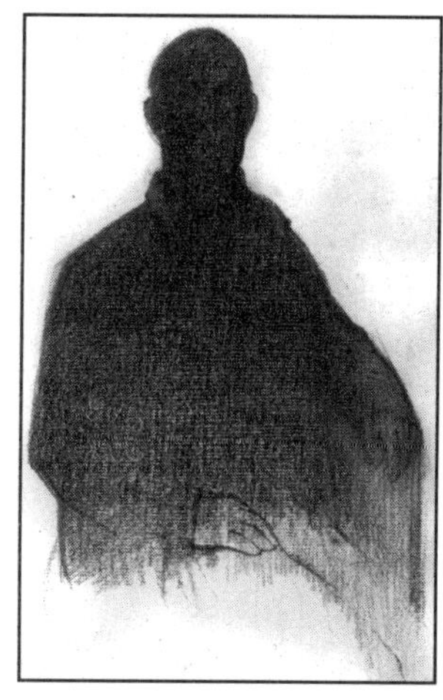

Garland writes about the old times of Gloucester and the Maritimes with genuine understanding. He knows about tides and weather and the way of small fore-and-aft vessels. He is familiar not only with the waters of Cape Ann, but with the vast northern fishing grounds where much of the action took place–Nova Scotia, Cape Breton, Prince Edward Island, Newfoundland and all the offlying banks and shoals.

He makes believable the sort of melodrama that a less competent writer would ruin with artifice and hokum.

He convinces us that this Captain Pattillo, a Nova Scotia Scotsman by birth, was a mighty man who conquered not only the northern storms and fogs, but terrorized whatever human opponents challenged him–jealous competitors, tax-collectors, custom officials, coast guardsmen: it would seem he was willing to take on the British navy itself.

–Boston Sunday Globe

One of the chief pitfalls Garland had to avoid was making Pattillo more than life-size. He has avoided it nicely, keeping his giant fisherman in perspective as he fights storms, ferrets out the schools of fish, protects his watery "claim" from jealous rivals and returns to port with the bounty of the sea. Pattillo was a lusty man, one of the best, and this is a lusty biography.

–Omaha World Herald

Mr. Garland has skillfully woven his biography of Pattillo into a fascinating story of the Gloucester fishermen, their hazardous lives, and struggle for fishing rights along the Canadian coast. A well-written story about a terrific personality and much local history.

–Library Journal

Aside from Gloucester, the book is set for the most part in the singular beauty of the waters and towns of the Maritime Provinces–in comparison with which Boston and New York were called Rogue's Holes by seafarers. . . .

Garland . . . gives us an immensely readable and well researched biography . . .

–Washington Star

Though Gloucestermen have lost their chief industry, they have never lost their sense of history, for they cherish the memory of their former greatness. Townspeople are quick to recall the colorful exploits of the men who once called Cape Ann their home. And the memory of none is so revered as that of James William Pattillo, a huge brusque, Bunyanesque rogue whose fabulous exploits are still a source of amazement and amusement to New Englanders. Now, thanks to Joseph Garland's spirited biography, Pattillo's picaresque career can be made known to the rest of America.

—*The Skipper*

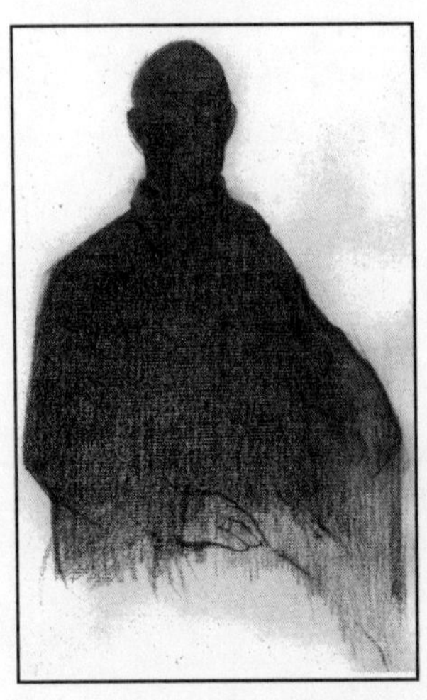

This "John Henry" saga by Joe Garland, a Gloucesterman and former Boston newspaperman, should leave us all forever grateful we were not around in the early 1800s when James William Pattillo was feeling his oats. The lot of us might have had our teeth cracked and our ears mashed.

Pattillo, who began as a Nova Scotia farm boy and wound up as a roaring Gloucester fisherman, never liked to walk around people. He preferred belting them out of the way or stamping through and over them.

And by the time you're one-third the way into this book, you'll be wishing your ancestors had held the splints-and-liniment concessions in all the waterfront joints Jim took apart. . . .

Where Pattillo went, trouble followed, even to the point of almost causing a war between the United States and Britain over his poaching and smuggling capers in Canadian waters.

As you read on, though, you realize that the story is fun-reading, and that for Joe Garland it was probably fun-writing. . . .

"This is a true story," says the author's foreword. "I am not a liar, I swear it."

Of course it's true, because it has to be. No writer would dare to chronicle the wild and monstrous adventures of the great Pattillo if they were not true.

—*Boston Sunday Herald*

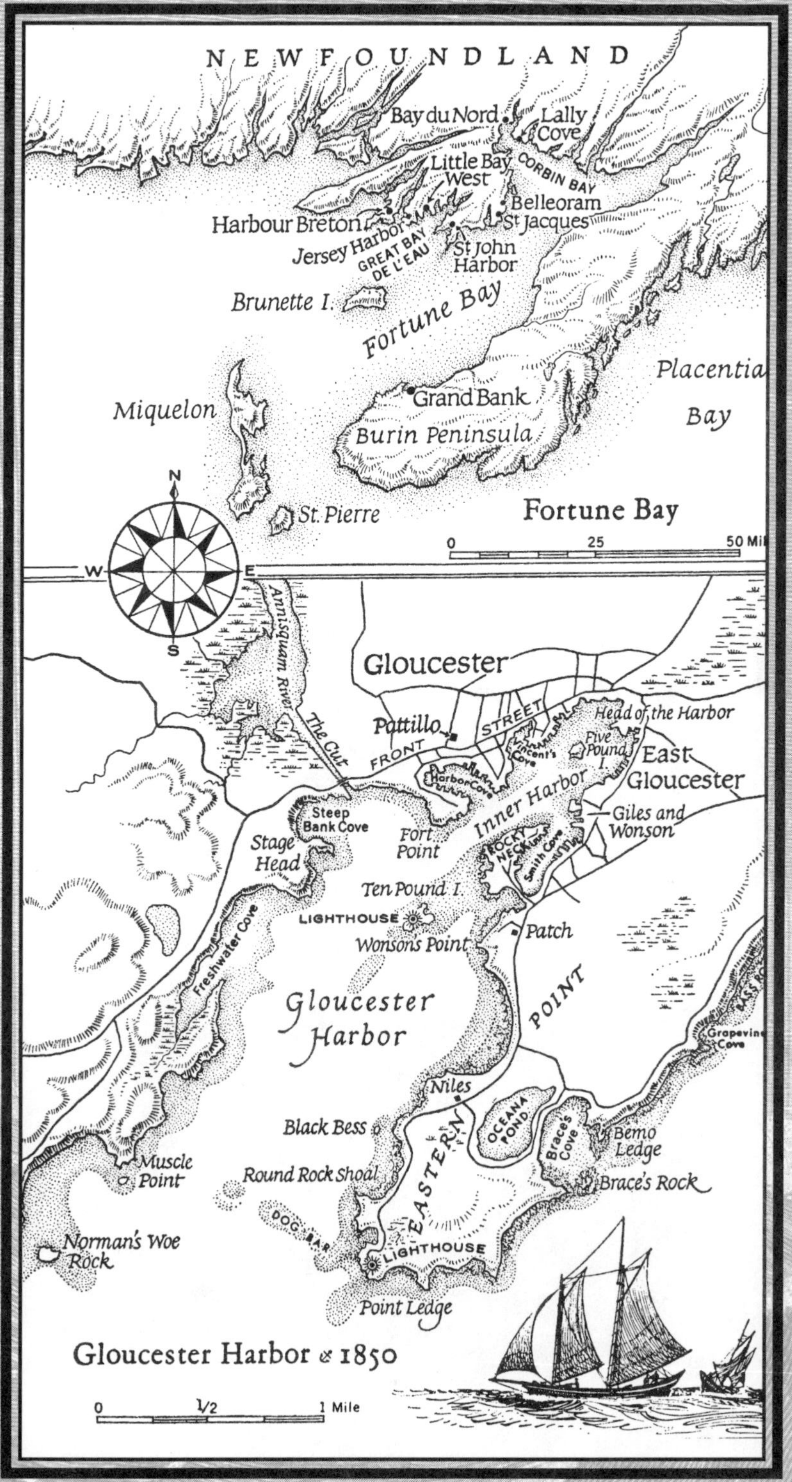
NEWFOUNDLAND
Bay du Nord
Lally Cove
Little Bay West
CORBIN BAY
Belleoram
St Jacques
Harbour Breton
Jersey Harbor
GREAT BAY DE L'EAU
St John Harbor
Brunette I.
Fortune Bay
Placentia Bay
Miquelon
Grand Bank
Burin Peninsula
St. Pierre
Fortune Bay
0
25
50 Mi
N
W
E
S
Annisquam River
Gloucester
The Cut
Pattillo
FRONT
STREET
Head of the Harbor
Vincent's Cove
Five Pound I.
East Gloucester
Harbor Cove
Inner Harbor
Steep Bank Cove
Stage Head
Fort Point
Giles and Wonson
ROCKY NECK
Smith Cove
Ten Pound I.
LIGHTHOUSE
Wonson's Point
Patch
Freshwater Cove
Gloucester Harbor
POINT
Gropevine Cove
Niles
Black Bess
OCEANA POND
Brace's Cove
Bemo Ledge
EASTERN
Muscle Point
Round Rock Shoal
Brace's Rock
DOG BAR
Norman's Woe Rock
LIGHTHOUSE
Point Ledge
Gloucester Harbor ≈ 1850
0
1/2
1 Mile

Bear *of* *the* Sea

GIANT JIM PATTILLO AND THE ROARING YEARS OF THE GLOUCESTER–NOVA SCOTIA FISHERY

Joseph E. Garland

Commonwealth Editions
BEVERLY, MASSACHUSETTS

Library of Congress Cataloging-in-Publication Data

[CIP data here]

ISBN 1-889833-23-1

Designed by James F. Brisson, Williamsville, Vermont.
Printed in the United States of America.

Commonwealth Editions is an imprint of Memoirs Unlimited, Inc.,
21 Lothrop Street, Beverly, Massachusetts 01915.
Visit us at www.commonwealtheditions.com.

CONTENTS

Foreword

BEAR OF THE SEA was initially published in 1966 as *That Great Pattillo: The Merry Misdemeanors of a Legendary Gloucester Fisherman.* It was a great read (and I *do* say so), sold short by my too-merry choice of a title and the not-so-merry, if well-meaning misdemeanor of a last-minute try at rescuing the cover from an artist who'd decked out my tempestuous antihero fisherman as a naval officer–cap, sea jacket and epaulets, necktie flapping in the breeze.

It wasn't the first time James William Pattillo had been miscast. James Brendan Connolly, the late Gloucester writer from South Boston, tossed off a couple of the exploits of "the famous Latin skipper Jim Patillo" in his 1940 *The Port of Gloucester* as examples of the contribution of Italian immigrants to the American fisheries of a hundred years earlier.

Setting aside that the "Latin" fishermen from Sicily didn't arrive in Gloucester for another fifty years, Jim Pattillo was born in Chester, Nova Scotia, in 1806, and was the son of an emigré from Scotland whose surname had evolved from Pittilock. As a young Goliath of a fishing skipper too handy with the bottle and quick with his fists, he fled the Canadian law for Gloucester, Massachusetts, which was in the way of being the great fishing port of the Western Hemisphere, where he would be a legend among the legendary.

When my friend Webster Bull of Commonwealth Editions resolved to republish *That Great Pattillo* in paperback, we agreed that a new alias was required and hit upon *Bear of the Sea,* felicitously truncated from the intriguing name of the big guy's first fishing boat in the Canadian Maritimes, *Lily of the Valley and Bear of the Sea.*

Novelistic as it may sound, this is a biography set in a rousing era of the historically contentious western Atlantic fishery. It is also a three-way collaboration spanning the eighty years from Captain Pattillo's old-age account of his life to Preacher Rakey (a talented interviewer who saw it as a temperance tract) to my rediscovery, verification, expansion, backgrounding and contextualizing of it. I took my first title rather too whimsically, perhaps, from Jim's engagingly innocent way, while spinning his tale, of referring to himself, as others had referred to him with awe, as "that great Pattillo."

When after uncounted hammerings of those unlucky or unwise enough to cross his headlong path, the Bear of the Sea fell so dramatically into a state of Grace for the first time, and for the first time foreswore strong drink forever, he more or less exchanged temper for temperance–even as I, who credited a leading brewery as one of my sources in the 1966 edition, found my own safe harbor a score of years later.

The result of the collaboration, I dare say, is as boisterous a temperance tale as the reader is likely to stumble across, and in the agony of redemption, as poignant a denouement. After thirty-five years of reflection I believe more firmly than ever that what I've recorded was intended for the truth long before I came on the scene. And yes, as I averred in my original foreword,

> I would ship to the poles with Pattillo [if I still had my sea legs!], for he is as honest as Lot Church. The heavy end of the yarn he has related on his oath in the witness stand. Furthermore, I have checked his references and will vouch for them. There really was a Constable Ham, and Officer McMullen and Tom Gaden, Miss Liza and Collector Bigelow, Captains Job Rowe and Steve Rich, fat Doctor

> Moriarty, good Master Moore, the mysterious Christie, poor Parson Arnold and all the rest.
>
> As for my end of it . . . the old man can't check up on *me,* but he *can* keep me on the straight and narrow just the same, because I have no desire to get into a controversy with him and risk a hammering in the hereafter . . . you see, he rests not the heave of a handspike from my family lot in Gloucester.

Our captain could barely write, though surely he must have been able to read, if with difficulty. Eleven weeks of schooling was all he had. Yet the Pattillo memory for names, dates, voyages, weather, catches and even the price of fish, events and encounters and conversations large and trivial, was encyclopedic, most particularly recorded in the memoirs dictated to Pastor Rakey and confirmed time and again by my research. They lurk in some of the deepest and broadest waters of inquiry I've ever sailed, verified by contemporary accounts of the highlights of his life published by the esteemed Gloucester journalist George H. Procter, by a brace of articles in the *Youth's Companion* magazine of 1883 for which their subject vouched, and by the nineteen pages of his sworn and colorful testimony in the proceedings of an international fisheries inquiry in 1877.

The Halifax Commission was created by the United States and Great Britain to determine what compensation, if any, the former should pay the latter for fishing the inshore waters of the Canadian Maritimes under the Treaty of Washington of 1873. Our whitewashed Yankee, as the Novie fishermen derided anyone who'd taken off for the "Boston states" and returned under the Stars and Stripes to catch Canadian fish, had come perilously close to provoking a shooting match between the neighbor nations with his daring encounters, blustery bluffs and close calls. So he was probably the key witness before the commission, transfixing all with the reaches of his memory and his gusto.

"This is a story of the old days, when a man could live out his life and think that some things were right, and steady as you go, from the beginning to the end." Thus I concluded my first, relatively youthful foreword to the book I reckon I've had more plain fun with than any other.

Thirty-five years later I'm not so sure about the "steady as you go." Thinking some things are right as a rule of life doesn't necessarily make them so, does it? But the fun remains.

Joseph E. Garland

Eastern Point, Gloucester, Massachusetts
February 2001

Bear *of the* Sea

To the fishermen of the Canadian Maritimes
and their families and descendants
who for generations have renewed
the life blood of Gloucester

My hero before conversion was a coarse, vulgar, profane man; a hard drinker; and when under the influence of ardent spirits, he was ungovernable, and like a young bear did not know his strength. If what is objectionable could be expunged and the mighty miracle of this man's conversion conserved, when his feet were taken out of "the horrible pit and the miry clay" and planted upon "the solid rock Christ Jesus," He who is mighty to save, I believe under God it could be made a powerful agency for good among seamen and people of that class.

REVEREND W. J. RAKEY

The Great Scotsman Tames the Wilderness and Is Captured by the Widow Bartlet

ALEXANDER PATTILLO was a pioneer of Canada. He stood straight and tall as an oar, and he could break one across his knee. He was broad enough to fill the doorway, and no man would pass. Jut-jawed and lank in the face he was, with eyes of ice, and bristling brows and the Celt's straw thatch of hair. His words were lean, and his deeds were long. Now dour, then droll, and ever dogged, he was a great Scotsman from the glens and crags of Huntly, off in the braes in back of Aberdeen, and all his kin that he left behind in the Auld Sod were the braw race of Highlanders from the beginning and before that.

He could do anything he had to do, and he did it. Stonemason, carpenter, woodsman, limeburner, boatbuilder, merchant, mariner, farmer, trader, distiller, lover and hunter he was . . . and whatever else was wanted to tame the wild wilderness that spilled down over the south coast of His Majesty's British North American Province of Nova Scotia, into the wild waves of the Western Ocean.

This hump out there in the cold sea belonged to the Indians.

Then came the French, and then the English, and the French called it Acadia and in the long wars set the tribes against their old enemies. But France lost her New World at last, and it lodged with the Crown, which invited the New Englanders to tame this New Scotland and fish in the spawning waters around it. The Yankees of Nova Scotia would not join the thirteen rebels in their Revolution, nor would they take up arms against their brethren either; but when the war was over, and a nation had been born, they welcomed those Tories who held their loyalty to George the Third and fled by the tens of thousands to the Province.

Trying to wean "that ill-thriven, hard-visaged and ill-tempered brat," in the words of Edmund Burke, the King urged his hardier subjects, with promises of land, to seek their fortunes there. And so it came to pass in 1783, at forty and a bachelor yet, that Alexander Pattillo, master stonemason, quit his job as the boss of a building gang, threw all over, broke all ties, and found himself in the township of Chester, awaiting the promised grant of land from his liege, a land so miserly of milk and honey that only a Scot or an Irishman or a Yankee would bother with it.

Still and all, it had its saving graces. Chester village bulged placidly into the head of Mahone Bay, certainly the most beautiful blue bay anywhere, a ten-mile basin of islands, each one a greener cushion of spruce than the next, sun and shadow parading across the Atlantic waters that shivered so deliciously in the breeze . . . enough to make the heart sing. Twelve miles across to the south was Lunenburg, where George the Second had flattered the Germans into settling. Forty farther on and to the westward was bustling little Liverpool. Up the coast in the other direction, to the eastward fifty miles, lay the great harbor of the small town of Halifax, outguard of empire. The rivers and streams rushed into the Bay from all sides, fed by the lakes of the hindland, all teeming with salmon, alewives, shad, trout and eel.

There was scarcely a wagon track in the township worth following when Alexander Pattillo and seventy-two other adventurers shared their twelve thousand acres from the Crown in 1785—nor even a wagon, for that matter; they packed all on sleds and their backs, winter and summer. And there were fewer than a

The waterfront in Chester, Nova Scotia, in the last quarter of the nineteenth century. (Provincial Archives of Nova Scotia)

hundred families. The settlement was strewn around the blockhouse–some rude cabins, a few ruts between, a tavern, general store, two or three wharves and a scattering of pretty little coasting and fishing vessels swinging at their moorings in the two snug harbors, Front and Back.

Behind was the wilderness. At the edge of it were the potato patches and the thin fields of barley, hay, oats, corn and wheat growing up from the lumbered-over burnt land. All in all, only four hundred acres out of a hundred thousand were under cultivation. Next over, or in some places deeper in the woods, was the half-land, the clearings where the virgin timber sixty, seventy, eighty feet tall and two or three across the trunk had been felled by the broad axes and dragged out or floated downstream for lumber; here was a stubble of brush, stumps and stones, no longer forest, not yet field.

Then all in back were the wild woods, thick and untouched as they were when God made them, copse, glen and grove, great stands of sugar maple, oak, white birch and ash, mast-high pine, hemlock and spruce, watered by brook, freshet and rapids flowing between the ponds and the lakes, beaver-dammed some of them, draining off to the sea, all in the state of grace. Here was the home of the lumbering bear and the big-nosed moose, caribou, white-tailed deer, rabbit, red fox, wildcat, otter and mink, the thumping partridge and the old hoot owl, eagle and wren. This was the primeval wilderness from Cape Sable east to Breton's Cape North three hundred and sixty miles long, from Chester north to Windsor on Minas Basin thirty-three miles as the crow flew, and who knew how far by the thread of the footpath that tied the two together?

It was this trek to Windsor that the doughty Scot Pattillo set out to make one fine day in the spring of the year. He had a matter to attend to there, and the folks in Chester told him (because he had not been long among them and did not know the wilderness) to direct his horse along the trail and to have no worry, however thick the forest closed in, so long as he followed the blaze marks on the trees–they would take him to his destination safe and sound.

So Alexander donned jacket and broad hat (for the men dressed light to save clothes), saddled horse, packed bannock cakes, oats, pistol, powder and ball, waved a goodby and plunged into the brush.

Soon enough the footpath choked and died. He pushed on through the elders and the catbrier, keeping his eye out for the blaze marks of the old-timer's axe. They faded, healed by time, and then he missed one. Horse and rider ripped on through the maze of shrub, and there was not another human mark to be found, not one–every tree around was a virgin, unscarred by man, and they were lost.

He spent the night beside his steed, and at the first light of dawn he resumed. Crackling, scratching through the thicket they followed the sun, forded Middle River, after that Gold River (though for him they had no names). Another day went by, and then another, and the last of the food had gone when they came out on the shore of Nine-Mile Lake (which he had never seen; he was groping west instead of north, deeper into the black woods with every hour).

Now this lake was a mile across. But the man's horse had a strong heart, and he swam, with his great master on his back urging him on. They came out dripping on the west shore where the deer looked up startled from the rim of the woods. The rider rested his horse, and they dove back into the forest. For two days they circled round and round, and when they came out, there was Nine-Mile Lake again.

"God mon!" muttered the Scot at the sight of it. He was filthy and cut by thorns, all scraggly beard and empty stomach. But he shook his head, slapped his weary horse on the rump, and into the water they splashed for the second crossing.

The poor beast stumbled up on the east shore of the lake where they had started from, but it looked to the man more dreary than ever. With an obstinate grunt and another shake of his head, he turned his wretched animal around and spurred him right through the mile of lake for the third time. This finished old horse, for he was near filled with water, bloated and broken of wind, and his spirit was spent. He laid down on the bank in the shadow of the wood with a sigh and died.

Master took off saddle and bridle, stirrups and all, and slung them over the limb of a birch, threw a last look at faithful friend, took his pistol and tramped forward–he knew not where–on foot. He had been nine days now in the wild woods, food gone for the last week . . . nothing to eat but berries and the bark of trees, no game within reach.

Into a glade he crashed, where the shafts of the sun shimmered down through the skylight in the trees. Wha' hae we here!–the lone cub of a bear, playing in the long grass! He pulled out his pistol, and was about firing, when a roar in his rear whipped him around in his tracks, face to face with mother, her hackles up, raring back, jaws wide open, preparing to spring on him.

Alexander aimed the pistol down her throat, stepping backward, and spoke to her softly:

"God mon, yer ladyship, ah weel mak a childe's barrrgin wi' ye . . . ye lemme be, an' ah weel le' ye be! Hoo's thet, ma sweet?"

And so he made his escape, neither bear nor cub offering to follow.

By the eleventh day he was crawling on his hands and knees. Face and arms were all blood and afire from the tearing of the branches and the bites of the swarms of insects, and puffed up from the poison ivy. He heard a chirrup, and he raised his head in time to catch the flash of a bluebird where she flew out from a little knoll. He followed her and found her nest with three eggs in it, sucked them, and they revived him, and he thought he was as good a man as ever he was, so he continued his wandering, praying for the way out of the wilderness.

But there was none. Three nights later, his fourteenth in the forest, the strengthy Highlander was sick and too weak to move. He fell on his face, and he knew he would not awaken when the sun came up.

Then a dog barked. He heard it. He hauled up onto his legs, and he blundered through the black woods and dropped senseless at the feet of an Indian and his hound.

The redskin worked the giant one's arm over his shoulder and dragged him to his wigwam. His wife gave the white man food and broth and washed his face and brought back the life all that night. In the morning he was somewhat revived. They supported him to the stream and laid him on his back in the canoe, and the squaw paddled him down the Lahave River to the folks at Bear Hills. When she left him with his people, Alexander Pattillo gave her a pound in coin from his pocket for saving his life, and himself set out for home.

Five miles to the east of Chester, beyond Scotch Cove, was Indian Point, rounding into the Bay between Eastern and Little Eastern Rivers. Alexander claimed a large piece of his Crown grant here, a hundred and fifty acres of the western flank of the point, all bounding on the land of the Micmacs. Along by the shore, which was the main attraction to him, were rich beds of brown limestone. He struck off his boundaries by guess and by God and built his kiln.

It was a cavernous rock oven, with a monstrous mouth and a hole in its crown for the smoke and gas to escape. The woods around about supplied the fuel, to the ring of the axe. The burly Scot mined his ore with pick and shovel, the soft limestone of a billion fossils compressed in the floor of the old receded ocean.

He stoked up a roaring fire in his kiln until he was all wet with sweat and hove in the chunks of the limestone. The heat drove out the gas, and the stone turned to quicklime. After this lumpy stuff had cooled, the perspiring burner raked it out and slaked it with a dash of water; it hissed and sizzled, seethed, frothed, and collapsed into a mound of white powder. Slaked lime this was, his product; he packed it into tight-staved barrels and headed them up, neat and dry. Add sand and water any time, stir, and the mason had his mortar.

Before he was fifty Alexander Pattillo had made up for his late start on the frontier in all ways but getting a wife and strong sons to share the hardness of his life. He owned more than a thousand acres of land, most of them in forest, but some on the islands in Chester Bay, and enough for his wants he had cleared already, burned over and put to agriculture. He gave the coin of the realm for his acres by and large, but there were times when he paid with the sweat of his back, as the two lots in the village for seventy hogsheads of lime.

Looking to expand his horizons, he built a shallop, a two-masted vessel of about forty feet with cabin and hold. The mystery was, where had the mason learned the ways of the sea? The Highlander was the sailor born, it must have been, because by 1791 a Connecticut Yankee merchant down at Liverpool by the name of Simeon Perkins was putting in his diary that Mr. Pattillo arrives in his shallop with cargoes of lime from Chester. For some years more he remarked these comings and goings–that Mr. Pattillo was bringing in lime or this or that, letting off passengers and taking them on, carrying one cargo and another back to Chester or on to Halifax . . . a restless man of unslakable energy.

One day in Liverpool Captain Pattillo met a big, buxom, handsome young woman known in the town as the Widow Bartlet and to her closer friends as Betsy. He was twenty years older, but she stirred the young blood in him.

She was born there to Robert and Margaret Roberts soon after they settled from New England. Her Pa was a mariner, and Simeon Perkins had little good to say of him, noting drily in the summer of 1767, when Betsy was five, that a man had been wounded in a scuffle with Robert Roberts down the coast at Port Joli–when the fishing's good, the fishermen "must needs go to killing one another . . . the fatal effects of rum."

But it was not rum that killed the parents of Betsy Roberts, it was the smallpox. Ten years later a small epidemic struck Liverpool, and they were carried off within three weeks of each other. The orphaned girl and her three brothers escaped it.

Elizabeth blossomed into comely womanhood, and a man entered her life, and left, under the scrutiny of the vigilant Mr. Perkins, who observed in April of 1789 that "Bartlet, that married Betsy Roberts, is missing. He went with (Captain) Ellenwood, and went on shore (at Boston), as they say, was seen crossing the mill bridge by Capt. Howard, and has not been heard of since. They conjecture that he may be murdered by one Bradley, that lived with Mr. William Smith, the winter past, for some reason they give."

Whatever the mystery behind it, Betsy Roberts at twenty-seven came to be called the Widow Bartlet, and in the course of time she met and conquered that great Chesterman Alexander Pattillo, and all agreed he was as likely a catch for a widowed woman with a small boy as there was on the south shore of Nova Scotia . . . with his lands and lime and his farm and vessel, and no one to share them with.

Inevitably–it was a steaming hot afternoon in August of 1794–old man Perkins took up quill and made all official: "Mr. Alexander Patillo is published at the Methodist Meeting to Elizabeth Bartlet. She was Elizabeth Roberts, and was married some years ago to Joseph Bartlet, who after living with her some months, went away, and left her. He was supposed to be dead, but has been seen by some of our people in the States. She has a son by him."

. . . And a daughter by her betrothed whom Simeon failed in his kindness to mention, if he knew of her, entered in the records of Chester, born the previous tenth of March and named Elizabeth.

The Scot was an upright man. At the age of fifty-one he made Betsy Roberts Bartlet an honest woman (and a bigamist) on the twentieth of September, 1794, and good Simeon Perkins penned them on their way: "Mr. Patillo sails for Chester, and carries his new wife, Mrs. Bartlet that was."

Alexander Pattillo carried Mrs. Bartlet that was and his two suddenly acquired bairns back to the best he could offer from his wilderness. He bought a lot of land where the breezes caressed and the water lapped the lovely east shore of the village, looking over Front Harbor. It was a few rods from the new Baptist meeting and the blockhouse, and here he built a home for his family and a wharf for his boat.

Already he had been having his troubles over at Indian Point. The usually easygoing Micmacs, whose land bordered his, disputed the lines laid out by the tall hard man with the tight fists. There was a fine how-d'ye-do over it and a most awful amount of grunting and growling and many a darkly muttered *God mon!* as Indian and Scot stomped through the woods, peered around trees and paced off their distances arguing the matter.

In the end Pattillo asked the Provincial Surveyor General to have his rightful claim determined once and for all. So on a brisk November day William Nelson lugged Gunter's chain and compass through the forest, in from one shore to the north, then westward to the bank of Eastern River. When he was through, he drew a map of the true bounds and filed it away in the Registry.

A neat X marked the location of A. Pattillo's lime kiln, some hundreds of yards over his east boundary on the land of the Indians. Did the stubborn Scotchman move his kiln? Family tradition implies that he didn't, that if there was a settlement or a truce between the Pattillos and the Micmacs, it was an uneasy one.

Betsy, a woman of ample size, and of strength sufficient to her tasks, often worked at the kiln. She was there alone one day, as the story goes, when out of the thicket popped a whole troop of Indians, one on the heels of the next–and as each came at her with his bloodcurdling shriek, Mrs. Pattillo pitched him headlong into the works.

The second child of Alexander and Betsy, born in wedlock, was a girl too, and they called her Margaret. Then followed Alexander in 1797 and Thomas Roberts two years after. The century turned, and in the dead of January, 1801, the third girl was born; but a week later her sisters Elizabeth and Margaret fell sick and died within twenty-four hours. The name of Margaret was passed on to the infant.

Five years went by, and on the twenty-ninth of September, 1806, while Napoleon massed his armies on the plains before Jena, their last one entered the world. Betsy was forty-four, and Alexander was sixty-three. It seemed fitting to call him James William Pattillo for two of his virile old father's brothers in Scotland.

About the best people could say of him was that he had blue eyes, a fair skin and a most lusty pair of lungs . . . and at a very early age showed evidence that he was gifted with uncommon size and strength. What he might amount to, if anything at all, was anybody's guess. For as everyone knows, heroes are made, not born.

A Dead Horse for a Set of Books

THE FARTHEST BACK Jimmy Pattillo remembered was when he was four years old. It was muster day in June, and the men of Chester were down in the square by the blockhouse for drill and parade. All the boys were on the fringes and getting in the way, when up went a shout, then a scuffle in the ranks and more shouts. Jimmy ran over in time to see Fritz Lawler pull a knife and stick it into Charlie Allen, right through the side of the nose. He fell down dead on the spot, the blood spurting from his face, and Jimmy skipped home to tell his mother what he had seen.

The next thing he remembered was how he earned his first dollar. His father was a Church of England man, but there was no church at all in Chester until after he settled, and that was the Baptist meetinghouse. The pastor since 1793 had been the Reverend Joseph Dimock (Father Dimock he was called through the length and breadth of Nova Scotia where he was a fervent preacher for his faith, sometimes against violent opposition). The year after Father Dimock came–in fact, the same month Alexander brought "Mrs. Bartlet that was" back to Chester–the Society for the Propagation of the Gospel of the Church of England sent the Reverend Thomas Lloyd to Chester to organize St. Stephen's Church. But this poor missionary had the bad luck that winter to freeze as stiff as a board during a blizzard, trying to fight through the same wilderness from Chester to Windsor that had nearly taken the life of the great Alexander. St. Stephen's had no regular rector until 1812, so the Baptist faith of Father Dimock held sway for some years in the township.

He was a man to be reckoned with. He, too, nearly lost his all one winter, searching after those blazed trees from Windsor to Chester. The silent snow drifted down through the branches, piling up deep on the forest floor, and when night came on the undaunted man of God kept himself from falling into a last sleep by pacing back and forth in his track, back and forth until dawn.

Father Dimock was of the stuff of the prophet, which is to say, when it was necessary he could clothe himself with a suggestion of the Second Coming. As he preached in new places salvation or be damned, the people were sometimes moved to heave stones at him; but these invariably missed their mark. One time a dozen men went out from a tavern to lay hold of him. They returned empty-handed, and to the taunts of the rest replied: "You couldn't touch him! There he stood like a child without any resistance!"

Father Dimock gave Jimmy Pattillo his first dollar. It was when the smallpox came on Chester. The boy was five. The preacher, who had some smattering of medical knowledge and hence doctored the township too, came to the house on the harbor to vaccinate him. But when the child was told to bare his arm, and he saw the needle, he put up a howl and would not let the good divine approach.

"Come now, Jimmy," said the preacher. "This will hurt you no more than the prick of a pin."

More screaming and kicking.

"I tell you, boy, here's a dollar if you let me vaccinate you."

A sudden silence. Then . . .

"Give me the dollar and you can stick me when you like."

The dollar went full circle for the Lord. There was a man in the town who was on his uppers—"one of God's children," as they said—and Alexander went about collecting money to buy him some clothing for the cold weather. Jimmy had a hard struggle to part with his first dollar. He took up a half-dollar and looked at it, thought it mean not to give the whole of it, as his mother knew he had it. So he gave it all for the poor man. She told him he was a good lad, and that made him feel happy.

It was about a year later that all of Chester had grandstand seats for one of the most spectacular naval chases of the War of 1812. Although the young United States made as if to wrest Canada from the mother country, the Nova Scotians were less concerned with this empty threat than with the movements of American privateers along their coast. One of these, the schooner *Young Teazer,* had been raising particular hell. She carried two deck guns and was a fast sailer, and with her sixteen sweeps she could be rowed at five knots, adding to the fear she inspired among coasting vessels in provincial waters.

The people of Lunenburg, therefore, saw with high anxiety a man-of-war and a frigate chasing another armed vessel into Mahone Bay on the afternoon of the twenty-seventh of June, 1813; it was during a break in the fog that had hung over the water most of the day. Immediately alarm guns were fired at the blockhouses and outposts around the Bay, bringing in the militia from all the countryside. When word reached Chester, Alexander Pattillo, though seventy years of age, must have grabbed up his musket and joined his townsmen on the high ground, with the women and children right behind, to watch the maneuverings of the three vessels as they approached, still a long way off. Surely they were British and American . . . but which was which?

Young Teazer had been slinking along the coast in search of a prize when she fell in with the English privateer *Sir John Sherbrooke,* an eighteen-gun brig, which gave chase for a while and then lost her behind a bank of fog. What the Yankee did not know was that the *Sherbrooke* was not her only pursuer; somewhere in or beyond the fog were also the seventy-four-gun man-of-war *La Hogue,* the frigates *Orpheus* and *Castor* and the brig-of-war *Manly.*

There was barely a stir of air as the fog began to break around the *Teazer* in the morning of the twenty-seventh. At about noon a cry from the masthead warned of a sail to windward. It was the *Orpheus.* All hands were called to make sail, but there was still scarcely a breath of wind, so they were put to work at the sweeps. At two another sail was discovered, this time to leeward.

So far it was no contest, for the air was so light that the strong backs of her oarsmen kept the *Teazer* away from her pursuers, far out of the range of their guns. But at four a breeze sprang up and, as luck would have it, favored the English first. They took the wind and commenced to get under way in style, and by the time it had reached *Teazer* and filled her sails, her hunters had her landlocked and forced the schooner to run for Chester Bay.

Behind the headland, with *Orpheus* hot on his heels, the skipper of the *Teazer* tacked ship from Sculpin Rock to Spindler's Cove, where he came about and ran with a fair wind behind Tancook, the island at the entrance of the Bay.

By now the sun was a fireball sinking toward the forest, and the wind was failing. *La Hogue* came to anchor and swung over five boatloads of boarders; she smelled the kill. The watchers on the shore could see the American privateer at a distance, her canvas adroop, the regular flash of her sweep blades in the setting sun. The Yankee was trying to keep her distance from the man-of-war's swarm, hauling hard after her on the horizon. Three miles separated them, but it was narrowing.

At that instant the southern sky blazed up with a blossom of flame as if a furnace door had been jerked open in the dark. It subsided, flared and fell back, shot through with arching rockets burning bright. The shock wave of the immense explosion struck the land and rocked it and reverberated, colliding with itself from shore to shore. A column of smoke rose vast in the evening sky.

Around the darkened semicircle of the Bay shore that night the people were full of foreboding, unknowing whether friend or enemy (were not enemies friends in this unwanted war?) had been blown to eternity in this nightmare all had seen, and the men lay upon their arms, waiting for the dawn. Not until the next day, when a small boat rowed to shore with eight men, two of them bloody and maimed, did the story come out.

As the British boarding party so slowly but relentlessly over-

Mahone Bay in the distance, about 1890, from M. B. DesBrisay's History of the County of Lunenberg. *(Provincial Archives of Nova Scotia)*

took the *Teazer,* an officer aboard the privateer—a deserter from His Majesty's service, and ironically from the pursuing *La Hogue* herself—was going berserk at the prospect of his fate should he fall into the hands of his former shipmates. Failing to bring the Yankees to his own pitch of desperate resistance, he put the torch to the magazine and blew all to kingdom come. Eight of thirty-six survived, blasted into the sea. One swam to her tender astern, cut the painter and picked up the others. They rowed ashore and surrendered.

The smoldering wreck of *Young Teazer* was towed ashore on Nass's Island, off Chester. George Mitchell bought the hulk for the good American oak in it, and when he built his store and wharf near old man Pattillo's, the east wall rested on her keelson.

In a while people were saying that the ghost of the Yankee privateer had been seen on black nights, reaching silently past Tancook, her ghastly crew at the rail; and the mysterious "Teazer light" caused many a heart to pound during midnight passages on Mahone Bay.

If the Bay was haunted, so was at least one of the islands. People said that Captain Kidd and his pirate crew had buried a fabulous treasure somewhere on Oak Island around 1700. A year or two later they took their secret to the gallows. But the search persisted for generations, and the romance in men's souls–and the cupidity in their hearts–transplanted the gold to every imagined hideaway and place of mystery on ten thousand miles of coast.

The legend attached itself to Oak Island, four miles to the southwest of Chester off the western shore of the Bay, around 1785, when a settler from New England found signs of a curious excavation; digging disclosed the remains of an undoubtedly man-made pit filled with dirt and curiously lined with tiers of logs and flat stones to a great depth. In time, droves of treasure hunters went out to the island, and a veritable treasure they spent there on the mystery. But never a doubloon did they take out of this strange and apparently bottomless shaft, which once was excavated to a hundred feet before water began to pour in from some underground source faster than it could be pumped out.

By a singular circumstance, Alexander Pattillo bought a piece of Oak Island at about the time the pit was discovered. Being a hardheaded Scot he probably took one look at the diggings and dismissed such nonsense from his mind. But his father's skepticism would not have kept Jimmy from going out there with his pals to poke around. While they oared back to Chester they could argue and speculate over what they had seen until they tired of Captain Kidd and his treasure, but the mystery remained.

When Jimmy was ten his brothers took him along on a coasting trip to Halifax. Alec was nineteen and Tom seventeen. It qualified as his first voyage, and his old man told him to keep his eyes open and make note of everything he saw.

The boy had been kicking around the wharves of Chester for long enough (he'd not yet been to school, having been put to work by his father almost since he learned to walk) that he knew most of the ropes; and with his size and strength being already half a man, he pitched in aboard and did his share to sail the small coaster the forty-five miles to their destination. He had the sea in his blood.

Halifax was a window on the world for an ignorant backwoods boy. Though a town of less than ten thousand souls, it was the bastion of Britain's western empire and the base from which she prosecuted the late war with the States and insured the defense of Canada. No would-be conqueror ever dared to test the fortress of Halifax. The town was on a peninsula dominated by Citadel Hill, from which brooded the great earthworks of Fort George, the lob of a mortar back from the waterfront. All its bustling life was crowded between the docks and the foot of the Citadel, conducted under those silent guns whose range swept the whole of the harbor and its island approaches, the Eastern Passage and the quiet reach of Northwest Arm in back. So big was this stormproof haven of deep water that between Halifax and the opposite Dartmouth shore every ship in His Majesty's Royal Navy could find scope for her cables; and if more was wanted, there was Bedford Basin farther in, as big again and almost landlocked by the Narrows. Truly one of the world's greatest natural harbors.

Past the ships of the line and the merchantmen, hustling sloops and shallops, slipped the Pattillo boys and brought their little vessel up to the wharf. And when all was secured, with time for a stroll, Alec and Tom took Jimmy between them for a look at the town. Leaving the docks and warehouses, they crossed Lower Water Street and passed by His Majesty's Fuel Yard and Customs House and buildings of the Royal Navy. The ground steepened as they walked up Prince Street by the Province Building, where the government offices were, through the crowds of townspeople and soldiers and sailors, carts, horses, wagons, drays and carriages, dogs, sheep, cows, pigs and chickens, all noisy and on the move, pressing in. Pulses and steps quickened when the wind carried above the street din the strains of a smart march from the garrison band, playing today before the guard inspection on the Grand Parade, a smooth patch of green marching ground in the middle of the town. The young Pattillos ran up and elbowed their way through the crowd at the edge of it to watch the soldiers, dashing in their red, gold and silver, muskets, swords and all, change the guard to the barking of the sergeant-at-arms, salute, wheel, troop to the colors and stand like statues to inspection.

Always there was this excitement in the air of Halifax, whose comings and goings were tuned to the thud of boot and the slap of stock, and nothing stirred the blood so as the ritual the sunset gun touched off, sending a column of soldiers behind fife and drum from the Town Clock, sharp-stepping down Barrack Street to the Government House or the General's quarters and back again to barracks.

The drill on the Grand Parade over, the Chester boys shoved and dodged on through the crowded streets toward Citadel Hill. This was the toughest part of the town, these streets below the Fortress. They were lined with dance halls, grog shops and brothels, frequented by Redcoats, jack-tars and the sailors of the world, and populated by drunks, trollops and procurers, thieves, ruffians and all the riffraff of a port on the edge of the wilderness. "The business of one half of the town is to sell rum," complained one disaffected citizen, "and the other half to drink it. You may, from this single circumstance, judge of our morals, and naturally infer that we are not enthusiasts in religion."

On pushed the frontier lads, holding close together, until they reached Barrack Street, skirting Citadel Hill parallel to the waterfront. Here was fresh air at last, and beyond was the sharp rise of the green sward and the harsh battlements of the Fortress high up the slope. Barrack Street had seen so many fights, robberies and murders that it was known to Haligonians as "Knock 'Em Down Street." But it was safe enough at midday, and the trio strode north along it to the Town Clock.

Now this was a unique building, standing in the field under the Citadel, only twelve or thirteen years old, erected for the sole purpose of raising up to the general view a great tower clock ordered for the garrison by the departing Duke of Kent. Above the dials stood a classically columned belfry from which the quarter hour was rung, and on the tip-top of the tower was a metal ball as big as a barrel. When the brothers approached, the hands were close to noon, and this sphere was raised on a rod several feet above the roof.

At precisely twelve, the big bell commenced to strike the hour, the noonday cannon boomed forth from the Fortress above them and the great ball dropped to the roof with a resounding clank. It was as good a show as the changing of the guard. But what did the ball do? Jimmy wanted to know . . . and thereby received his first lesson in navigation.

If you were a shipmaster, explained Alec, way out there in the harbor, and wished to set your chronometer to the nearest second before starting on a voyage, you could see the ball with your bare eye, or through your glass, and set your timepiece to noon when it dropped. But if you counted on the sound of the cannon, it would take a few seconds to reach your ears, even on a fair wind, and that is all it requires to throw you off a few miles at sea when you're shooting the sun.

The young Pattillos circled back to the waterfront. There was a battle-scarred man-of-war at a slip not far from where their boat lay. Jimmy was not shy, and he struck up a conversation with an old salt lounging about at the rail who had nothing else to do. Shortly he was invited to come aboard. The grizzled Jack showed the boy around under the towering spars and amongst the dead-black deck guns and the rigging every which way. It didn't take him long to find out where the kid was from, and what he was doing in Halifax, and that he already had the sea fever, and that he had never been to school, so that he could not read or write, which was bad enough for such a big lad, but could not even box the compass, which was infinitely worse. This called for a remedy, and so the veteran sat down with his young visitor, lit his pipe and told him a story about the very vessel they were on board of, and he instructed his pupil gravely to learn it by heart if he ever hoped to ship before the mast:

"She was a lucky ship and never was captured, and she sent in prize money enough in four years to pay each of her crew five hundred pounds prize money besides their wages–that is, if they were able seamen and could box the compass, but one old Jack could not do so, so they cut him down to an English shilling.

"The crew boarded with a widow woman by the name of Brown. It was but a very little while that the man with only the shilling was minus cash, so the old landlady asked him if he was sick. He said he was not sick, but his money was about all gone. She said to him, have you spent all your five hundred pounds already? He said he had no five hundred pounds but only a shilling. She wanted to know the reason. He said the reason was because he could not box the compass. She asked him if he could steer by the compass. He said yes. Then she inquired of him if he could do everything else on board of a ship required of an able seaman, except boxing the compass. He said yes, he could.

"Now, she said, come along with me and I will teach you to box the compass. So she taught him the words of a song. After he had learnt it she told him to go to the Lord Admiral and demand his prize money.

"So he presented himself as directed, but his demands were rejected, he receiving the answer that all the affairs pertaining to the voyages had been settled according to the laws of England.

"The sailor then entered an action against the Lord High Admiral, and the jury was empanelled, and old Mother Brown and her lawyer and the sailor also attended. The Judge asked the Lord High Admiral the reason why he had not paid that man his five hundred pounds prize money the same as the rest of the men. And he answered him, because he could not box the compass.

"Then the Judge asked the sailor if he could do so. He said he could. The Judge told him to stand up and box the compass in his own way. So he began:

North a point easterly
North easterly
To the nor'ard of north
No ship can lie,
For old Mother Brown she told me so
To the nor'ard of north
No ship can go.

"The Judge said there never went a vessel to the northward of north, so say on:

East a point southerly
East southerly
To the east'ard of east
No ship can lie,
For old Mother Brown she told me so
To the east'ard of east
No ship can go.

"The Judge said there never was a ship went to the eastward of east yet, so say on:

South a point westerly
South westerly
To the south'ard of south
No ship can lie,
For old Mother Brown she told me so
To the south'ard of south
No ship can go.

"The Judge said there never went a vessel to the southward of south, so say on:

West a point northerly
West northerly
To the west'ard of west
No ship can lie,
For old Mother Brown she told me so
To the west'ard of west
No ship can go.

"And the Judge said, there is the whole compass. Pay the man his five hundred pounds prize money."

When they returned to Chester, Jimmy told his father and mother of all he had seen at Halifax and repeated the story about old Mother Brown that he had heard from the old tar aboard the man-of-war, word for word as it was told him.

The next winter, in January of 1817, Alec the oldest died two months short of his twentieth birthday. His share of the jobs fell on Tom and Jimmy, and Tom was some of the time in school. The auld Scot was seventy-five, hard and tough as ever, and he expected the work of men from his boys.

At eleven Jimmy was much beyond his age in size and strength. His old man saw to it that he kept his nose in the dirt, lime, sawdust and manure, so he had no schooling, books or anything. In the winter his first chore was to turn out of bed before dawn, light the fire in the kitchen stove, make his breakfast, harness the horse, go into the woods five miles, cut down trees, trim them into stove lengths and haul the load back to the woodshed.

On this one bitter cold black morning in February of 1818 he got up as usual to find it had snowed all night so deep the road would surely be blocked, making the sled of no use. After kindling the stove and bolting some porridge, he bundled himself up, went out through the drifts in the dark to the shed and harnessed the old horse, putting on collar, hames, traces, saddle and bridle, hitching whiffletrees to drag behind, and taking axe and wedge. Along the whole five miles out to the woodlot, hunched over the saddle as the horse labored through the snow, blowing out clouds of vapor, he met not a soul, it was that cold.

When he reached the lot, he went in along the logging road a way, dismounted, felled a hemlock, trimmed it, hitched it to the whiffletrees, climbed back in the saddle and started for home. But boy and horse were barely off, dragging the log in the snow, when it fetched up between two stumps and wedged in fast.

He worked to free the timber, cut a sapling for a handspike and tried to pry it loose, but all to no avail. The horse was stubborn and wouldn't help, and the boy of eleven sweated and strained in the drifts of snow there in the frigid woods by the dim light of the dawn for an hour. He cursed the log and the snow and his old man and the horse, and suddenly overcome by a blind rage he seized the axe and threw it at the animal. The flying weapon struck the horse on the temple and knocked it down in the snow, the blood pouring from its nostrils.

What was the boy to do? Too late for regrets—the poor brute

was no good for anything now—he gave it two whacks on the side of the head to stop its suffering and left the carcass in the snow—collar, hames, traces, saddle, bridle, whiffletrees and log all attached. Then he slung the bloody axe over his shoulder and waded off through the drifts the five miles for home.

"Jimmy, where is hoss?" was the greeting of his white-haired old man when the boy came stomping in the kitchen door, shaking off the snow, his face pinched and blue, nose dripping.

"Pa, he's all right enough," he mumbled from under the coat he was getting out of.

Betsy was at the stove, heating him some barley soup.

"You poor boy," said his mother. "You're almost frozen. Was there no one on the road?"

"No, Ma, it's dreadful out—I didn't see a living creature."

Alexander was patient but persistent. He let him eat, and as the lad was making for the kitchen stairs he repeated the question, this time with more than a hint of suspicion.

"Jimmy lad, where is hoss?"

The boy hesitated. Then he turned back and faced the great towering old man.

"I killed him with the axe, Pa, up on the lot. He's laying there—collar, hames, traces, saddle, bridle, whiffletrees and the log all with him."

"God mon! Wha' ha' the boy been aboot!"—and his father made a lunge to give him a crack.

Jimmy stood his ground.

"Tom can go to school day and night," he bellowed, "and I have to work day and night doing all the work around the house, and it's not fair!"

This gave old Alexander and Betsy Pattillo pause to think. Were they neglecting their youngest, a child doing a man's work? And the two of them old enough to be his grandparents?

So the auld Scot went off and bought a set of books for his son and sent him to school with Mrs. Hawbolt.

The boy thought it was the best job he'd ever done, killing the horse, for without it he'd have had no schooling at all.

Lily of the Valley and Bear of the Sea

MRS. MARGARET HAWBOLT had the first day school in Chester in her home. She started when she was sixteen helping her father, a Scotsman from Glasgow. The year Jimmy Pattillo went to the schoolmarm's–1818–was the same year the Countess of Dalhousie paid her memorable visit to Chester and afterwards sent Mrs. Hawbolt some schoolbooks from Halifax. It was the undoubted high point in the life of the town's lone teacher, and many was the time she used to say of her noble patroness: "She was a lady, I tell you, and she was Scotch and that was all the better."

Jimmy stayed for eleven weeks and went through the elementary arithmetic. School then closed for the season, or else he was expelled (or more likely his father hauled him back to work), and that was the beginning and the end of his formal education.

That summer–he was still eleven–he went to sea for good as crew for his brother Tom coasting cargoes between Chester and Halifax. He kept at this summers until he was thirteen, working on the farm and burning lime the rest of the seasons. He got to be such a big lump of a lad that by New Year's Day of 1821, being fourteen years old, the time had arrived for the first serious test of his merit. In short, this was the occasion of that ancient rite, the first fist fight, and it must be admitted that the cause of it all was drinking.

It is unpleasant, so shocking early in our tale, to record that our lad fell in with liquor at the age of fourteen. Yet he will have to stand, falter or fall on his own, whether under the influence of ardent spirits or not, for it is beyond our power to alter the record. We can only plead certain extenuating circumstances in his behalf and let the reader be the judge, if judge he must.

It is a simple matter of logistics that no tight-fisted Nova Scotian shipowner was going to permit any vessel of his to sail to the West Indies with a hold full of lumber, fish or potatoes and return in ballast. The most plentiful and profitable of all West Indian offerings in the export trade came in barrels and was called rum. The stuff was easily made and easily acquired, easily stowed below, and once arrived at its destination, easily disposed of.

Now this was a pioneer age of hard-drinking, as every age is. Rum, whisky, brandy, Madeira, beer or what will you have were universally popular among all classes, but especially rum. For rum was what fueled the West Indies trade, made England strong and America great and kept the Provinces alive, and it oiled the wheels of commerce so nicely, and made all run so smoothly and every man so happy with his lot, that indeed it achieved the status of a liquid currency. What could be more advantageous to the expanding capitalist than to foster among the working men a disposition literally from childhood to take their wages more in rum and less in cash . . . and the more of the one, of course, the less demanded of the other.

A case in point was the first bridge to be built over the Lahave River around this time at Bridgewater. The men logged so many hours going to and from the tavern some distance off that the boss of the job concluded the stream would never be spanned unless strong measures were taken. Did he forbid his men to drink? On the contrary. He had a rum room partitioned off in the tool shed at the works, laid in a supply and charged each man's drinking against his wages. When the job was done (and it was a good bridge, too) many were in debt to their employer. It took twenty-seven puncheons of rum first and last–two thousand gallons more or less–to build that bridge.

It was so nearly universal in Nova Scotia to accept part of one's wages in rum that the man who didn't drink wasn't thought much of, and the earlier he started, the more to be admired. Rum flowed copiously on muster days, during court sessions and at launching and hauling parties, and every other occasion, work or play. No farmer would think of asking the neighbors to lend a hand at the raising of his barn without providing a bucket of rum and a tin half-pint to dip it with. Like as not, the male guests at a wedding and the groom were drunk for two days just to rouse things up for the arrival of the minister and the happy bride.

Occasionally abstinence was forced on a young fellow by circumstances beyond his control. One such youngster who lived to the south of Chester Bay was so poor he had to walk into town barefooted when he went. The people used to be so thick in the taverns that they would tramp on his feet and hurt him, so he had to give up going in until he got shoes.

Well then, it was a hard mold of the backwoods and the sea that Jimmy Pattillo was forced into, scarcely schooled at all, and for better or for worse (though Father Dimock might rail against it) he who could hold his liquor and use his fists—besides tackling the work of the world—was the one to be reckoned with.

So it came about that Jimmy, at the age of fourteen years and three months, was having a little celebration of the New Year with a few friends and a bottle or two in the tavern kept by Lot Church in Chester. Their host was a big, affable political type of gentleman who came up from Massachusetts with the Loyalists when he was six and established such a solid reputation in the county for patriotism and honesty ("as honest as Lot Church," people said) that he was even now serving his first term as an Assemblyman.

Jim and the gang were in the taproom having a few, minding their own business and not bothering anyone, when they were joined by a fellow named Murphy, a regular brawler, twenty-seven, known as the bully of Lunenburg County and proud of it.

In a confidential way Murphy got all heads together and said how about that bunch with their girls upstairs—wouldn't it be a great joke to start off the New Year by cutting off their supplies?

Hot from liquor and hitherto peaceful but now spoiling for a taste of battle, Jimmy Pattillo and Jim Gorman and George Millett and the others sailed into one of the young swains from above named Corkum, who was on the way back up with a tray of crackers and gingerbread and bottles of shrub and aniseed, and they tipped the lot on the floor, about seventy-five cents' worth. Poor Corkum went hollering up the stairs that Pattillo and Gorman and the gang below wouldn't allow anything up from the tap.

Meanwhile, the villain Murphy had slipped upstairs himself and joined the party in progress. When Corkum raised his cry, the bully was all innocent rage and burst out of the room with "Leave it to me–I'll fix'em!" and charged down the stairs. The girls all rushed with a squeal from the chamber and lined the stairway to see the fun.

Murphy, the rogue, went for Jim Gorman first, but Gorman was seventeen and a quick thinker and told him to wear off as he had three brothers in the tavern (which he didn't). So next in line was the Pattillo kid, and Murphy hauled off and gave him such a crack on the jaw that he staggered across the room and out the door and collapsed in the porch. Murphy was after him like a bull, and as the boy was trying to get up he was on him, half hauled him to his feet and threw him out into the street. Jim struck his head on the frozen ground, skinned his nose, drove pieces of gravel into his palms and ripped a brand-new suit of broadcloth in the bargain. He struggled to his feet again and Murphy, waiting for him, slugged him in the mouth and down he went on his back.

There he was, sprawled out on the frosty street in front of Lot Church's tavern, with his young belly full of New Year's liquor, the grinning bully hulking over him, all the gang and the girls in a crowd waiting to judge whether Jimmy Pattillo was just an overgrown kid after all . . . or a man according to the lights of the world.

"Jim, what are you afraid of?" . . . the voice of George Millett, half mocking, half encouraging, drifted through.

And he shook his head and pushed himself to his feet for the third time. He squared off and with a hard left hook split Murphy's ear open (Lot Church later put in five stitches).

Murphy didn't go down but wheeled around on his heel and came back at Jim with a blow on his forehead that raised an egg. He followed this with looping rights and lefts as fast as he could throw them, but Jimmy was seeing straight now and warded them off with his arms, ducking and parrying and working into a spot on ground higher than his opponent, who like a madman was exhausting himself.

When the opening came Jim was ready. With a great blow he knocked Murphy down; and as soon as the man was on his knees the boy knocked him down again, up and down, down and up for two hundred yards through the frozen street to the shouts of the crowd, until the bully of Lunenburg County lay where he was and gasped out that he'd had enough.

The fight got to be the talk of the township, if not the county, and no one was prouder of this chip than the old block it came from. Alexander now commenced to look for opportunities to show off the brawn of the son who was sixty-three years younger than himself, and one was not long in coming.

A few weeks after the New Year's brawl father and son loaded the shallop with seventy-five barrels of lime and set sail for Lunenburg. On arriving there they found a vessel taking out dried fish from Labrador on the other side of the wharf. Mr. Oxner, who was having the fish weighed off and trundled into his store, jabbed a finger in the direction of the crew who were busy at it and commented slyly to Alexander that they couldn't produce such stout men as those over in Chester. There were eight in the crew, all Lunenburg Krauts, and not one of them under six feet.

The old man looked them over, and then he said to the storekeeper: "God mon, I hae a mere lad aboord ma vessel wha' can carry in yon han' barrow moor than ainy wan o' yer Dutchmen."

Oxner proposed a trial of strength and the wager of a new silk hat on the outcome, which was accepted. Father took son aside:

"Jimmy lad, carry yon barrow wi' th' best o' th' Dutchmen, an' if ye dump 'em ye hae silk topper from Mister Oxner an' anoother t' match it from me. Noo gae ahead, boy, ye can do it!"

All gathered round to see what this big youngster from Chester could do, and they picked Adam Hebb, who was six feet three and weighed two hundred and seventy-five pounds to carry with him. George Tanner, skipper of the vessel in from Labrador, who knew the Pattillos, took over the loading of the barrow, which was but a wood frame between two sets of handles. As he kept piling on the fish, putting as much on one end as the other to make it fair, the giant German told Jim to say when, but the boy only replied:

"Well, I don't know how much I can carry; if you know when there's all you can handle and you can carry it and I can't, why then I'm beaten."

At that point Captain Tanner said there was enough for two horses and stopped. Hebb gave Jimmy his choice. The boy took the front, grasped the handles and asked the man if he was ready. Hebb said he was. Jim picked up his end in a quick motion and threw the weight over onto Hebb, but the man rallied, and they carried the barrow with its swaying load of salt fish thirty feet up the wharf to the store.

There was a three-inch step to get inside. Jim entered, and just as Hebb put his foot on the step the boy gave his own end an extra hike up, which threw the weight on Hebb for the second time and he dropped it.

They weighed off the fish and it came to seven hundred pounds, plus ten more for the barrow. Jim left Lunenburg with two fancy silk hats–one from Mr. Oxner and the other from his beaming old man.

Back in Chester, Jim signed as crew for Harry Hawbolt aboard his small coaster, *Lily of the Valley and Bear of the Sea*–a boat which, whatever other virtues she boasted, had the longest name on the south shore of Nova Scotia. *Lily of the Valley and Bear of the Sea* was a fine little vessel, and during the two months he shipped with Hy Hawbolt, the young fellow concluded that he must have her as his own. He had saved twenty pounds huckstering fish and other merchandise during the three summers he sailed with brother Tom, but Hawbolt wanted a hundred for the boat. So Alexander agreed to lend his boy eighty pounds, and the deal was made.

Thus, at the age of fourteen and a half, Jimmy Pattillo was

owner and master of his first vessel. His first voyage as captain of *Lily of the Valley and Bear of the Sea* he made to Halifax that spring of 1821, her hold stuffed with a hundred and fifty thousand shingles and a deckload of barrels (lumber now accounting for the greater part of Chester's business, with a half dozen sawmills in the township). After *Lily of the Valley and Bear of the Sea* had been brought in neatly alongside Fairbanks Wharf, her young master went into town to arrange for the sale of his cargo. While he was gone a large bark warped in to take on lumber for England, laying clean across the ends of Fairbanks and the next wharf over, sealing off the dock.

This was all right. When it came time to leave, Jim simply walked over to the master of the bark and asked him to slack off his stern docking line so the square rigger could swing away from the one wharf and allow room for *Lily of the Valley and Bear of the Sea* to slip by and out. The captain was agreeable, but for some reason one of the owners who happened to be on hand wasn't; so when the captain ordered his mate to slack off the fast, the owner countermanded him, which left *Lily of the Valley and Bear of the Sea* more in the valley than on the sea.

For a solution, Jim grabbed his axe, strode up the wharf and with one blow cut the fast in two, jumped back aboard his vessel and began to haul out by the bark, which was already easing off from the wharf. At this, the mate, a powerful man of about two hundred and forty pounds, dropped from his vessel to the deck of the smaller one, walked up behind Jimmy, knocked him down on the taffrail and gave him a few kicks for his insolence.

When the boy got clear of the mate he bawled at him: "By God, if there is any man around here that will show me fair play, I know I can hammer you!"

Captain Tom MacDonald from St. Mary's, who happened to be there with his vessel and was acquainted with all concerned, came up and offered the lad fair play, meaning he'd guarantee a square fight, no interference.

The boy and the man jumped on the wharf and a ring was formed. They squared off, and with one crack Jim knocked some flesh over the mate's right eye so he couldn't see and floored him in the bargain. Half blind from the blood, the man withal got back on his feet, and the boy floored him again. That ended it and a beefsteak was found for the loser's eye.

Although the loan from his father was agreed for two years, Jim paid it back in six months, and for four years he coasted in *Lily of the Valley and Bear of the Sea* until he was eighteen, when he sold her to Tom in the fall of 1824. The following spring he went skipper of a schooner for George Mitchell, who owned the store in Chester that was built on *Young Teazer*'s keelson. In due course they beached the vessel to scrape her bottom and paint her, and when the time came they brought her around to the Pattillo wharf for refitting.

The day was just right for the job, dry and no wind. The schooner carried a main topmast which had been lowered to be oiled and painted. Billy Smith went up in the bosun's chair to the mainmasthead to reset the spar. Jim hauled it up to him by the tackle, and when the butt was seated properly in the withe, he sat down on the quarter rail to splice the stay while Billy secured the mast.

A yell from aloft, and he jerked his head up. The spar had slipped and was dropping straight as a spear right for him. He froze. Down it came, raked the rim of his cap, skinned his nose and struck between his feet, smashed clean through the deck and fetched up below on the cabin floor, the top of it quivering in his white face.

It was a late afternoon the winter after he was almost impaled by his topmast that Jim, nineteen now, and his mate were in Halifax in George Mitchell's same little schooner, about to sit down to supper in their snug cabin. Outside, a regular nor'wester was whirling down from the Arctic, carrying a swirl of snow along with it. Vessels, wharves, sheds, harbor and town—all muffled in whiteness—were disappearing with the last light of the day. But down below, warm from the forecastle fireplace, about to dig into their dinner, Jim and his man discovered after some rummaging around that they had no candles to see by.

Said the lad: "I'll just trot up to Winton's shop above the Fuel Yard, buy some candles and be back in a jiffy while you keep the grub hot."

He pulled on his boots and coat, climbed out on deck and over onto the wharf and plowed through the drifts across Water Street, up Prince Street by the Fuel Yard of His Majesty and into Winton's, where he purchased two pounds of candles. As he was leaving, who should he fall in with but John Rogers, a butcher friend, who invited him up to the confectioner's shop below the Parade for a quick nip and a hand of cards.

Some hours, several games and six rounds of brandy punch later, the friends called it a night. Young Jim, remembering the long forgotten purpose of his errand and his mate back in the dark cabin with no light to see by, tucked the candles under his arm and hurried somewhat unsteadily down the street through the snow. All was dark and the flakes pelted him as he careened on, head down, when just as he turned the corner above the Fuel Yard a voice through the howling wind stopped him in his tracks:

"Halt! Who comes there?"

"The King of England, you whoreson! Go ——, you whoreson ——!" replied the boy captain thickly.

The next instant the sentry loomed out of the blizzard, collared this drunken rascal who dared to offer him such a hard time and marched him into the sentry box. Jim pleaded with the soldier to let him go and apologized for his insolence, all to no avail. The sentry was in a dark and unforgiving mood; it was a hard night to be on outside guard duty all alone, hard enough in the storm without being accosted by saucy drunks.

Jim offered the Redcoat a dollar for his release, then doubled it, but the man would not be bribed, arguing that once freed, his prisoner would report him and get him flogged for his kindness.

Perish the thought, protested Jim, and again he groveled for his saucy answer to the challenge, but the sentry was as cold inside as out this night.

"Well, at least let me walk with you," implored the prisoner. "I'll surely freeze to death in this box of yours. It's terrible cold–and look at me–I'm not dressed for it!"

So the sentry relented and let the culprit come and walk his post with him. Since the platform he trod was too narrow to take both abreast, the two fell into file, and when captor walked to the north his captive was in front of him, but when he about-faced and retraced his steps to the south, then the tables were turned and Jim brought up the rear.

Naturally he started to sneak off into the night on the southward march, but the soldier wheeled at the movement, poked the muzzle of his musket in his chest and ordered him back to the sentry box, offering to shoot him the next time he tried such treachery. However, once again he relented and let Jim walk with him.

Now here was a sobering situation. On the one hand was a soldier who'd as soon put a bullet through him as not if he made a wrong move; on the other, he could hear the Town Clock strike every quarter, and it was nearing midnight, the time for the relief. That, he thought to himself as he paced up and down with the sentry, would be the signal for his captor to hustle him off to the guardhouse, where without doubt they would rob him, as he had thirty pounds in his pocket.

The time to make a move is now or never, he decided, before the relief comes; and that means he must strike the soldier in order to make good his escape. But with what–his fist or the candles?

James gave this question of weaponry serious consideration, walking there in the snow, first ahead and then astern of his captor, and he concluded to keep the artillery in reserve and give the fellow just a tap with the candles, for after all, he had nothing personal against the sentry, who was just doing his duty.

He waited until the next southward march, and when the sentry reached the end of his beat in front of him and was wheeling to about-face, Jim gave him a little touch with the candles that knocked him down in a heap in the snow. The lad took to his heels, and just as he turned the comer of the Fuel Yard the soldier picked himself up and regained his wits enough to fire after him. The ball whistled past Jim's head, and he heard it thump into a board fence across the street from Winton's.

Sober as a saint now and struck through with the fear of God and the troops, he kept running up Prince Street looking for a place to hide, turned into Granville Street and remembered that directly across from the Province Building there was an auction room with a broad access platform that crossed over the open gutter into the street. He made for it and crawled under.

By this time the guard had turned out in force and was hunting the area high and low for the mad giant with the candles, cursing and hallooing, and some of the soldiers tramped past a dozen times, ten feet from Jim's refuge. The wind whished bitterly by above him and drifted the snow in over him; he was numb and blue with the cold but dared not move.

Some time after two in the morning a pair of soldiers clumped by in the snowy street, and he heard them say the guard had all returned to quarters, thoroughly tired of the search, for that fellow must be past Bedford Basin by now.

He lay there for another hour, close to perishing from the cold and listening for footsteps, but he heard no more. The time had come to make a break for it or freeze to death. He pulled off his boots and left them in the gutter so as to be as silent as he could, crawled out into the street and put his coat on inside out.

Walking furtively to Duke Street, Jim turned down and struck the waterfront near Collins Wharf. He took a skiff belonging to a coaster laying there and rowed over to his own vessel, quiet as could be, and snuck aboard as the Town Clock struck a muffled four in the morning–still carrying his two pounds of candles, what there was left of them.

4

A Chapter of Collisions

> The old stock comes from New England, and the breed is tolerable pure yet, near about one half apple-sarce, and tother half molasses, all except to the Easterd where there is a cross of the Scotch.
>
> —Sam Slick

JIM SAILED FOR George Mitchell until the summer of 1827, when he shipped with George Tanner in the *Susan* after a cargo of mackerel. While up the coast that way they took the time to ferry Father Dimock across the Gut of Canso to Cape Breton; the tough old missionary was on a tour of the Province, giving his all for the souls of men, and he was bound to hold a revival up at Mira Bay.

That September Jim crossed the threshold into manhood. Like his old father of four score years and four, he filled the doorway. He stood six feet in his boots and weighed two hundred and thirty pounds, and every ounce was bone, sinew and muscle. His strength was as the strength of ten, though not necessarily because his heart was pure.

A person could see that this young giant had a cross of the Scotch, all right; it was carved all over his fair and clean-shaven face, with its unexpectedly fine proportions for such a great braw laddie. He brushed his dark hair straight across, giving it a roguish curl over the ears. Eyebrows arched quizzically above canny blue eyes—half closed with some private amusement if the mood of their owner was benevolent, shut quite tight when he laughed. And when Jim laughed he laughed, no two ways about it; he opened wide and gave forth with a whole-hearted, full-throated rumble of roars that started right from the belly.

As for the nose, it was long and well built for its purpose and undamaged yet in battle. Stark cheekbones gave a Celtic lift to his countenance, as if drawn high by the tilt of the brows, leaving the cheeks and chops lean and hungry looking. These romantic features were anchored to reality by the obstinate breadth of the chin, which was fashioned of granite and hinged to a mouth of surprising fullness, at once self-indulgent and whimsical. Sticking out of it most generally was a cigar or pipe, for he was a slave to tobacco.

This great, coarse, vulgar, violent fellow was able to read with difficulty and could only barely write his name. Intemperate in the extreme, he waxed tempestuous, unpredictable and as totally ungovernable as a wild beast of the forest when under the influence of strong drink (in which condition he was to be found increasingly). Nevertheless, at twenty-one Jim possessed certain germinally redemptive attributes: he had his own peculiar brand of honesty, a turn of humor, the loyalty and leadership which invariably come in twos, flashes of tenderness or sentiment, a kind of earthy camaraderie, an exceeding sharp eye, natural seamanship of the first order, courage most certainly, and possibly other qualities which still lurked in the recesses of his personality.

Whatever may emerge from this singular minglement of Scotch, applesarce, molasses and rum, only time and patience can bring forth. But of that great glory of his young manhood . . . that Olympian strength . . . Jim was entitled to be (and was) extravagantly proud to a degree that exceeded the farthest reach of contradiction.

Such, indeed, was the conclusion of a gentleman whose veracity is beyond question and the evidence of whose eyes in this particular matter has already been recorded elsewhere. This observer was one day standing on George Mitchell's wharf in Chester watching young Captain Jim Pattillo prepare to take out a cargo of salt fish from the hold of his vessel. For what he saw he could scarcely credit his sight. But his eyes had not deceived him; there were other witnesses, too. After lengthy cogitation and with the utmost gravity–and throwing behind the statement the full weight of his reputation for sobriety and truth–the gentleman pronounced that in his considered opinion Pattillo was one of the strongest men ever born on the continent of North America.

Each of these barrels of fish weighed approximately two hundred pounds. Jim grabbed each in turn by the rim and lifted it up through the hatch onto the deck. When all were out of the hold and ready to be taken ashore, he seized a barrel, raised it to his right shoulder and shifted it around until it rested on his back and neck, steadying it there with his left hand. Then he bent over, embraced a second barrel with his right arm, tipped it onto his right shoulder, and, as he straightened, worked the first barrel over to his left.

In a trice he had them balanced to his satisfaction. He stepped over the rail onto the wharf and walked the length of it, easy as you please, a two-hundred-pound barrel of salt fish on each shoulder. And so, presumably, he went about it with the rest.

Inevitably the thoughts of such a man as this should tire, from time to time, of salt fish, rum and the rigors of the sea and turn instead to the charms of the hearth and home–in short, to love.

Hence, on the nineteenth of the next February after coming of age, it being the year 1828, James William Pattillo took Anne Gorman for his lawful wedded wife before the altar of the little Church of England church of St. Stephen's on the windswept hill above the town. The Reverend James Shreve united them, and brother Tom stood up with the great groom . . . or held him up, for if the wedding was like most of them, there was hardly a sober man besides the rector in Chester for a week fore and aft of it.

And what can we say of the bride? Was she as pretty as the old picture, wearing her grandmother's taffeta gown on this marriage day in the dead of the Nova Scotian winter? Was she tall or short, plump or slim, and did she have dancing Irish eyes and a dimpled smile that set the heart of her swain to pounding?

Anne was the next to the oldest of the ten young Gormans (it was her big brother who put the bully Murphy onto Jim in Lot Church's tavern that day), and she was almost a year the senior of her husband. They had known each other since childhood, for Pat Gorman, the father, came over from County Wexford, married Susannah Lynch (daughter of Tim the blacksmith) and settled down as a farmer and cooper over on what they called the Peninsula, a short stroll from the Pattillo family. The Peninsula was an island all covered with spruce, and it hung off in the Bay only a spit to leeward on a windy day from Chester across the causeway. Pat was a jolly one over a drop or two, and his barrels carried many's the ton of old Alexander's lime. But his wife died in the flower of her life in 1825, so Pat found another mother for his houseful, a slip of a girl named Mary Ann Frail, the same age as Anne, making stepmother and daughter more like sisters.

Then Anne Gorman up and married that wild Jim Pattillo, and the women in the town shook their heads and clucked their tongues. This is all that's known of Anne—except that the Fates did not love her.

They settled in Chester. In the summer Jim bought the *Resolution,* a happy little schooner, to go coasting. At the end of November Anne bore him a son. They called the skinny thing Alexander for his grandfather Pattillo, who was eighty-five—hoary and strong as ever—a wee baby to come from such great stock, and he would be their only one.

One night the next fall *Resolution* was running out of Halifax Harbor, the wind abaft, having delivered a cargo of mackerel. She was headed back to Prospect (halfway to Chester) for another load. The breeze was sharp but steady from the northwest, near midnight, and all around was blackness. Jim was asleep below. At the helm was his man George Millett, the same who taunted him to get off the ground and whip Murphy that New Year's. There was nothing at all to be seen and nothing to be heard but the rush of the water and the creak of the spars as the schooner plunged along, free and easy, a lonely lord of the sea.

At that instant, out of the dark, Millett caught the riding lights of a vessel—a sizeable one, much bigger than their own—bearing down on them, coming right for the *Resolution,* less than a cable length off the starboard bow.

He cried out for his skipper.

Jim vaulted from his bunk and scrambled up on deck. They could hear her now, the spray flying off her bow and the thumpeting of the wind in her canvas. She was a tall brigantine, beating toward Halifax on the port tack, sticking to her course like an arrow; she couldn't have seen them yet.

The two were now so close that it was too late for the schooner to swing into the wind and cross the bigger vessel's stern. So Jim grabbed the helm, kept off all he dared short of jibing and yelled out to the captain of the brigantine to luff, for God's sake, luff!—and come into the wind and lose way so the *Resolution* could scud past his lee.

But the other skipper—either misjudging Jim's intentions or figuring there would still be room for the schooner to cross his stern if he bore away from her—sang out to his helmsman to hard up. The wheel spun and his vessel fell off the wind and was picking up way just as the *Resolution* desperately tried to hurtle herself across his path.

With a fracturing crash the runaway brigantine angled into the schooner's side as if to mount her, bearing her over in a fearful shudder of splintering wood and cascades of water. Her long bowsprit speared over the rail and with the swift strike of a battering ram snapped the *Resolution*'s mainmast off at the deck. Her prow followed as she climbed with her bobstay, out of the water part way, crunching along her victim's flank, smashing through the bulwarks like matchwood and cutting away three stanchions before she fetched up fast, driven hard against the schooner, her sails filled and half a gale pushing her on, trying to sweep the smaller vessel aside and be on her way.

Lucky to be alive, Jim and his man with one thought leaped into the bowsprit rigging of the *Lady Ogle,* as she turned out to be, crawled on deck and made for the pinrails. In a mad fury they let go topsail and topgallant and jib halyards and braces and sheets and every other piece of running rigging within reach. In this they were joined by the stunned crew of the brigantine, and after a few more moments of stumbling and cursing about the decks in the darkness, all hands had shortened sail enough to take the wind out of her. Aloft her canvas slapped and snapped, and the yards careened and banged; she lost her way finally, and they got her clear of her tangle. The two Chestermen jumped back aboard their vessel, damning the brigantine, her master and the night that brought her, and afraid of what damage awaited them as the *Lady Ogle* bore off and slid past.

Feeling down on her starboard planking, Jim found to his relief that it was not cut through, and a hurried look below showed *Resolution* had not sprung a leak. But her broken mainmast, along with boom and sail—though they had fortunately not gone by the board—were leaning perilously over on the port side. So they wore her around, and when she gave her port quarter to the wind, it lifted the mainsail, which jibed to starboard and righted the mast. The port shrouds and spring stay now held it erect, and as luck would have it, the wedges at the deck kept the broken butt from slipping. They hauled down the mainsail and tied one of the parted starboard shrouds to a stanchion on that side, bringing the other aft to the mainsheet horse to keep the mast from pitching forward. Again they wore around, double-reefed and hoisted the mainsail, and under this jury rig hobbled that morning into Ketch Harbor, where they brought the crippled *Resolution* alongside of Jack Martin's stage.

Two spars served for sheers as Pattillo, Millett and a few friendly helpers slung the mast clear and hoisted the broken butt out of the hold. They cut a new step at the break, lowered the mast in place, wedged and rerigged it. Now the mainmast was seven feet shorter than the foremast, making it a mizzen, and *Resolution* resumed her voyage as a ketch.

Seven more trips the skipper and his mate made between Prospect and Halifax, their vessel dragging her heels and hanging her head with mortification every mile of the way, but when the last of the mackerel had been taken out, Jim bought her a tall new spar, and she was her old self again.

In the meantime he took the first opportunity to call on John

Stairs, master of *Lady Ogle,* where she lay at one of Sam Cunard's wharves in Halifax. Though only forty-two, Cunard owned or controlled forty vessels and had a finger in everybody's pie, for above and beyond his large mercantile operations he was expanding into whaling, lumbering, shipbuilding and ironworking and was the agent for the East India Company. The wharves of this diminutive son of a Philadelphia Loyalist were getting to be the center of the port's commerce. With the launching at Dartmouth two years earlier of the 140-ton *Lady Ogle,* named for the spouse of Rear Admiral Sir Charles Ogle, His Majesty's local fleet commander, Cunard inaugurated the first regular mail packet service between Halifax and Boston. It was to be on the basis of his successful experience running *Lady Ogle* to Boston and her sister ship, *Lady Strange,* to Bermuda that Cunard would contract with the British government to carry the mail between Liverpool in England, Halifax and Boston and thereby establish the first scheduled transatlantic steamship service.

Pattillo, however, was less interested in the extent and future of this tycoon's activities than he was in getting compensation for damages to his schooner. Captain Stairs was amiable and gave the young man a soft answer when he demanded that amends be made. He would do his best to make him whole, he swore, but since *Lady Ogle* was owned by Cunard and not himself, Jim would have to represent his case to his boss. In any event, he trusted that Captain Pattillo did not think he had run down the *Resolution* intentionally.

"I'm damned if I know whether you did or not!" was the heated reply from his visitor. "You took charge of both vessels, for we kept off the best we could and told you to luff, and you sang out to hard up helm and ran into me, carrying away my mainmast and three stanchions in the bargain!"

Captain Stairs arranged an appointment for Jim to take his case to the owner. Up in his office in his great stone warehouse at the head of his wharves, Sam Cunard heard the whole story of the collision, and the details were confirmed by the master of his own vessel. And who was in the right? If either had turned the other way, they would have passed in the night.

The founder of the world's most famous steamship line was described at this time of his life as "a bright, tight little man with keen eyes, firm lips and happy manners."

Bright and tight Sam Cunard certainly was this day, but happy he was not.

"Captain Pattillo," he concluded curtly, "I will not pay you a cent. If I did, it would set a precedent for every other vessel on the seas, and their masters would be running them into each other as often as they liked. Good day, sir."

Afterwards Jim wanted to take Cunard to court, but brother Tom, who had moved to Liverpool and was in the way of becoming a bit of a shipping magnate himself, advised against it.

"A suit will cost you more to prosecute than you'll ever gain," he told the young hothead, "for they have the power and the money in their own hands."

So Jim sold the *Resolution* and went to work for Tom, running his schooner *Rival Packet* in the coasting trade between Liverpool and Halifax that winter. But by the spring of 1831 he was back in his own vessel, the *Eleanor,* a stout schooner of sixty-five tons he acquired for coasting and carrying coal.

Along in May Captain Lynch employed Jim to sail to Halifax for a hundred and eighty hogsheads of salt to put aboard his brig at Chester, which he was readying for a salt fishing trip to Labrador.

When they got back with the salt and some other cargo, his mate, Ned Bone, disappeared and Jim couldn't find hide nor hair of him. So he hired David Evans, a Chester fisherman, in his place, and the two of them transferred the salt to the brig. Then he heard tell that Lynch had coaxed Bone away to ship with him for Labrador. When all the salt had been stowed aboard Lynch's vessel, Jim and his new man made the three-mile run over to Chester Basin, where they unloaded five casks of rum and molasses and twenty barrels of flour for David Crandle. They loaded three cords of wood, sailed back to Chester and took the wood out on the same wharf where the brig lay.

After these labors, master and mate went below. Evans was a

Liverpool waterfront, 1890s, where at least two schooners prominently displayed the American flag. (Provincial Archives of Nova Scotia)

middle-aged Welshman, and the very best of company, an old Navy man who had served on the great *Bellerophon* in the battles of the Nile and Trafalgar. He liked to call himself "one of Nelson's bulldogs," and was full of stories of the wars. Between them they drank six quarts of rum. Then with bursts of song, they unsteadily cast *Eleanor* off from the wharf, let her drift out into the harbor and succeeded in anchoring. Evans staggered below and fell asleep, but Jim took the tender and rowed noisily back to the wharf. There, lounging at the rail of the brig with a sassy look on his face, was Ned Bone.

"Is Lynch aboard?" asked Jim, doing a slow burn at the sight of the man.

"Don't ask me," sneered Bone.

"Has he got all his crew for Labrador?" inquired Jim fiercely.

"I guess he does–and the best crew he ever had, too!" Bone smirked.

Jim ticked off the names of all the men he could recall had shipped with Lynch in late years, and then he roared:

"I see you ain't among 'em, but now you've left me flat for Lynch, and I suppose you think you're the one makes it the best crew he ever had, you son of a whore!"

Bone replied with an oath, leaned over the rail and shook his fist at his ex-skipper.

At this Jim sprang from the wharf, hurdled the rail in a leap, and knocked Ned flying into the scuppers, bellowing the while:

"By God, Bone, I can hammer you and Lynch and the whole lot of you and I will!"

The Pattillo half of the six quarts of rum was beginning to work.

The commotion brought Captain Lynch and Mr. Lovett, one of the owners, out of the cabin and onto the quarterdeck on the run, and when Lynch heard this challenge and saw Bone sprawled out in the scuppers and the dark look on Jim's face, he wagged a finger at him and warned:

"Jim, if you hurt any of my crew so as to injure my voyage, I swear I'll make you pay for it through the nose. Now get the hell off my vessel and go stick your head in a bucket of water!"

Pattillo sauntered with drunken dignity over to where Lynch and Lovett were standing on the quarterdeck.

"Now I'm just here on a little piece of business. I come for my nine pounds for the hundred and eighty hogsheads of salt I brought down from Halifax and put aboard of this brig."

"Get out of here and go to the owners and get your money!" growled Captain Lynch impatiently.

"Now lissen Lynch–you're the one hired me and by God this vessel don't leave the wharf till I'm paid!"

To settle it and get rid of this troublemaker, Lovett stepped forward and paid him the nine pounds, and as quick as he stepped back, Lynch gave Jim a shove with his foot and toppled him off the quarterdeck, which was a foot higher than the main deck. The big one fell and struck his head against a hatch coaming, and as he lay there half dazed from the blow and the rum, Lynch's crew, who had been standing around watching this exchange, piled in–

all fourteen of them—and jumped on him and gave him a few pelts and kicks, raising an egg on the right side of his jaw, and then Lynch called them off.

Down but not out, Jim hauled himself to his feet and told Captain Lynch he thought that was pretty hard treatment, considering that his father had brought him up after Lynch's stepfather threw him out of his house, and many the night they had shared the same bed.

And then he let himself back down on the wharf, stripped off his shirt, took a position and roared up at the sixteen of them crowding the rail to come down and take him on, one or two at a time or any way they had a mind to.

Down they came from the brig and at him, and he hammered the lot, sending some reeling and rumbling across the planks of the wharf, dispatching others directly into the harbor. Poor Lovett should have stayed aboard, for Jim broke his jaw with one blow.

Putting on his shirt, he strode in an irregular but resolute fashion up into town and entered Billy O'Brien's tavern, identified for all by the sign that swung outside in the breeze, showing a milkmaid at her rustic task, with the invitation: "Come in, good friends, and you will see what beautiful milk my cow gives me."

Jim had no sooner demanded a bottle when panting and pounding up the road in hot pursuit came Constables Mills, Walter and Robinson! He took a long draught by way of girding up his loins, burst out the door with all the righteous indignation of a bull entering the ring and positioned himself in the road by the corner of the tavern, as this was the traditional arena in Chester for settling differences of opinion. Scraping a circle in the dust with his foot, he squared off and warned the three officers in the King's name to keep away.

For two hours he kept them at bay while a crowd gathered to witness the humiliation of the law by that great Pattillo, so drunk that staying on his feet was a miracle, but with fists as dangerous as ever. Then one of the crew he had beaten stood off a few paces and challenged. Jim fell for the trick and made for him. At last the three constables had their opening; Mills jumped on his back and Walter caught him round the legs, but the unlucky Robinson—a cooper by trade—was on the bottom when they all went down and had a couple of staves knocked in.

Surely they had the wild man now, and even Jim's old friend George Mitchell, who was Justice of the Peace, moved in to help. However, the rum was not through with him yet, nor he with it. He flung them all off, stretching Mitchell in the ditch with the rest, stumbled unmolested down to the wharf, oared out to the *Eleanor* and collapsed in his bunk. When he had slept it off he came back ashore and surrendered, for Jim was a peace-loving man when sober.

Mitchell the Magistrate was always strong for temperance, and more than ever now as he rubbed his bruises, so he put the culprit under bond to keep the peace until October, when he should appear before the Inferior Court of Common Pleas for the Middle Division, which would be sitting then in Lunenburg.

The case of James William Pattillo versus every man within reach was called the second Monday of that October, and six indictments were handed down against him—one for assaulting Mitchell the Magistrate, one for part-owner Lovett, one for Captain Lynch, and one each for Constables Mills, Walter and Robinson. Lynch's crew that he manhandled brought no charges, for they knew 'twas all in good fun.

Jim had engaged two of the best lawyers in the county—John Creighton, Queen's Counsel and an Assemblyman, and Judge of Probate George Solomon—and after the session he took his witnesses and hurried to their office. The barristers were less than encouraging; they thought they could get him acquitted of four, but the other two would likely stick, and if they did, the judge would salt him pretty thoroughly. So they advised him to plead guilty to the lot and throw himself on the mercy of the court.

There were fifteen solemn men in their wigs and robes on the bench the next day—fourteen magistrates led by none other than Chief Justice Thomas Chandler Haliburton, the creator himself of Sam Slick, Nova Scotia's famous humorist who some thought was more interested in jokes than justice.

James stood in the dock and pleaded guilty to the six indictments. The judges withdrew from the crowded courtroom, and when they had filed back in Justice Haliburton pronounced sentence. Pattillo was to be fined a hundred and fourteen pounds and bound over in two thousand pounds to keep the peace for a year.

Did the defendant wish to make a statement? Yes, yer honor, he did. Well make it then, here's your chance. So Jim looked the bench up and down, pounded the rail of the dock with his huge fist and bellowed for the whole courtroom to hear:

"If I had the same thing again I'd do it over tomorrow, yer honors! When sixteen men, three constables and a magistrate can't handle one man with three quarts of rum in him, then by God they ought to go in the woods where the sun will never shine on them!"

"That's enough!" said Sam Slick from the bench, looking as grave as he could in the face of this embarrassing indictment by the prisoner and the burst of horselaughs it drew from the spectators. "Sheriff, do your duty!"

Sheriff John Kaulbach, known far and near as Hy but very official and imposing today in his cocked hat and sword that whacked his knees when he walked, stepped down from his box to the dock to collect the fine.

"Hy," rumbled Jim, stabbing a finger against the sheriff's chest for emphasis, "I've fifty pounds in my pocket and a load of coal in the *Eleanor.* You send a man down to the wharf where she lays to sell the coal, and with what he gets for it I'll pay him his time and you your hundred and fourteen pounds."

While Kaulbach was cogitating this proposition, a friend of the Pattillos named Snow Freeman, the agent for the American Consul in Liverpool, stepped up and paid the fine himself in gold, whereupon the Sheriff steered the defendant out of the dock to the door and inquired where they would be going next to get his bonds.

"What the hell d'ye mean, where are *we* going?" his charge burst out. "I never in my life walked the streets of Lunenburg County or any other with any officer, and I don't propose to begin with you, and more than that, any men I'd ask to go my bonds, you wouldn't accept their names. By God, I haven't brass enough in my face to ask any man to go my bonds for two thousand pounds, and if you're afraid I'm going to run away, go ahead and lock me up in the jail!"

"All right, Jim, all right." Sheriff Kaulbach slapped him on the shoulder. "Where will I meet you tomorrow at nine in the morning?"

They agreed on the tavern kept by John Fredericks and parted.

Jim walked straight to the tavern in the morning, slumped down at a table in some dejection and called for two quarts of gin. What a fix! By thunder, Haliburton had salted him good! Where the devil was he going to find anyone to go his bonds? Keep the peace for a year . . . he might as well go to jail and be done with it . . . him with a wife and kid. . . .

"Hey, Jimmy! They salted you pretty hard today!"

He looked up. It was Joe Webber, an old family friend from Chester, in Lunenburg on business and one of the lookers-on in court earlier.

"Yes, they did that," he grunted. "The fine is nothing, but they're going to lock me up in jail for a year; there ain't a man alive fool enough to go my bonds for two thousand pounds."

Webber regarded the gin bottles for a moment.

"Jimmy," he said suddenly. "Promise me just one thing, and I'll go your bond for one and find another man in ten minutes for the rest. Get off the bottle from the time the bonds are signed until you're released from them, which is a year. Can you do it?"

The other way was jail. The big fellow gave his promise. Webber and Jasper Zink, a leading citizen of Blandford, signed the bonds. Jim sold his cargo of coal, repaid Snow Freeman for the fine and had eighteen pounds left in his pocket when he sailed back to Chester. True to his word, he allowed not a drop of hard liquor to touch his lips for a year from that date on.

More Collisions, with a Look at the Rogues' Hole

CAPTAIN PATTILLO was twenty-five when he made his first trip to the United States, and it came near being his last anywhere. During the course of it he learned why seafaring men from the Provinces called the place the Rogues' Hole.

This enlightening experience occurred in March of 1832 while he was still bound to keep the peace after his free-for-all with Lynch and the bunch in Chester. He had a load of potatoes he wanted to sell in New York if he could locate a buyer, and to that end he got letters of recommendation from friends in Liverpool to Messrs. Bartley and Livingstone on lower Broadway.

The voyage was not remarkable, and six days out of Nova Scotia the *Eleanor* skipped through the Narrows and along by the Brooklyn shore, tacked amongst the confusion of shipping into the East River, and with the Battery still close on her port quarter, hove to and brought up smartly at the Old Slip.

Her canvas had hardly collapsed on the deck when she was boarded by an old acquaintance of Jim's, Captain Grahamson, master of a vessel belonging to Halifax that was lying in the same dock. After the usual pumping of hands and talk of their respective passages, it developed that Grahamson was himself consigned to Bartley and Livingstone, and he offered to conduct his countryman to their offices and introduce him, a courtesy gratefully accepted.

Leaving his man in charge of the schooner, Jim set out with Captain Grahamson, taking marks of the journey so as to find his way back. Old Slip was one of the very earliest landing places in the oldest part of Manhattan, and it still maintained its ancient appearance even as the working waterfront consumed more and more of the shoreline of the island up the East River and around the Battery and along the Hudson side, for New York was bound to surpass Boston as the great port of the East–its growth fed, ironically, by Massachusetts money, vessels and cargoes.

South Street was the trunk from which most of the East River wharves branched, and what a thrill it was to pause in the middle of it and look up or down either way–keeping clear of the crying, cursing, calling, clattering crowd of hustlers, hostlers and hawkers and their beasts and vehicles that rushed or loafed the length and breadth of the thoroughfare from pier to pier and back and forth to the almost solid wall of sturdy warehouses and maritime establishments facing the harbor on the city side. The greatest sight for sailor or landsman, though, was the prickly barricade of tall masts and crosswise yards that pierced the sky from the slips as far as the eye could see, while right overhead and then on down the length of South Street the bowsprits and jibbooms of the packets and schooners angled a third of the way in above the cobbles, an honor guard of knights for the passing pedestrian, their lances at salute. No wonder they called it the Street o' Ships.

Through the busy back lanes of the commercial district and out onto Broadway this Saturday afternoon the two Nova Scotians walked, and in short order they were being ushered into the presence of Messrs. Bartley and Livingstone, to whom Captain Grahamson introduced Captain Pattillo before departing on business of his own. The partners scanned the young skipper's letters of recommendation, inquired for their friends in Liverpool and questioned him about sundry matters pertaining to conditions in the Provinces and his cargo of potatoes in particular. By the time they had finished, dark had fallen.

Captain Pattillo could find his way back to his vessel, they supposed.

Jim thought so, thanked them and took his leave. He walked and walked, and walked some more, but everything looked strange to him, especially so since the day had gone and the streets were only dimly lighted. At length he decided that he had lost his bearings completely, and rather than go further astray, he stopped a passerby who looked to be a gentleman and asked the way to the Old Slip.

The New Yorker said he could do better than that; he would conduct him there personally if the captain–as he was plainly a seaman–would merely pay him for his time. Jim offered him twenty five cents, which was accepted.

The Good Samaritan took him by the arm, and they walked and walked, and walked some more, up this street and down that, through one alley and across another. At about eleven o'clock Jim was suspecting that his guide was either as lost as he was or was deliberately drawing him away from his vessel instead of towards it and told him so.

"Come now, Jack," broke in the New Yorker with a show of indignation. "Do you take me for a man of that kind, eh?"

"Your appearance looks well enough," said Jim with exasperation, "but I am satisfied that I have walked fifty times as far as I should have from where I met you to the Old Slip."

By now they had for some time been shouldering their way through as tough and squalid a quarter as Jim had ever been in. The streets and alleys were littered with filth, and all about were wretched tenements, flophouses and roaring joints. Even at this late hour, and dark as it was, ragged urchins scampered across his path, and in every shadow lurked a hard-looking character with malevolent eyes or a baggage who reached for him as he strode past, the unwilling companion of his guide, whose intentions he was beginning to seriously question.

As if reading the big one's thoughts, the New Yorker nudged him toward the doors of a saloon with the suggestion that a drink would help speed them on their way. Full of smoke, stink and cursing low-life, this was a den of thieves, thought Jim, and he told his pilot that he wanted nothing to drink, only to get aboard of his vessel at the Old Slip.

But the New Yorker insisted. He hauled his sucker over to the bar and ordered a brandy while Jim, mindful of his pledge but more urgently of the need to have his wits about him, called for a spruce beer, which besides being only mildly alcoholic was a wholesome sailor's drink, having been taken against the scurvy long before the limes were ever thought of.

They stood around for a few minutes, and then they had another round, the New Yorker inviting several blaggardly looking ruffians in the place to join them. Big Jim took out a half a dollar and slapped it down on the marble top to pay for the house, and while he was returning the change to his pants pocket his guide, to his amazement, reached over and brazenly as you please stuck his hand in the sailor's vest pocket and took out two Spanish dollars.

"Friend, don't make yourself quite so free until you're better acquainted," muttered Jim, maintaining his composure and pulling off from the fellow. "You can just hand me back what you took."

The New Yorker wanted him to tell what it was first, and Jim complied, upon which his guide up with his fist and struck at him. Jim partly countered it, but the blow cut his lip and made the blood run. He wiped his mouth with the back of one huge hand and said in a slow, quiet voice full of warning: "My friend, two can play at this game, but I have not come here to fight. Give me back my two dollars and direct me to the Old Slip as you agreed to, and that is all I ask."

"I'll Old Slip with you!" yelped the con man with a curse and made another crack at him.

But Jim was at the end of his patience. He knocked the blow aside with his left as if it were a feather, and with one quick flick of his right he laid the rogue out in the sawdust on the floor, stiff as a pilcher. Then he jumped on him with both knees in his stomach, reached into his pocket and regained the two Spanish dollars.

Here was a turnabout, and the rest of the gang pulled off their jackets; they dragged their fallen comrade to one side and made for the intended prey.

Pattillo, however, was now so disillusioned by his reception in friendly little old New York that he stationed himself in the corner where the bar met the wall, and each and every one of his attackers who ventured to come within range, he stretched out across the room. One big mucker sneaked around behind the bar, thinking to catch him with his back turned. But Jim eyed him in time, reached across the marble, grabbed his shirt with his left hand, pulled him halfway over and hit him such a whack with his right that the rascal crashed almost the length of the shelves in back before he fell out of sight, sweeping kegs, bottles, glasses, mirrors and a fine double flint decanter to the floor in an ear-shattering explosion of breaking glass and splintering wood.

The proprietor ran out into the street, yelling for a watchman. Soon one came on the run and burst in at the doors, cudgel in hand. The white-faced owner pointed a quivering finger at the Nova Scotiaman, who was catching his breath in the corner, lord of all he surveyed (which was a shambles), and shouted with high-pitched hysteria:

"There he is! There he is! That's the one! Arrest him! Arrest him!"

"Yes, by God!" panted Jim. "Here I am sure enough, and sorry to be here! But don't lay a hand on me," he warned the constable, "or by God I will stretch you out the same as the rest and that bag of bones there who promised to take me to the Old Slip and stole two dollars from me and struck me and cut my lip, and there he is laying there and all those other fellows who tried to pepper me, with him! Now I will go with you, and I want you to direct me to the Old Slip or to prison, one or the other. But I have letters to Bartley and Livingstone on Broadway, and by God see if I don't get some satisfaction come Monday morning if I have any more hard times tonight!"

The watchman looked at the great lad, and he surveyed the debris, and the bodies sprawled out on the floor that were starting to come back to life, and he told the sailor his guide had taken him into a section called Five Points, the cesspool of New York; he was a lucky young fellow to be alive and should know better than to trust strangers, for he was beyond twenty blocks from the Old Slip.

And then he said, "Come along with me, Jack," and walked with him to the edge of his beat, where he wrote on a piece of paper, "Direct this man to Old Slip," which Jim handed to the next watchman, who steered him true, and at two in the morning he boarded the *Eleanor* at last.

Rogues' Hole, right enough! And a cut lip to show for it, too!

The next week Captain Jim sold and took out his cargo of potatoes and, through the good offices of Bartley and Livingstone, chartered the *Eleanor* to Smith, Wood and Company for several voyages to Joggins, Nova Scotia, after grindstones. Joggins was way up in Cumberland County near New Brunswick, beyond Fundy and most to the head of Chignecto Bay, and it was famous grindstone country due to its extensive sandstone deposits, which were quarried close to the low-water mark, where the action of the tides had exposed the beds.

A good Joggins grindstone was greatly in demand wherever an axe or knife needed a most particular fine edge. Captain Sylvanus Smith used to tell the yarn about Mr. B, the Cape Ann storekeeper who, as he said, "like the ancient Greeks, kept his accounts by characters representing the article sold, and while often these meant nothing to others, they were full of meaning to him. In settling an account with a certain customer there was a dispute as to the article charged (which happened to be a cheese) and the customer showed Mr. B conclusively that he could not have bought a whole cheese. After considerable talk and discussion, and many references to his book, Mr. B recalled that the circle he had drawn represented a grindstone, but that he had neglected to put the hole in it. The customer recalled having made such a purchase, and matters were settled satisfactorily."

Pattillo pursued the trade in grindstones all that summer of 1832, and at the expiration of the charter in the early fall, being stranded in New York without a cargo, he thought he'd try his hand at smuggling . . . an avocation to which was attached very little opprobrium back in Nova Scotia, where one measure of a seafaring man's stature was the quantity of contraband he had the ingenuity to move undetected past the ever-suspicious noses of His Majesty's Customs Officers.

Jim ordered four hundred dollars' worth of rum, brandy, tobacco, tea, boots and shoes, to be delivered on notice. He and the old Portuguese he had engaged to sail with him (who knew nothing of his intentions) next built a rough wooden platform across *Eleanor*'s keelson at the bottom of the hold. Then he had about twenty-five tons of mud and stones hauled alongside for ballast.

He gave his man a dollar and told him to go have a little spree. While the old salt was gone he hired a wagon, brought his goods down and spread them out on the platform in the hold, built another platform over the whole business and hired three Irishmen to shovel the mud and stuff on top.

His man staggered back aboard in the wee hours, none the wiser and glad to see that the dirty job of ballasting had been done in his absence. At dawn *Eleanor* stood out of New York Harbor with as fair a wind as vessel ever had, for seventy-two hours later she was back at her wharf in Chester, nearly six hundred miles.

Jim paid off the old Portuguese, took out a barrel of flour and some things he had bought for Anne and his mother and went home. To give himself a couple of days of house and hearth before he disposed of his contraband (and to put it out of harm's way the while), he slipped the word to Timmy Gorman, one of his young brothers-in-law, and Tim Smith to bring another lad and take the *Eleanor* across by Peggy's Cove or anywhere they liked that was out of the way and fish for themselves until Sunday—but to hustle up and leave, which they did.

And in the nick of time, for there were a few men in Chester bound to get even with that Pattillo after the way he had used them on one occasion or another between his temper and his drinking and his fists. No sooner had the *Eleanor* come sailing into the Bay than something made two or three of these former friends smell a rat. So they sneaked into a skiff and rowed clear across the Bay to Lunenburg, a distance of twelve miles, where they fetched Dan Owen, the Customs Officer, and offered to bring him back to seize the schooner, for they were sure Jim Pattillo was smuggling.

Twelve miles back they rowed, with the Customs man in the stern, half-frozen from the autumn chill on the night water. They glided into the slip at about eleven o'clock, but no sign of *Eleanor.* They stepped ashore for a little conference in the dark. Meanwhile, the object of all this passing to and fro had been informed by someone what was up, and not wanting to miss the fun, he slunk along by the inside of the fence, crouching low, past his house to where they were huddled at the head of the wharf.

"The vessel was here when we left," protested one.

"Well, she ain't now!" growled Owen. "What kind of a wild goose chase is this, anyhow?"

"He's given us the slip, that's what! He's smuggled in a load o' stuff, I'm sure of it. Pattillo ain't fool enough to leave the vessel, that's all. He's had it taken off somewheres, which is evidence enough o' what he's been up to."

Of course they had to take the grumbling Customs man back to Lunenburg and return again, forty-eight miles all told in the coming and going twice, every stroke of the way for nothing.

The lads were back with the *Eleanor* and a good fare of fish Sunday afternoon, as planned. They took out and Jim took over and set sail for Sydney, up around the bend of Cape Breton, where the coal mines were. A few miles short of his destination he put in near Bridgeport and laid a proposition before John Young, a tavernkeeper he trusted: Young should have the smuggled rum, brandy, tobacco, tea, boots and shoes–along with the invoice for the stuff–for the four hundred dollars it cost in New York . . . if he would give Captain Pattillo an order on his own account at Sydney for all the coal the *Eleanor* could carry.

Young was delighted with this deal, for he had ways of passing off the contraband at a profit that would far surpass the cost to him of the coal, which would serve the triple purpose of hiding the entire affair under a cloak of legitimacy, providing Jim with a ready cargo at Sydney and a hundred per cent profit when he sold it, no questions asked.

Sydney shipping piers, about 1871. (Beaton Institute, Cape Breton)

So the ballast was dumped. The rum, brandy, tobacco, tea, boots and shoes were removed from under the false bottom during the night and carted off to John Young's. Pattillo took the four hundred dollars and the order for the coal from his partner-in-evasion, sailed on to Sydney and filled the *Eleanor* from the mines with all she could carry. Decks near awash, they coasted down to Liverpool, and what he got for the coal was clear profit.

For the rest of the fall of 1832 Jim worked his schooner freighting coal out of Sydney. When the winds backed around from the Arctic northwest in November and brought snow, and the salt ice was forming along the north coast, he abandoned the trips around Cape Breton and bought two hundred cords of firewood from old man Knickle (Ku-nickle), figuring to carry it in lots from Chester to Halifax, where there was a ready market.

One cargo of twenty-seven cords he sold to the footman of Lady Sarah Maitland, the wife of Lieutenant General Sir Peregrine Maitland, the Lieutenant Governor in charge of Nova Scotia, to heat their residence, Government House. When the wood had been measured and certified by Fielding the Surveyor and delivered, Jim made out his bill and twice plodded through the snow to call for his money at the great stone mansion in the south end; but neither the Governor's lady nor her footman was in, and no one else could pay him.

Impatient to get about his business, Jim set up watch nearby. About four in the afternoon, zipping down Granville Street on the hard-packed snow, came a fine covered sleigh drawn by four horses at a spanking clip, hoofs pounding and bells jingling, a coat of arms on the door, the liveried servant he was looking for sitting up in the box beside the coachman, haughty as you please.

Just as this equipage was about to pass by, Jim jumped out square in its path, caught the bridles of the leading horses and brought the sleigh to a startled halt.

Lady Maitland was the daughter of the Duke of Richmond. She was very charitable, very musical and very unaccustomed to such a confrontation in the very street before her house. She put her head out the window and inquired with some asperity why the horses had stopped.

Jim came around and tipped his cap.

"Your Ladyship, I sold this man up here" (pointing to the footman in the box) "twenty-seven cords of wood for yer house. I've been round twice for my pay, but I couldn't find him nor you nor anyone else who knew about the transaction, and I want to get home and about my business."

Was he a married man? she asked, looking him up and down. He replied that he was. And so Lady Maitland dismounted from her sleigh then and there, went into Lawyer Johnson's office for the money and paid him on the spot. And as she was assisted back into her conveyance, she turned and looked him full in the face and declared with warmth:

"Captain Pattillo, I glory in your spunk!"

Some weeks later *Eleanor* was back at Market Wharf in Halifax with another cargo of this irksome wood. Jim and his man Mike Clancy had piled a cord and a half on the wharf, and while the skipper was off on some business nearby, one of the associate police court judges came by, an officious individual by the name of John Liddell, inspected the neat stacks and found one of the half-cords "a stick too short," as a woodseller would say. So he confiscated the half-cord and called Welch the truckman to cart it off to the Poorhouse.

Clancy ran across two wharves to where his captain was and told him a man was taking a half a cord of wood and wouldn't pay for it. Jim came back on the run with fire in his eye.

Where did Welch think he was going with that wood?

To the Poorhouse.

Who ordered it?

Judge Liddell, over there.

Jim walked over to the police justice.

"Are you going to take this wood to the Poorhouse without paying for it?"

"I am."

"Then look out for yourself!"

And Jim up and knocked the judge down. He jumped at Welch the truckman and stretched him out likewise, and then he grabbed hold of a wheel of the wagon and with one heave tipped it right over on the wharf—wagon, wood and horse all together in a heap.

The next thing, four soldiers and a sergeant had surrounded him with their bayonets and were marching him up across Water Street to the police court.

In short order he was standing before Mr. David Shaw Clarke, the other police justice, who had the distinction of being without dispute the fattest man in the town of Halifax and also one of the most amiable.

"Well' m'lad, d'ye know that man there and who he is?" inquired Shaw Clarke, nodding at his dishevelled colleague of the bench, who was almost speechless with rage and shaking like a leaf.

"Yes, yer honor, I know him."

"Well, did ye strike him?"

"I did."

"And what did ye strike him for, Captain?"

"Because he was stealing my wood!"

"Ah now," said Judge Clarke with a trace of satisfaction. "Tell me the whole story in your own way."

"Yer honor, this load of wood was not measured when I took it aboard, but it has to be measured out when I land it according to the surveyor's certificate. Now if every Tom, Dick and Harry who comes by steals a half a cord, what kind of returns can I make to my customers? As long as I have my health and strength, by God no man shall take my wood while I can defend it! So I knocked him, Welch, wagon, wood, horse and all down onto the wharf, and here I am to answer to the charge!"

Shaw Clarke stared at the big Pattillo, and then he said:

"Case dismissed. Ye can go about your business, Captain. If I had a hundred men like you I could make my way through the world!"

His first trip to Halifax of the New Year, in January of 1833, Jim was one frosty morning piling cordwood on Market Wharf when an elderly man with an official look about him strolled by, saw the name *Eleanor* on the stern of his schooner and came over. Identifying himself as Edward Duckett, His Majesty's Light Duty Collector and Surveyor of Shipping for the port, he requested a pound for the previous year's light duty (an annual fee based on tonnage, levied on coasting and fishing vessels for the maintenance of lighthouses and beacons in the Province).

Now Jim Pattillo had a chip on his shoulder when it came to officials generally and a particular grudge against the Customs men of his native land. He was contumacious by nature and by no means above baiting the King's men for the pure pleasure of it. So when Collector Duckett dunned him for the back light dues, he boarded the *Eleanor* and brought up from his cabin four packages of coppers which he handed the official, knowing well that the market at the time was so glutted with this particular coin that it had been suspended as legal tender.

Duckett reminded him of this, so Jim said he would have the coppers changed and to come back tomorrow morning. Both kept their promises, and next morning the Customs Officer was offered two half sovereigns, equal to a pound; but meanwhile he had changed his tune and now demanded another pound for the year that was beginning. Jim tendered four more packages of coppers. Duckett demurred and reproached him for trying to load down an old man with heavy coin. Jim told him he would have them changed and to return later.

Collector Duckett dropped by Market Wharf several times, but on each occasion the master of the *Eleanor* happened to be absent. He decided he was being put off. And so the next Jim knew, his man Mike Clancy came hustling to where he was a wharf or two off with the news that Constable James Ham was aboard with orders to collect the light money or seize the *Eleanor* then and there and take her across the slip to the King's Wharf.

This wouldn't do at all. Pattillo hurried back, jumped aboard and invited Ham below to his cabin, where he offered him the two half sovereigns and a pound note from his sea chest. But when the constable demanded an additional half sovereign for his services in coming down to make this collection, Jim exploded:

"You will not get another penny from me. If Mr. Duckett hired you, since he's in the pay of the government, then you'll have to go to him for your fee. Either you take the two pounds here and now or you must leave this vessel immediately or by God I shall put you out very quickly!"

Officer Ham was a big fellow and not used to being crossed. He reddened and suggested, with an appropriate oath, that Pattillo wasn't man enough to carry out this threat.

Jim bellowed for Clancy and Danny Ryan, his other man, to come below, and when they stepped into the cabin he growled at the constable:

"Will you agree to put the law aside while we see about that?"

"Sure!" Ham squared off with another oath. "Just try it!"

"All right, look out for yerself!" roared Jim, and he knocked the policeman into the fireplace. Then he pulled him to his feet and slammed him against the cupboard, caught him by the nape of the neck and the slack of his breeches and put him up on deck, jumped after, gave him a few more thumps and threw him over the rail onto the wharf.

Constable Ham was a tough nut, but he'd had cracks enough in the line of duty for one day. Beaten and covered with fireplace ashes, he picked himself up. There was a brawny Irishman standing by watching the fun, just spoiling for a brawl, so Ham mumbled at him to go aboard and take charge of the vessel, and then he staggered off to the Police House for help.

Already a crowd was coming on the run from all about the waterfront to see what was up. Jim warned the Irishman off, but thinking to make a grandstand play, the fellow ignored the advice and sprang aboard. The captain of the *Eleanor* picked up a stick of wood from the quarterdeck and gave him a clout that returned him reeling where he came from.

Officer Ham reappeared at the head of Constables O'Brien, Glazebrook and Clines, and they went for the docking lines to seize the schooner and move her to the King's Wharf.

"The first man casts off that fast I'll split his brains open!" bellowed the captain, raising his cudgel. "She's my vessel, and if there are any demands on her I'm ready to pay 'em, but by God yer not taking her while I'm here!"

The constabulary hesitated and drew back; Mr. Ball the grocer, who was in the crowd, took advantage of the moment to invite the parties into his store at the head of the wharf to see if the dispute could be settled without further bloodshed. They agreed. Pattillo threw down his stick and picked up his money and went with Ham and Mr. Ball.

Inside the store the grocer asked the officer what was the least he would take for his trouble (more than he had reckoned on, perhaps) in coming down, and he replied a dollar, so they settled for that and the light money for two years.

But this day James William Pattillo was half Scot and half mule. He begrudged every penny of that dollar. Taking his receipt, he stomped the block up George Street to the Police Court and stated his case to Shaw Clarke. The fat judge, however, was far too amiable to get in the middle of such an altercation and declared that he could not venture an opinion, that it was a matter for the Customs, for he knew nothing about it.

So Jim strode down Bedford Row to the Customs House and

stated his case to J. W. Madden, the Collector of the Port of Halifax. The Collector of His Majesty's Customs, however, was much too much the civil servant to get in the middle of such an altercation and declared that he could not venture an opinion, that it was a matter for the Governor, for he knew nothing about it.

So Jim marched up Prince Street to the Province Building and stated his case to Michael Wallace, the Acting Governor during the absence in England of Lieutenant General Sir Peregrine Maitland. The Provincial Treasurer, however, was too skillful a politician to get in the middle of such an altercation and declared that he could not venture an opinion, for he knew nothing about it at all.

Jim told the Acting Governor that by God he would go to somebody who did know something about it, and he pounded off to see Mr. John Johnston the lawyer, known far and wide as the Poor Man's Friend.

He gave the attorney a sovereign and stated his case and at the barrister's suggestion brought Mr. Ball the grocer who vouched for every word of it.

"Good, good!" exclaimed Lawyer Johnston, a smile overspreading his kindly face. "Now, if Mr. Shaw Clarke the Police Court Justice knows nothing about it, and Mr. J. W. Madden the Collector of the Customs knows nothing about it, and Mr. Michael Wallace the Acting Governor knows nothing about it—then see if I don't know something about it! Captain, go on with your business and leave the matter with me!"

Three months later Jim received a letter from the Poor Man's Friend enclosing a doubloon and informing him that this was eightfold compensation for the dollar he had paid Officer Ham.

6

In Which Jim Burns His Bridges

OLD ALEXANDER, the snowy-haired patriarch of the Pattillos, died that New Year's Eve of 1833 in the house he built on the ice-packed shore of Chester Bay. He was ninety. The ancient Scot's little grandson and namesake Alex, just turned five, was taken by his father Jim to the bedside, and never forgot the ghostly vision of the once powerful figure, gaunt and hoary as Father Time himself.

The auld one, the hard-handed and hardheaded frontiersman of New Scotland, was finally gone to his rest. He left Betsy, nineteen years younger but an old woman still, land-rich and money-poor. Two daughters and a son had gone before him to the grave. Of his living offspring, Tom was wedded to the Widow Perley and making his way in Liverpool. Margaret was the wife of Tom Bennett, a good farmer in Windsor. And Jim, the youngest–born when his father was sixty-three–was on the way to being a drunkard, a violent, moody giant married to a sickly and unhappy woman. What was to become of them and their spindly child?

After the service the family huddled in the snow-drifted churchyard of St. Stephen's, noses pinched, lungs tight from the January gusts that swept the hilltop. Behind was the spruce forest, green muffled in white; far down the blanketed slope and beyond the burdened roofs was the blue, the white-capped, the islanded Bay of the wilderness. Bitter and sweet were the feelings that filled their hearts as the long pine box sank into the earth.

Within a week of burying his father, Jim was off in the *Eleanor* for Port Joli, thirty miles to the westward of Liverpool, to take on twenty cords of wood. When they arrived, the sea was too rough for loading, so they anchored to wait for calmer weather.

Instead of steadying, the glass dropped and a gale of wind sprang up. At the height of it a vessel scudded into harbor under reefed lowers and dropped her anchors near the *Eleanor.* She was the brig *Rambler,* Captain Humphrey, bound for Halifax on the last leg of a voyage from Berbice, British Guiana, with a cargo of rum.

This wasn't the *Rambler*'s day. Her anchors found no good holding ground to bite, and with the full force of the gale gripping the brig, they bounced and dragged along the bottom until sure enough she fetched up on the beach. Fortunately she struck, or eased herself into the sand, in a favoring position, little damaged, and the storm abated before she took a pounding from the waves. Late in the afternoon the surf had subsided enough for Captain Humphrey to set about the formidable task of getting the *Rambler* off, the first order of business being to lighten her.

By nightfall all hundred and ten casks of rum had been taken ashore, rolled up on the beach and ordered under a strict watch.

What an optimist! The light of dawn revealed that two hundred gallons were missing from various casks, and Port Joli was jolly in deed. Captain Humphrey thought that this would not do. He persuaded Captain Pattillo to forgo his twenty cords of wood for the time being and in their place to fill the hold of the *Eleanor*–and her decks if need be–with the hundred and ten casks before another night should fall, delivering them forthwith to the consignee, Mr. Thomas Laidlaw of Halifax, at the rate of a dollar and a half per cask.

The *Eleanor* loaded and sailed. Off Liverpool the wind shifted ahead, whistling in from the northeast, so they sought shelter in harbor.

No sooner had the schooner full of rum nudged with a gurgle against the wharf when His Majesty's Customs Officer, John

Freeman by name, was aboard. Looking to swell his collections, he sized up the situation in a twinkling and announced that neither vessel nor cargo was to be moved until the full duty had been paid on each and every cask. Captain Pattillo fulminated in vain; in the end he stayed put, for he was not about to pay another man's duty from his own pocket. A keeper was stationed on board until such time as Captain Humphrey should succeed in getting his brig off the sands of Port Joli and proceed on to Liverpool to take charge.

For two weeks the *Eleanor* lay at the slip in Liverpool on demurrage until the *Rambler,* having been floated on a high course tide, worked in alongside. Before agreeing to return her cargo to the brig, however, Jim drove a hard bargain with Captain Humphrey: though he had not completed his voyage, he should receive his dollar fifty a cask as originally agreed, since it was not his fault that he had been detained for a fortnight in Liverpool; also, the day's passage and another for unloading that it would have taken had he gone on to Halifax should be deducted from the demurrage, making the whole due him thirty-seven pounds in the mixed currency of the times. It was agreed. The cargo was reshipped from schooner to brig, and since the Customs man would not permit the *Rambler* to proceed to Halifax without a pilot, Captain Pattillo was engaged for the job.

Jim left *Eleanor* in the charge of his man John Mullins to take her to the same destination (with his old drinking partner, Nelson's bulldog Evans, for crew), and the two vessels stood into the stream in company.

Now, the chances of getting two days of good sailing weather to rub together in the month of January are about as rare as a day in June. The brig and the schooner were only off Lunenburg when the breeze again turned contrary and kicked up a choppy sea from the northeast. Since home was just up the Bay, they reached across and came to anchor in the lee of the Chester Peninsula. Jim rowed ashore to share his father-in-law's hearth and bottle, which between them might put some warmth in a winter's evening.

He was welcomed with open arms as always, and the walls of

Gorman were ringing with mirth and jollity when there came a knock at the door and in tumbled a young gallant from the village, well along in his cups and determined to pay court to Mary, one of the girls. There was that about the cut of his jib that backwinded Jim, himself three sheets in the breeze (which always aroused the chivalry in him), and he advised Mary in the strongest of terms to have nothing to do with the vagabond.

This brought a torrent of invective from the object of Jim's disapprobation, and there was an exchange of words between the two which ended when the young lion, ever the guardian of house and hearth, caught hold of Mary's spark by the nape of his neck and the slack of his breeches and threw him out the door.

It was a portentous act.

Again the welkin rang with rustic laughter. Late in the evening Jim wound up a most pleasant sojourn with the Gormans, undisturbed by further amorous invasions; he staggered down the embankment to his skiff and rowed back to the brig, cleaving the stillness of the night with a few rousing bars from a chantey that might better have been left unsung.

Next morning, the wind continuing contrary, he returned on shore with the intention of paying a visit on his widowed mother. He was striding through the snow past Mitchell's store, minding his own business and not bothering anyone, when up stepped a constable with outstretched hand as if in greeting; but the greeting was from William the Fourth, for the officer clapped his great townsman on the shoulder and announced that he James William Pattillo was his prisoner in the King's name.

"For what?"

"For abusing that man (pointing to the ejected suitor who was watching from a couple of hundred yards away) and throwing him out of Pat Gorman your father-in-law's house last night." The constable pulled a writ from his pocket, cleared his throat and commenced to read.

He was talking to the wind. His prisoner took off up the road with a roar and an oath. The complainant showed his heels, but Pattillo bore down and collared him. In less time than it takes to tell, the fellow (who was white with fright) promised to have the summons withdrawn, pay for the expense of its service and do anything else required if Jim would not hit him, for God's sake! Besides, he had been put up to it, for he was not the kind of a man to do such a thing to a man like Jim on his own hook—as Jim surely knew, eh?

So his captor unhanded him. They walked over to the constable, who was joined by a second officer, and all went up before George Mitchell the Magistrate.

Then came the rub. The fellow found his courage in court; his promise, he declared, had been made under duress (as indeed it had), and the law should take its course or no man in Chester would be safe from that great Pattillo. Magistrate Mitchell, who had taken some lumps from the defendant himself, was inclined to agree and ordered the prisoner held until he should raise bond, pending trial for assault.

Since it was for the sake of his sister-in-law Mary Gorman (her virtue and all) that he was in this mess, said Jim to the constables, let us go to Pat Gorman for the bonds. So taking each of his guards by the elbow he directed his steps toward the Peninsula. When they were crossing the causeway, one of them remarked that their prisoner no doubt could take and handle the two of them about as he had a mind to—to which he nodded agreement but reassured that he had no disposition to injure them so long as they went no further than their duty required. Thus were the ground rules established, in case there should be a game.

After the three came stamping through the snow up to Gorman's and had been let in and welcomed and brought before the fire, Jim told his father-in-law about the scrape he was in for putting that loafer out last night. The old man said sure, he'd go his bonds, so the son-in-law hustled one of the lads in to town to quick bring back a couple of quarts to celebrate.

In two shakes boy and rum were back, and one and all had a round and then another, including the constables of course. Along the line somewhere, the prisoner went aside and passed the word to the girls that he would be leaving before long and when the time came they should be ready at the doors to let him out, as he might be in too much of a rush to open them himself.

The rum went and the time came. Jim rose to his feet and addressed his captors:

"My lads, I'll say this much: I've given all the bonds in the British North American Provinces that I ever expect to."

The announcement caused not a ruffle nor a ripple; the constables judged this would be the case when they came to the house with him and said so.

"All right, boys, then there's no need for you to break your necks after me. I'll just take my leave and you can stay by the fire for a while, and when you make out your report just say I ran away and escaped."

No, no–the proposition was too bare-faced, Jimmy. It wouldn't do, not at all. They had been sworn to perform their duty to the King without fear or favor, and they said so.

"Boys, you know me well enough. You have no need to fear me, and I don't ask you to favor me. So watch out for yourselves!"

The constables looked at Jim and they looked at each other . . . and they called on Pat Gorman and his two sons to assist them to take James William Pattillo in the King's name (so as to clear themselves).

The prisoner threw them all off and hurtled himself toward the doors, which were opened in a wink by the girls. He ran towards Gorman's cooperage by the road but slipped on the ice going downhill, toppled and brought up against the shop door with a dreadful crash. This stopped his flight enough for one of his pursuers to catch up and jump on him. Jim rolled over and regained his feet. He swung the officer around and picked him up, walked him along and threw him over the stone wall into a snowdrift. This was sufficient to keep the other at his distance. Their prisoner waded through the snow down the embankment, got into his skiff and rowed out to the brig, again with a merry song on his lips.

Back into Chester walked the constables, nursing their lumps, and reported that Pattillo had knocked them down and escaped without putting up his bond. Justice Mitchell and the town fathers conferred and thought it the better part of caution to raise reinforcements. They rang the bell for the militia.

And so twenty-five of Jimmy's townsmen picked up their muskets and left their homes and their work and marched down to the beach. When they saw the great drunken bear out there, standing at the quarter rail with a marlinspike in one hand and a big grin on his kindly face, shouting cheerful insults at them across the water, they set about quarreling over who should be the first to board the brig and lay the hand of the law on him in the name of King William. None of them being anxious for the honor, however, they dispersed and went about their business, leaving Pattillo in possession of the field, as it were, and reminding of the little verse he had learned as a child:

> The King of France went up the hill
> With twenty thousand men;
> The King of France came down the hill,
> And ne'er went up again.

Next morning came on sunny and clear, with a fair wind for Halifax. The *Rambler* and the *Eleanor* ran up all their canvas, weighed anchor and sailed out the Bay. By nightfall they were at their destination. Captain Pattillo took charge of his schooner again where she lay at Strachan's Wharf and the following day walked up into town to round up orders for a cargo to Liverpool.

On his return in the afternoon he was swinging down Sackville Street, down under the brooding Citadel all in winter white, his boots crunching in the snow pack, whistling a tune to himself and not a care in the world, when Dan McLean stuck his head out of the door of his place, gave a call and beckoned him over.

Jim crossed the street and drove McLean half to his knees with a knock on the back.

"What's up?" he roared.

The proprietor recovered his breath and told him to pipe down, for God's sake, the constables were after him; they had been down aboard of the *Eleanor* looking for him, an army of them.

"For what?" asked Jim. "I don't owe any man in Halifax a dollar, and by God I'll tell you something else . . ." He trailed off in mid-sentence. Three constables were cutting across the way, headed for the door. Too late to escape. He vaulted over the bar and hunched up underneath in back.

The police came in and walked over to the bar. Had Jim Pattillo been in here?

He had.

"Well, if you see him Dan, tell him to come up to the Police Court and we'll make it as easy as we can for him. A party came in this morning had hiked all the way from Chester to swear out a warrant against him . . . said Jimmy had beat him up and thrown him out of his father-in-law's and then abused a couple of officers and resisted arrest and jumped his bonds and stood off the militia and escaped in a vessel. He must be on a binge again."

They had a drink and departed. Jim unfolded himself from under the bar and coolly asked Dan's brother Hector if he wouldn't like to go down to Strachan's Wharf and bring back his man John Mullins off the *Eleanor,* as he wished to have some conversation with him.

Just to take in the slack while waiting, Jim had a little drink, and soon Mullins came on the hobble up the street, for he had a terrible rheumatism in his back. With furtive glances to right and left, he ducked in the door. Outside it was starting to snow.

The mate was overjoyed to see his skipper; he was sure they had nabbed him. There was a frightful lookout; five constables came aboard, searched the whole vessel from stem to stern, all through the cabin and forecastle and lazarette. Yes, yes–he was glad to see him, but what now?

Captain Pattillo took his man by the arm and moved him back out of sight of the street.

"Jack, here's what you must do. Go down on board of Captain Phillips's brig at Long Wharf and get the two MacIntosh boys to come over and lend you a hand to haul the *Eleanor* out of the slip and across to the head of the wharf into the wind. Have the fasts all singled ready to cast off. Tie a reef in your main and your foresail and hoist them and take bonnet off your jib. Now when you're all done here's a dollar for to treat the boys and then come off and let me know and the hell with the constables."

Just to take in the slack while waiting, Jim had another little drink, and in an hour Mullins was back up the street again, humping along, all hugger-mugger. He slipped in and gave the report that everything was ready as ordered, and there was a brigade of constables combing the waterfront for his captain. The snow now was settling in thick, and there was a regular southeast gale in the making.

Pattillo cogitated this information and studied the deepening stone. He turned to Mullins.

"The hell with the constables. Get back to the vessel, Jack, and stick the axe in the capstan on the wharf and take a stand by the foremast with the jib halyard in your hand, all set to hoist away. When you've had the time to get ready, as I reckon it, I'll start down and the devil take anyone tries to stop me."

His mate went off in a swirl of snow, and the fugitive called for a pint of gin, which he poured down his throat without ceremony. The time had come.

Near the door was a tub of axe handles. He pulled one out and hefted it.

"I'll just borrow this, Danny," he muttered.

"Jim, you can have it," said McLean, with a look of consternation. "But I hope to God you'll do nothing you'll be sorry for after!"

"Not me, Danny boy, I'm not the type." Jim grinned. "I'll trouble no man if he don't trouble me." And with a hearty goodby and a wave of his axe handle, he stepped out and disappeared into the storm.

Nearly down the hill to Lower Water Street and abreast of old Johnny Brown's he saw all five of the constables coming up at him. He kept right on course in the middle of the road. Two of them crossed through the snow over by Robert Noble's place, apparently as a matter of tactics to engage his flank. The other three came for him.

Jim kept on as if to crash through them, when one of the three called him his prisoner in the King's name and raised his staff to club him. But the prisoner-supposed-to-be wrenched away the descending stick with one hand and tossed it off in the snow. He

Halifax in the 1820s. The Citadel dominates the town and harbor. In the foreground is Dartmouth Cove, where Jim and the Eleanor *took shelter in their flight. (Haliburton's* History of Nova Scotia*)*

let fly with his axe handle and stretched all three out in a drift.

Immediately his flank was attacked. The remaining two constables rushed on him from the side; one gave him a crack with his staff behind the ear that spun him right around, but he recovered and knocked his assailant senseless at his feet with a clip of the handle.

Now only one officer stood between him and his vessel. He swung at him, but the last of the constables was bound not to go the way of the other four if he could avoid it and caught the weapon before it struck.

Unfortunately for the forces of law and order, two could play this game; Jim caught the handle also, with his left hand, jerked the policeman toward him and hit him with his right. He broke a knuckle, and the officer's nose in the bargain, and the man went down beside his fallen comrades.

Jim sprinted the rest of the way to the wharf where the *Eleanor* lay, her sails faintly visible at the end of it through the flying snow.

"Up jib!" he shouted to the faithful Mullins, who for all the world like a snowman was well-nigh frozen to the foredeck. But old Jack could move at that, and while the jib climbed its stay to join the rattling reefed-down main and foresail, the great captain seized the axe from the capstan and slashed the bow fast with one stroke. Her head fell off from the wharf as the wind caught the jib, and the schooner filled away on the starboard tack. Jim jumped for the stern line, severed it with a blow and leaped aboard.

A cable's length from the wharf they shut the door and were gone in the storm without a trace, the snow was driving in so thick.

The two men worked the straining schooner across the harbor, close as could be to the wind. They came about with a flap of sail the instant the shrouded Dartmouth shore materialized out of the flying wall of snow. They beat back again on the port tack, but what a hard chance! Two legs against a southeaster blowing dead into Halifax Harbor and they just barely weathered Georges Island, so close it was visible in their lee in spite of the thickness of the storm. At this rate the hard-pressed *Eleanor* would be all night clearing Halifax; the wind was dead ahead, and the helmsman could see naught but snow beyond the bowsprit. There was a most awful risk of collision or of going ashore, with other islands to clear.

So Jim eased her a trifle and crossed the harbor for the third time, hove to just under the Dartmouth shore and they hauled down the mainsail and foresail. Hard down helm and turn her tail to the gale. *Eleanor* skittered behind the bosom of her jib into Dartmouth Cove, right across from the hidden Halifax docks, and they dropped both anchors for the night.

Pursuer and Pursued

NOW WHAT? Jim asked himself the question over and over, lying in his dark bunk aboard the *Eleanor,* tossing, trying to sleep, trying to stay awake, trying to think his way through the clouds of booze that fuzzed his brain.

What a stew he was in this time! It was the end of coasting to Halifax for sure, for they'd salt him good if they ever caught him now. Getting soused and hammering the constables . . . God knows he might have killed one. And that fellow of Mary Gorman's . . . that whoreson! He was the cause of it all, running around after him now with a writ in his pocket . . . Chester wasn't safe anymore, nor anywhere else on the coast, for the vagabond seemed sworn to hound him to the ends of the Province. . . .

Such thoughts as twisted and squirmed through his mind this night! Here he was, twenty-seven years of age already, and look at him . . . with his ancient father fresh in his grave, and his mother talking of moving away to Liverpool to be with her people . . . Annie so often sick, and acting so odd sometimes . . . married six years . . . only one kid . . . in debt . . . afraid of himself drunk . . .

It would not be prudent to scratch below the surface of this man as he struggled with himself in the blackness of *Eleanor*'s cabin where she rode serenely to her anchor in the lee of Dartmouth Cove, the gale all howling outside. Suffice it that it dawned on him, even as the dawn slipped her rosy fingers over the snowed hills of Dartmouth, that if he were to remain a free man he must leave the land of his birth, perhaps forever, without the luxury of fond farewells and as quickly as possible.

And where away? Why, to the Rogues' Hole, where else! Onward to the States, the shores of opportunity!

The prospect so revived his flagging spirits that he sprang from his bunk, knowing now what he had to do. He washed down his breakfast with a glass of rum. Leaving the trusty Mullins in charge, he dropped into the skiff and rowed ashore to a remote part of the Cove. He hauled the boat above high water, flipped it over and hid the oars in the snow behind some bushes. With all secured for his return, he plowed into the village to await nightfall amidst the amenities of Tom Medley's tavern and bowling alley.

He was still warming his backsides at the hearth, glass in hand, when in out of the cold walked an old acquaintance, a Captain Lane, whose vessel was on the ways for repairs at Lyle's, the yard at the point of the Cove where Sam Cunard had the heft of his fleet built. Lane, too, had the day to kill–if for a different reason–and was an affable companion; the two whiled away the hours over a bottle or two of rum before the great fireplace, shared a hearty dinner and rolled ninepins until dark, which came on in the late afternoon.

Bidding Lane goodby, he left Medley's and walked down to the foot of Ochterloney Street where Skerry's Ferry came and went.

For two generations John Skerry's boats had taken passengers, stock and cargo by sail and oar across between Dartmouth and Halifax. But the steamboat *Sir Charles Ogle* had come and was hissing him out of business. Skipper Skerry was seventy now and retired, though still hanging on with his regular ferry, and he kept a man and a small boat at the slip for special calls.

Jim hailed him and brought him out of his shack; after some bargaining the ferryman agreed to take him over to one of Cunard's wharves for a dollar. They reefed the sail and shoved off.

In thirty minutes our wicked friend was back in Halifax, hurrying along the darkened waterfront toward the scene of his latest misdemeanors. Down Lower Water Street (he had walked almost a mile) and up Sackville he quickened his pace, traversing the very spot where twenty-four hours earlier he had cracked five skulls of the town's constabulary and left their owners groaning in the snowbank. He pushed into the McLeans' place, as cool as might be, and called for a gin.

Shock, dismay and solicitude overspread the countenances of the brothers and of his old friend Captain Phillips from Liverpool, who happened to be present.

"My God, Jim, what the devil are you doing back here!" exclaimed Dan (setting the bottle on the bar). "Where is your vessel? Is she down in North West Arm?"

"I shouldn't wonder," replied Pattillo, taking a drink.

"Well, she's not there, then. So she must be down to the Eastern Passage back of Lawlor Island, eh?"

"I shouldn't wonder," repeated her owner, taking another drink.

"In that case, good luck to you," broke in Hector, "because if she's up in the North West Arm or down in the Eastern Passage, there's an army of soldiers marched to both places to take her, and you've lost your *Eleanor.*"

"Maybe so," said Jim calmly and took another swig.

Captain Phillips urged him to come down to Long Wharf with him and spend the night on board of his brig, but the great fellow grunted that he still had business to attend to. He finished the bottle and walked out.

Under cover of the winter darkness he went first to Thomas Laidlaw, the merchant who owed him thirty-seven pounds for carrying the rum. Laidlaw protested that he had not that much money with him, and the bank was closed, and why could not the captain come around in the daytime during business hours anyway?

The fugitive assured him that it had not been convenient for him to stop by during the day. So Mr. Laidlaw dug down and gave him ten pounds on account.

From the merchant's he ducked over to the shop of Crawford the watchmaker, below the Parade, and collected two watches he had left to be repaired. Thence he steered a course down George Street, past the Police Court (with collar turned up), and down onto Market Wharf. A little schooner from Tancook Island in Chester Bay was laying along the end of the slip. She had a cargo of potatoes. Jim knew the vessel and the men who were working her, by the names of Mason and Richardson. They invited him aboard for the night. Once below and snug before the fireplace with his boots off and some supper in him and a bottle to go all round, he told them of the scrape he was in; they had heard some of the story already but were eager to get it from him, for he was known up and down as a grand spinner of a tale.

While Mason cooked up breakfast next morning, their guest pressed a coin on Richardson and sent him to the head of the wharf for a bottle. The three then settled around the mess for a nourishing feed washed down with a glass of rum and bitters. When finished, Jim hauled up in front of the fire and was just putting a light to his pipe when there was the sound of boots on the deck above; a familiar personage appeared in the companionway and started down the ladder.

Who should it be but Mary Gorman's lad who had hiked the forty-five miles from Chester to Halifax through the worst of the winter to take out the writ! When he turned in his backward descent and recognized the hulking figure in the dancing light of the fire, he reversed himself and scrambled back up toward the deck.

But Jim, for all his size, could strike with the swiftness of a cobra. He jumped up with an oath and caught their unwelcome visitor by the seat of the pants, just as this despised individual was about to make a getaway, pulled him down off the ladder and knocked him flat on the cabin floor.

"Now, my friend," he rumbled, standing over his victim with the appearance of Satan before the fires of hell, "here's your chance. If you have anything you want to repent of, do it quickly, for your time has come!"

Bloody-nosed and blubbering, the poor wretch floundered to his knees and begged for mercy. Under the persuasive influence of one of those rocklike Pattillo fists poised six inches from his

The oldest part of Halifax seen from the Citadel, 1880s. On the left is the old town clock, on the right St. Paul's Anglican Church, built 1750. (Provincial Archives of Nova Scotia)

head, he proposed to swear on a pile of Bibles that he would do anything Jim wished and settle the affair any way he directed if only he would not strike him again. As he had cried in a similar emergency in Chester, he had been put up to the whole thing.

Though Jim longed to pound his enemy to a pulp, he dared not molest him further; any more commotion might rouse the curiosity of the soldiers in the guardhouse by the head of the wharf. So he contented himself with grinding his teeth in a most menacing fashion and kept the pitiful creature his prisoner in the cabin until after dinner, trying to figure out his next move.

Neither his captive nor his friends could read or write, and he knew that what he scrawled in his primitive script and they put their marks to would have no standing with the authorities, who would think there was something fishy about it (as well they might). Then Richardson offered to go up town and fetch Dan McLean to come down and draw up the document of absolution,

Jim to dictate in a general way and his prisoner to put his X at the bottom.

Good idea . . . and the prisoner was released (at his own suggestion) to go with Richardson and use his powers of persuasion on Dan McLean. The two climbed on deck and were off.

A minute or two later the air was rent by the blast of a conch shell, followed distinctly by the familiar cry of *Over! Over!* announcing the imminent departure of Skerry's Ferry from the slip, which was one to the northward from Market Wharf.

With the wind the way it was, Jim knew the little sloop would have to pass close by the end of the wharf entering the stream, probably in about five minutes. Here was his chance, he told Mason, to make a break for it across the harbor, bring the *Eleanor* back from out of seclusion under the Dartmouth shore and have her standing by for a fast departure, just in case.

Out on the deck of the Tancook schooner the air was fiercely cold, though the wind was only moderate. Dusk had come on. Jim took a stand on the outside rail by the main shrouds and waited.

Suddenly with a swish of water and a ruffle of canvas the sailboat was nearly on him, heeling briskly. In that second when it came abreast, he crouched and made a prodigious leap across the gap and landed safely all in a heap in the bottom of the ferry, much to the surprise of the passengers. He pulled a spare sail over himself in a rather vague attempt at concealment, and soon they were at the slip in Dartmouth.

Throwing off the sail and slapping a coin in the ferryman's hand, our captain bounded ashore and hastened up Ochterloney Street and through the drifted fields to the Cove. The skiff and oars were where he had left them. He shoved the boat in the water and rowed out to the *Eleanor.*

Old Jack Mullins was happy to see his skipper, for the rheumatism was bad on him, and he was having a most terrible time getting about. They raised sail, hove in the anchor and reached back across the harbor. A few fathoms off the end of Market Wharf they came into the wind, anchored again and dropped sail.

Telling his mate to be ready to sail without warning, Pattillo rowed into the slip. He tied up and climbed back aboard the little schooner from Tancook, expecting to find Danny McLean and the rest waiting for him.

But below in the cabin there was no Dan McLean, nor the enemy from Chester either—only Mason and Richardson with long faces and a short story. Mason told it:

"Fifteen or twenty minutes after you jumped aboard of the ferry, Jim, back comes your pal from Chester, asking where is Jim? He says he's got Dan McLean and he pokes around in the hold and looks up the lazarette, calling all the time for you to come out.

"Well I told him you left right after he did, and then I went on deck and by God there's no sign of Danny anywhere around! I'm just asking him what the devil's up when down come four soldiers and a sergeant with their bayonets drawn and they march aboard. It turns out that on the way to McLean's your friend gave the slip to Richardson and walked into the guardhouse and told 'em if they marched aboard quick then they'd have you fixed for good! So they searched all over, but they got tired of waiting after a while and the whole lot left. And that's the story."

Jim decided not to await their return. He stole up into the town and paid another after-dark visit on Mr. Laidlaw in the hope of getting the balance owed him. The merchant was beginning to have certain reservations about Captain Pattillo's manner of doing business, but he thought it wise to keep them to himself. So to get rid of the giant mariner with the nocturnal habits, he gave him another fifteen pounds on account.

And now, exulted our friend (for he was filled with a sudden thirst), now for one final fling in Halifax! Which one of his old haunts should it be? Ah! That was it! To Tom Landragan's, where he had enjoyed many the drink and dance and good times with the girls!

No sooner said than done. Off he went, and through the doors he burst with a shout. There was good old Tom in his place behind the bar.

A variety of hair-raising stories about Jim's current escapades were flying about Halifax already, and Tom ventured to caution his unpredictable patron that he would take it as an act of friendship if he could bring himself to behave while in the Landragan place of business. The giant mariner gave him vigorous reassurances, along with two dollars he owed him, and pushed into the back room for a dance or two with one of the ladies. When he emerged he accosted Landragan with a crunching handshake and announced that he was off and away, bound for the Rogues' Hole.

This news that one of his most loyal and athletic patrons was leaving Halifax (perhaps for good) moved Landragan deeply. He confided with a sly poke in the ribs that he held a writ against Jim himself (on account of some exuberance, no harm meant), but he would not trouble him with it after all, for the captain had put a good many dollars into his pocket first and last (and was finally being run out of town, thank God).

Let bygones be bygones, said Tom, and he wished him Godspeed and told him he must have a drink on the house. Just as Jim had poured himself a tumbler of gin and was putting the water to it, drop by drop, who should come into the place with two others but his old enemy!

Pattillo bolted down his gin, lunged across the room and caught his nemesis with such a clout that he crashed clean through the partition and into an adjoining shoemaker's shop, which fortunately for the owner was not occupied. In a lather of rage, Jim dove after him.

Immediately the two that came in with his enemy set upon him from behind, and one of them hurt him enough to make him leave off pelting the rascal. Jim turned and with a blow somersaulted his assailant clear over the bar and into the ample form of Mrs. Landragan, who until that moment had been enjoying the rumpus. With a scream she was swept backward against the shelves of bottles and glasses by this human projectile, and both landed on the floor in a heap–shelves, bottles, glasses and all.

In the meantime the young rogue, whose gall in offering tipsy suit to Mary Gorman had launched this epic in reverse, recovered his wits enough to rise from the rubble while the wild one was distracted from him. He staggered to the door, all battered and bloody and his jacket torn, and made a break for the guardhouse.

Out of the corner of his eye Jim caught the fleeing figure. Instantly he flattened the second of his enemy's companions and took off through the snow in hot pursuit. Landragan was left standing in the door, mouth ajar, surveying the shambles of his place, seemingly deaf to the muffled cries of his spouse who, out of sight on the floor behind the bar, was out of mind.

Pursued and pursuer panted down the street. The distance between them closed, and Jim was about to lay hand again on this bane of his existence when out stepped a sentry from the shadow with a cry of "Halt! Who comes there?" Pursued was too breathless to reply and fell at the astonished soldier's feet.

That does it, thought Jim. The guard would be out in a flash. The time had come to go to sea.

He sprinted down to Market Wharf, dropped into his skiff and pulled like a demon in the night for *Eleanor.*

Start the sheets, jump to the halyards and sway away from main to jib, up with the anchor, run for the helm, hard down and let her stand out! The schooner was off, gaining way, heeling to the wind, working out the harbor, leaving the old town astern. And her master was her crew, for old Jack Mullins was below all the while, groaning in his bunk with the miseries.

To the southward and close to the coast that night beat the *Eleanor,* into Ketch Harbor where he anchored to get his breath, for Pattillo was on the run now for fair.

In the morning he made sail again and drove her across to Liverpool. He put his crippled mate ashore, shipped two men in his place and ran posthaste back along the coast to Lunenburg. He hustled into town to hit up Matt Arnst for money owed him on a load of coal, but the old Kraut talked Jim into taking instead an order for twenty-five cords of wood, which a yoke of oxen dragged alongside over the ice . . . it was that thick in the harbor.

Jim stacked her hold with wood to the overhead and turned the *Eleanor* westward for the second time. He put into Liverpool once again, for supplies and passengers.

Once again he put back to sea, in full flight from his native shores and his people, a fugitive, a man without a country. He pointed his schooner through the sparkling sunlit waves of the winter Atlantic.

For the Rogues' Hole . . . for Boston.

8

At Cape Ann Jim Finds His Fame Has Gone Ahead

DROPPING ASTERN the dunes of Cape Sable, the last of Nova Scotia, Captain Pattillo prodded the *Eleanor* across Fundy's tidal swirl and set her head for Cape Ann, the first of New England. Afar off the coast of Maine and out to sea the schooner worked her way on to the westward. In due course the cry *land ho!* went up; it was the low profile of the Cape on the horizon. Jim had made his landfall right on the nose.

This northern sentinel of Massachusetts Bay was a mailed fist of granite, poised against Cape Cod's long crook'd arm of sand. As if it had struck a knuckle and bounced off into the Atlantic, Thacher's Island hunchbacked out of the ocean a half a mile away. It was a windy pasture, thrusting aloft twin beacons ninety feet above the tide, two cable lengths apart, built by the Colonial Government four years before the Revolution. The Cape Ann lights had warned mariners off from their first night on, except during the war itself, when the patriotic fishermen seized the Tory keeper and doused his lanterns as a foil to English men-of-war.

Eleanor gave Thacher's a broad berth to starboard, keeping clear of a partly submerged pinnacle of rock to seaward marked

Londoner on the chart. *Secured by an ironbound shore* was the way Blunt's *American Coast Pilot* described the island, and that fitted most of the outward side of the Cape. To those who crowded the windward rail for a look at the coast of New England this February day, there was something about the sight and sound of the long Atlantic swells bursting white against the rocks of Eastern Point, the screaming gulls on the wheel and the dip a feather above the explosions of the surf . . . something about it that said bear off. Down from those dread ledges, down below low water and the brown kelp and seaweed and under the churning undertow, where they had heaved up and fallen back, broken, into four fathoms, it was a boneyard of men and ships.

On to Boston, steering from Cape Ann lights southwest half south (eight and a third leagues to Boston Light), cutting across the Bay past bold, barren Halfway Rock sticking out of the sea so solitary to the starboard, gray with guano of gull and shag, cairned, spindled and topped off with a two-foot copper ball (every outbound Marbleheader leaned over the rail and flipped his penny at the rock for luck). All to the north of Boston was to Jim an indifferent shore of rocks and reefs, harbors, inlets and seaside clumps of white houses and church spires, and he stood well off it; these waters were unknown to him with their ledges and outcroppings sometimes visible only when the tide was out, and he had no wish to pile up on one so near his destination.

Entering Boston Harbor from the northeast, he ran *Eleanor* up to a parcel of dry rocks marked on the chart The Graves. Following Blunt's directions, he left these two cable lengths to larboard and sailed southwest by west through Broad Sound between Deer Island and the seven-foot lantern of Long Island Light, illuminated with its ten patent lamps. Now Boston came into view four miles up ahead, the golden dome of the State House on the crown of Beacon Hill a rival orb in the rays of the setting sun. The schooner sailed easily and briskly through the anchorage identified as President Roads, energetic tiller and sheet work being required to thread the stream as it thickened with vessels swinging at their cables.

Broad off Castle Island, the *Coast Pilot* brought them in:

"When abreast of the Castle, steer N.N.W. one quarter of a mile, to clear the Upper-Middle Ground, which has a black buoy on it in two fathoms water, that you leave on your larboard hand; if the buoy should be removed, run N.N.W. till you bring the two northernmost steeples in Boston a handspike's length open, then steer N.W. by W. 2 1/2 miles, which will carry you opposite the town."

Jim drifted his schooner into one of the busy docks that lifted a long block of warehouses from Atlantic Avenue out over the harbor and disembarked his passengers.

So here he was in the Rogues' Hole, all ready to turn over a new leaf!

First off, he sold his cargo of firewood, and then he sold the *Eleanor* to John Anderson of Liverpool, who promptly departed for the Provinces in her with a promise to pay him two hundred pounds as he could. Gone now was the snug home of the last three years. The big man shouldered his sea chest and walked with long strides up into North Market Street, a few steps below Faneuil Hall, where he found a berth in a seamen's boarding-house kept by an old fellow named Frankson.

It had been a fair enough exchange, he supposed—his vessel for his freedom. He could not have worked her out of the States because the law said that every vessel of more than twenty tons had to be licensed and owned and commanded by American citizens. A Yankee he was not, so that finished the *Eleanor,* and left him a common Jack like all the rest. No more "Captain Pattillo this" or "Captain that."

Boston was booming—"the hub of the universe," any Bostonian would assure you—and the evidence to support the boast was all about, from Beacon Street to Boston Light. The day of the fast sailing packet was dawning, and you had to get up early in the morning to beat a Yankee. Some dozens of vessels daily cleared the port to and from every part of the world, the best of sailors thrown into the forecastle with the sweepings of the waterfront; few captains were particular in their choice of a crew, as a young Harvard College student named Richard Henry Dana was to

Boston, with the State House atop Beacon Hill, as seen from South Boston, 1840s. (Author collection)

learn that very summer, sailing on the brig *Pilgrim* for two years before the mast.

Now to find a site on some ship off for far-off ports, and he was not long at it. There was a bark bound "up the Straits," as they said, meaning the Mediterranean; Jim drew his thirty dollars for a month's pay in advance and signed the articles, and then up came the law again: two-thirds of the crew had to be Americans, born or naturalized, and Pattillo was still a British subject, even if in disfavor with his King.

Landlord Frankson was one of those characters essential to every port, like bondsmen, pimps and pawnbrokers; his sideline was useful to captain and motley crew alike. He was a *naturalizer.* That is, if his palm were satisfactorily crossed, he would convert a foreigner into a Yankee in a twinkling. To be blunt about it, the old rascal kept a great cradle in his back room. The alien who longed to ship as a Yank merely climbed aboard for a perfunctory lullaby, and Frankson would swear to his citizenship . . . in fact, he had rocked him in the cradle with his own hand.

James William Pattillo, however, declined his host's offer to oscillate him into a berth on the bark, for he was unwilling to add

American perjury to his Canadian sins. As it turned out, her captain was able to round up enough thus retroactively rocked to make up his two-thirds, so Jim was shipped as a foreigner.

The day before sailing he was lounging against a capstan on Long Wharf, smoking his pipe, when he was hailed by an old acquaintance from the Provinces whom he recognized as Richard Wilson. His countryman was clad in the tarpaulin hat, pea jacket, guernsey frock, red flannel shirt, satinet trousers and cowhide boots of the Gloucester fisherman, and wore a look of contentment besides. He hove over to Jim and related with enthusiasm that he had been fishing out of Cape Ann for some few years now and would exchange it for no other life or location. So where was Pattillo bound for?

"Up the Straits in that bark over there," replied Jim, pointing with his pipe at the three-master lying alongside the wharf.

"What! Go to sea in that hulk and get flogged for it?" Wilson cursed and spat. "Why Jimmy, the first week out you'll take on a skinful and hammer the mate and land in the brig! All these here merchant skippers are quarterdeckers and slave drivers. There'll be three months of your life not worth the living on board of that bark, if you don't get blown off a yard first and break your bloody neck. I tell you, Jim, you come down to Cape Ann with me!"

He would get him a good chance in Gloucester, Wilson promised. Truth was, one of the fleet of sail owned by Giles and Wonson (that he shipped with) was right now fitting out for fishing off of Whitehead, down home; they wanted a pilot, and Jim was just the man. He could board with Wilson and his missus between trips while he looked the place over. There was a future in Gloucester for a Bluenose; the people there were the finest kind, and they took to Novie folks like bread to butter.

The proposition appealed mightily to Jim, but he was committed to the bark; he had signed articles and accepted his month's pay in advance.

"Let's see if we can talk the old man out of it," said Wilson. They hustled aboard to interview the master, who was a decent sort after all and released Jim from the voyage on the return of the thirty dollars.

Pattillo shifted his sea chest to the pinkey *Augusta,* Captain Charley Story, where she lay discharging fish. Three days later, on the eleventh of March, 1834, they cast off and raised sail for Cape Ann. The little schooner with the high pointed "pink" stern was a smart sailer, as most of her type were. Pushed on by a fair southwest breeze, she scooted past the long arm of Nahant and Marblehead Neck, by the harbors of Salem and Beverly deep inside the coast, and their guardian Baker's Island, and on past Halfway Rock. Late in the afternoon Eastern Point bore directly off the starboard bow, and the harbor it gave Gloucester lay dead ahead.

Since he was a young shaver Jim had heard tell of Cape Ann and the fishermen who had already been sailing to the banks for two hundred years from there. Sometimes off his own coast he had spoken one of the small, old-fashioned bluff-bowed schooners they called Chebacco boats or dogbodies, according to whether the stern came to a high V like the *Augusta*'s pink or more rarely was square and flat, sawed-off like. He admired their skill with a handline as the Yanks jigged for mackerel over the rail, and there was always a swap of banter as the vessels passed.

The first Nova Scotian had settled in Gloucester only in 1828, so Wilson was a pioneer there, and Bluenoses were welcomed as first-rate men with sail. Now that he was about to take a try at Cape Ann fishing, Jim looked and listened curiously while his friend and Captain Story sang out a running account of their passage into the port.

There, right off the brick-colored ledge of the mainland, they were passing Norman's Woe Rock, a bare and brutal way to end a trip. Once clear, however, you could hold a northeast course into the Harbor, keeping the length of a cable and a half from the West Gloucester shore, which was mostly bold and free of shoal.

Jim had stood off the back shore of Eastern Point on the passage down in the *Eleanor,* but its harbor shore was new to him. This point was an arm that hung off to the southwestward from the body of Cape Ann, close on to three miles into the Atlantic, and it provided the old port with its magnificent harbor.

His shipmates told Pattillo that the government had lately

erected that lighthouse there on the rocky tip of Eastern Point. Keep off if you're passing to and from the eastward, well outside a ledge to the southward marked by a red spar buoy, another called Dog Bar across the harbor entrance with a white buoy on its western edge, and a third obstacle, a shoal called Round Rock, square athwart the entrance, from which a black spar buoy bobbed and swayed.

Augusta was now running broad off a crown of rock and pasture crested by a cheerful little lighthouse and keeper's cottage identified to Jim as Ten Pound Island, which in colonial times may have been divided into ten sheep pastures called "pounds." Steer for the light and then bear off to port short of it and so pass by. Abreast now on the other hand was Stage Head, a once fortified bluff under which the English settlers had landed their catches and cured them in the field behind, two centuries before.

Up ahead, as the eye swung to the right, was the sandy arc of Pavillion Beach, split by a canal called the Cut, dug through the mud to connect the Harbor with the dead end of the Annisquam River. This was not really a river at all but a tidal stream that wound through the salt marshes and clam flats and past the fishing village of Annisquam to its origin in Ipswich Bay, on the north side of Cape Ann. The Cut made an island of the Cape, but not much of one; the old decaying draw had been replaced by a fixed bridge, and now only small boats could pass under it from Gloucester Harbor through to Ipswich Bay.

Off at the east end of the beach was a familiar long and low shedlike structure that Jim knew as a ropewalk. Directly beyond and on a slight rise whirled a windmill–strange place for one–while the next eminence contained the remains of a second crude citadel, called Fort Point.

Augusta slipped through the narrows between Fort Point and Rocky Neck, a bold pastured promontory on the starboard hand, and entered the Inner Harbor. A neat feather of spray dashed off her bow, as a playful squall skipped across the water from the town that rose on low hills back of the wharves to port, a charming cluster of white clapboard and weathered shingle homes, punctured by the steeples of the churches.

Captains Samuel Giles and John Fletcher Wonson. (Alice E. Babson)

Here indeed, his mates told him with pride, was the securest anchorage on the coast; and so it seemed, for this Inner Harbor was crowded with every kind of vessel, and on every hand was a bustle of activity. Here is the home of the fleet and the heart of the town, they exulted—drop your hook here and you are safe against all winds that blow . . . even a hurricane if your neighbor's ground tackle is as strong as yours.

Working smartly round Rocky Neck, the fishermen tacked across the short mouth of Smith Cove (for an anchorage, safer than your back yard) and brought up on the luff at the stubby wharf of Messrs. Giles and Wonson.

The pastoral and sparsely settled community to the east of the Harbor Village known as Eastern Point existed for fishing. Two or three farms that shared the uplands extending out on the peninsula were cultivated with diffidence; the soil of Cape Ann was almost as poor as the enclosing sea was rich. This out-of-the-way jut of land and its people, separated from "over town" by the intervention of the Inner Harbor, already proclaimed a characteristic eccentricity and ingrown distinction usually associated with islands. The ascendent family here were the vigorous and prolific Wonsons.

The leader of this Wonson clan was Samuel, son of Samuel the settler from Sandy Bay across the Cape, and the partner of Sam Giles, a retired Salem shipmaster who had pledged his capital to the Wonson fishing interests and his troth to his associate's daughter. The family owned and fitted out a fleet of ten or a dozen handsome schooners built in the Essex yards round the Cape to the landward of Ipswich Bay, launched and floated down the salt marshes and around to Gloucester, with names such as *Augusta* and *Forest, Eagle, Lucinda, Tiger* and *Nautilus*—the last being the vessel fitting out for a Nova Scotia trip on which Wilson had assured Jim that a site awaited him as pilot.

The newcomer was hardly ashore before he had been sized up by the partners and signed on by Captain Fred Gerring. He went to store his gear with Dick and Mrs. Wilson up the hill on Mount Pleasant Avenue overlooking the Harbor, and then he joined the rest of the crew getting *Nautilus* ready for sea.

After the usual chores of maintenance had been completed, she was stored with barrels of salt for preserving the catch. Each of the six members of the crew went on his own hook, purchasing on credit from Giles and Wonson's store his fishing gear and provisions for a ten weeks' voyage. These consisted of hard crackers, salt pork, molasses, flour and such—and a sea store of rum or gin, each man to his own poison. Jim bought a five-gallon keg of gin and tossed it in his berth. The schooner was taken out and anchored in the stream, and he returned to his room to pack his cuds.

In the middle of this, in came Wilson with a message from the owners: the new man was to go aboard the *Nautilus,* take ashore all of his things and pick up the pay owing him.

"For why?" asked his boarder all taken aback at this turn. Wilson didn't know the reason, so Jim stamped down Highland Street to the partners' store at the Square. He accosted Captain Gerring and demanded to know the reason he was being let go after having signed articles which he was fully prepared to honor in every way according to agreement.

Well, explained the master of the *Nautilus,* pulling at his ear with some embarrassment, Captain Giles had been aboard and seen the five-gallon keg of gin in Pattillo's berth. Thinking this was enough and more than enough for one man, he had mentioned it to some countrymen of Jim's who were going in another vessel–just as a matter of curiosity–and they told him in so many words that if Pattillo had five gallons of gin and got half drunk he would throw all hands overboard. When this news of their pilot's reputation reached the *Nautilus,* the crew to a man declared they would not go in her if he did. Furthermore, Captain Giles was vice president of the Gloucester Temperance Society.

"What!" roared Jim, crashing his fist down on the counter. "Is that all the trouble?"

Gerring assured him that was the sum and substance of it–the owners would not risk having him and the gin in the same vessel together.

"All right, by God, all right! I am going in your vessel according to agreement, and I give you my word, so help me God, here and now that I will not drink a drop of liquor of any kind from the time we drop Cape Ann until the time we pick it up again! Now, if that don't suit you I will go up to Mrs. Wilson's boardinghouse and stay there and make you pay for my board and my share as the next highest line out of Gloucester. I tell you I'm ready to go on board and do my part as I shipped for! And all the trouble, you say, is the five gallons of gin?" Jim pounded the counter and set the floor to shaking again in a towering wrath of righteousness.

"Yes, yes–that's it," allowed Gerring dubiously.

"By God, then, come along on board with me, Skip, and we'll settle this here and now!"

The great Nova Scotian shoved Gerring out the door and hustled him down through the flake yard, where the split fish were drying pungently and the flies buzzing in the early spring sun, and onto the wharf, and he rowed him out to the *Nautilus.*

On board, he jumped into the forecastle and jumped out with his gin in one hand and a hatchet in the other. He dropped the keg at the feet of the astounded captain and knocked in the head with a blow. Then he picked up the dripping cask. He looked at it balefully, and he muttered–"If you belong to the devil, you shall go to where you came from!"–and tossed it over the side into the harbor.

Which Winds Up in a Holiday Chowder at Eastern Point

FIT AND READY FOR SEA, the fleet lay in Gloucester Harbor for nigh onto a fortnight awaiting fair wind and weather. On the eleventh of April a favorable westerly sprang up, and the seventy sail of schooners hauled anchor and filled away for the eastward, clearing Eastern Point by the middle of the morning and leaving Cape Ann a smoky line on the horizon by noon.

The heft of the fleet shaped a course for the Grand Bank of Newfoundland, the greatest of the North Atlantic codfisheries. The pursuit of old *Gadus morrhua,* that big fishy-looking fellow of near thirty pounds with his chin whisker and his sometimes fatal habit of gulping at anything that resembled dinner in the murk of the ocean bottom—the pursuit and the catching of the cod on these vast shoals of the Newfoundland banks and on the continental shelf of the New England coast was so much the life of Massachusetts that for exactly fifty years his image in gilded pine had hung for all to see in the place of honor in that State House with the golden dome.

But the Sacred Cod was more than a graven image; it was a real power, even unto the halls of Congress, which in 1792 placed a bounty on its head. This subsidy was supposed to be by way of compensation for the parlous sufferings of the fisheries during the Revolution, a stimulant to their regrowth and a kind of acknowledgment of their role as "the nursery of our Navy." Here was a favorite theme of the New England politicians, who used it whenever they talked about the fisheries with rather more enthusiasm than accuracy; Yankee fishermen were too cussed independent for Navy discipline and mostly stayed clear of the quarterdeck and all it represented in those days of forty lashes and the brig.

There was also the tariff on salt, shiploads of which were imported under heavy duties, mainly from Cadiz and Liverpool; this was used for the curing of fish, and the bounty was intended as a drawback on the duties for the benefit of the fishermen, the right hand returning what the left hand had taken away. The government paid the bounty according to the tonnage of the vessel, regardless of the size of its catch, provided it was employed in the codfishery at least four months of the year between March and December. At the end of the season the bounty was divided three-eighths to the owner, the balance to the crew. Yankee ingenuity wove such an intricate web of abuse around it that in a few years all concerned were thoroughly sick of the subsidy and harangued for its repeal.

After a few days out *Nautilus* parted company with the fleet and was piloted along the Nova Scotia coast by Jim until they found fish within the fifty-fathom line, six or seven leagues southwest of Whitehead off the under side of Cape Canso. There the schooner came to anchor, and the men dragged themselves through the next six weeks handlining from the rail for Mister Cod, sun up to sun down, day in and day out. At the end of each stint they split the fat green fish down the midline of their gray bellies, gibbed out their guts and slewed the rough salt on their flesh. Spreading their sides like wings, they packed them in even, flat layers in the hold. Each man cut out the tongues of his catch and kept them. Each night, before they hove themselves into the dank bunks that lined the smoky forecastle, Skipper Gerring counted cod tongues by lantern light and entered their day's luck in his book against the names of his crew; every other tongue would belong to the vessel when they settled, as men and boat shared fifty-fifty.

Thus it went in hard and unvarying grind through fair weather and foul that spring until the middle of June, when the last pickled clam was impaled on its hook and the last barrel of coarse Cadiz salt was wet. Then with the first fair wind, it was up sail, up anchor and point her for Cape Ann. Lashed on deck was a mysterious and vaguely disturbing derelict that had floated up on them one day. It was a long mast, square-rigged with yard, sail, shrouds, sheets, braces, blocks and all; Captain Gerring had it gaffed and tackled on board, and whether the good ship it had once driven was on the bottom with all hands, or where, no one ever knew.

That great Pattillo from Nova Scotia with the wild reputation was as good as his word and mild as milk from start to finish. Not a drop of spirits touched his lips during the whole trip, so that when *Nautilus* wore around Rocky Neck and groaned all heavy with salt fish to her berth, he was dry as a sponge. The Fourth of July was a couple of weeks away, and all the fishermen were home or on the way for the holiday. Happy times were in order, but Jim swore to himself that he would hold to his good behavior; damned if he didn't like what he saw of Cape Ann and her people, and he was bound to make good here.

Others had different plans for him, however.

While he was off on his first trip out of Gloucester there had been some powerful talk from his old countrymen along the water front about Jim Pattillo's gigantic strength and his monumental bouts with fist and bottle–more of the same that had scared his mates into a shore mutiny before they ever sailed with him.

So the men of Giles and Wonson thought it would be great fun to see the newcomer in action, and they had their eyes peeled for the *Nautilus* to round the Point. It occurred to these schemers that the Novie might be the means of silencing a noisy bantam rooster named Percy Mathews, a fisherman from Blue Hill, Maine. There had been a difficulty between him and the owners with the result that he went over to Ben Parsons's wharf across the slip and had been crowing loud and long how he would flog them or any of their gang that crossed his path.

Jim had no more than walked ashore when the men gathered round and pointed out Mathews to him across the way. Take the rooster on, they urged, and stop his noise. But thinking of all the trouble his fists had brought him, even to fleeing from his homeland, he shook his head and pushed them off and would have none of their troublemaking, as he said–good, bad or indifferent.

Two of the Giles and Wonson skippers, Job Rowe and Stephen Rich, were the ringleaders in this affair. When they saw it was useless to push their man or pull him, they resolved to get to the windward of him. There was more than one way to shape a course. They would bide their time.

The Fourth of July in this fifty-eighth year of the United States held a promise of boisterous political goings-on. It was all owing to Old Hickory.

The Common Man had swept President Andrew Jackson and his Democrats to such a swamping victory over Henry Clay in 1832 that it demolished the tottering National Republican Party. The hoary hero of the War of 1812, with his ramrod principles and spoils system, his strong-man view of the Presidency and hatred of the Federalists, had amputated the tentacles of the monopolistic Bank of the United States by vetoing its recharter and now was squeezing the blood of government deposits from the body. These battles with privilege entrenched the old general's popularity with the common men, none more so than the Gloucester fishermen; and they drove his political enemies to regroup under the shield of a revived Whig Party early in 1834.

Faced with this new threat to Jacksonism the Democrats of Cape Ann in the days preceding the national birthday laid plans to whomp the Whigs with bombast in absentia at a mass gathering in the bucolic seaside environment of Eastern Point, the favorite locale for the celebration of the Fourth as long as anyone could remember. It would be a gala, a circus, a display of numerical and oratorical strength that would set the Whigs to rout. All the Democratic politicians would be there, the rum would flow, and the attraction of the day, as touted by the *Gloucester Telegraph,* would be a fish dinner "consisting of halibut, codfish, haddock, hake, cunners, lobsters, etc. etc., which will be stewed, boiled, fried, baked, roasted, chowdered, hashed, minced, etc., and be on the table at precisely one o'clock. Salutes will be fired and the bells rung, morning, noon and night, in honor of the day." Tickets were on sale at Giles and Wonson, from whose premises the affair would radiate.

It was here that the conspiracy of Captains Rich and Rowe to test the mettle of Jim Pattillo was to unfold.

In the midst of the preparatory activities–and as if to escalate the pitch of excitement–a whale wandered into the Harbor one morning and went snooping somewhat absent-mindedly amongst the innermost recesses of the fleet and docks, where he suddenly announced himself to the public by surfacing and blowing a lazy cloud of vapor into the June sunlight off Five Pound Island, a few rods from the establishment of Giles and Wonson.

What a bumbler! Still, how could he have known that a long harpoon's throw from the spot where he came up for air lay the enemy of his race, a whaler fitting out for her second voyage? She was the ship *Mount Wollaston,* 325 tons, Captain David L. Adams, just returned seventy-five days out from the South Atlantic islands of Tristan da Cunha. It had been a disappointing maiden voyage of fifteen months with a mere sixteen hundred barrels of oil and thirteen thousand pounds of bone. She was only the third (and would be the last, it must be admitted) vessel ever to go a-whaling out of Gloucester. The local company formed to invade the territory of Nantucket and New Bedford was determined to have one more try at it.

So it must have been the crew of the *Mount Wollaston,* taunted by the presence almost in their berth of the huge prey they had sailed halfway around the world for with such indifferent success, who leaped in their whaleboat, eager for vindication in the bosom of their home port.

The men pulled with strong strokes across the few feet of open water, swinging their oars to the lusty shouts of the steerer.

Harpooner poised taut and tense in the bow, weapon at the ready, they bore down on the basking quarry. Now they were almost against him, and the harpoon sang and thudded into the expanse of glistening back.

Suddenly the quiet balm of the June morning was rent by the fierce and frenzied thrashing of the wounded leviathan. He whipped the water into a churn of spray flecked with the red of his blood and bore off with a thunderous smash of his tail whence he came. The line zipped through the chocks, and when it fetched up, off they dashed, whale and boat at a steaming clip, through Gloucester Harbor at the utmost hazard to themselves and the fleet.

Out the length of the Harbor the furious whale towed his shouting entourage at breakneck speed–Gloucester fishermen on a regular Nantucket sleigh ride, their boat careening and plunging in the boiling wake of their steed. But when they found themselves outside of Eastern Point after a few incredibly short moments, headed for the open Atlantic, their velocity undiminished, and with no means at hand of dispatching their victim (who seemed to take on strength as he entered his mother waters), they held a quick conference and voted one and all to cut the line.

This was immediately tended to. Old whale sounded and disappeared in a maelstrom of bubbles and froth, taking with him one harpoon and a length of severed Manila. His pursuers drifted to a stop and then dejectedly rowed back into the Harbor, reflecting on the irony of the encounter and the jeers it would provoke on their return.

Church bells a-ringing and a resounding twenty-four-gun salute by a detachment of the Gloucester Artillery Company roused the sun and raised the curtain on a grand and glorious Fourth of July. By mid-morning the crowds were gathering from all about the Cape and the North Shore, arriving by boat, carriage, wagon, horse and foot. Some inspected the wharves and schooners, sniffed the fish drying acrid on the flakes in the rising heat or stood idly by under the trees kibitzing on the prepa-

Gloucester's western harbor in 1830. The windmill was erected in 1814 on the height occupied later by the Pavilion Hotel (for which the beach to its left was named) and now by The Tavern. Behind and to the left of the schooner was the ropewalk built in 1803. (The Fisherman's Own Book)

rations. The old men with their cigars and whiskers talked politics and slapped gnarled hands on thin thighs and pined for the good old days. The ladies snapped open their parasols as the sun mounted overhead. Lovers strolled over the rocks and along the beach. Others picked wildflowers and berries in the upland meadows, and the youngsters played merry, high-pitched games across the fields.

As the morning wore on the dignitaries and politicians staged their arrivals–the Honorable Robert Rantoul, Jr., handsome young Gloucester lawyer and the main speaker of the day who would be a national figure of promise in Congress; Jonathan Cutler, Theophilus Herrick and John Wonson, Representatives in the Legislature; General John Webber, Addison Winter and jovial Dr. John Moriarty, all three hundred and fifty pounds of him.

Over in Giles and Wonson's cooper shop Job Rowe was hard at it, cooking up the chowder that was to be the mainstay of the fish dinner. But he kept one eye on the door, and when big Jim Pattillo lounged past, hands in pockets and pipe in mouth,

Captain Rowe called him inside, informed him with a wink that he was one of his lads, and gave him two long drinks from his black bottle.

At this moment Captain Steve Rich dropped in to observe the progress of the chowder. The plotters fell to talking about this and that, and before long their conversation worked round to the subject of strong men they knew of. Rich approached Jim and felt the muscle in his bulging arm and said to him:

"Jim, you must be a mighty strong man yourself, I'd say."

"Well, I suppose I am," acknowledged the object of this innocent observation with some diffidence, taking another swig offered from the black bottle.

"How much d'you spose you could lift, Jimmy?" Captain Rowe inquired. He threw a panful of onions in the chowder.

"Lift? Oh, I don't know exactly, Cap." Jim cogitated the matter. "I can say this: from the time I was fifteen in the Provinces I never hired a horse to take a barrel of flour from any store or wharf up to my mother's. I carried 'em on my shoulders. Now that's about all I can do–and I can do that easily."

Rich glanced slyly at Rowe:

"That's pretty good, but I know little men that come to your chin, Jimmy, what could take up barrels from the ground like winking and put 'em on their shoulders. . . ."

Our friend flushed. Then he took the hook thus baited:

"Skip," said he, "if you can produce such a man, large or small, as can bring a barrel of flour up from the ground and put it on his shoulder as you say, I'll pay for it–but if he fails, by God, then he and you can go to the devil together and it belongs to me!"

The wager was accepted and off went Captain Rich for his man in high glee, spreading the word of the contest all about, and whom did he fetch but the same Percy Mathews who was going to whip all hands at Giles and Wonson!

The best barrel of flour in their store, value eight dollars, weight two hundred pounds, was rolled out, and a ring was formed in the sun over by the flake yard, the people coming on the run from all over to see the fun as the word went out.

Mathews peeled back his sleeves, cocky as you please, and took hold of the barrel with slow deliberation, commenting that if it contained pork or beef or fish or something that had weight in it, the effort would be worth his while, but flour was nothing in his hands.

And then he straightened up, flexed his arms and looked at the great barrel lying in the dust. Beads of perspiration appeared on his face, but he still did not offer to lift this object of his contempt.

"Haw!" whinnied a voice from the crowd. "I could whittle a better man out of a piece of pine!"

This set up a laugh, and someone else chimed in:

"A piece of pine! Why I could go over to the graveyard and dig up a better man!"

A roar of laughter this time, and a few catcalls. Mathews glared around him furiously and looked uncomfortable. He still did not touch the barrel.

"All right boys, don't be too hard on the poor jack!" Jim was beside himself with mirth. "Give him time! Give him enough time and he can shoulder the barrel–if his mother makes the flour into bannock cakes so he can eat 'em. That's how he'll shoulder it!"

Such a fanciful jibe raised a howl of delight, and the crowd whistled and jeered and made all manner of fun of Rich for wasting their time with his blowhard. Captain Steve put on a mock show of embarrassment, but the humiliated Mathews danced up and down and shook his fist at Jim:

"You're a bag of wind–you can't do it yourself!"

"What! What was that?"

Mathews suddenly grinned.

"A gallon of rum says you can't shoulder that barrel yourself!"

"Stand clear!" roared Jim. With a leap he sprang to the barrel, caught hold of it by the chimes, hove it up on his shoulder, strode over to the shop with it and knocked in both heads on the rock that served as a doorstep, sending up a cloud of flour that drifted down like snow.

All dusted with white, he made for Mathews, who was retreating into the crowd. Jim knocked aside five or six spectators that stood in his channel, plucked up Mathews by the neck of his shirt and the slack of his britches and tossed him off the wharf into the mud.

The gallon of rum Jim won was passed around amongst his admirers and lasted until chowder time.

During the dinner and after it and all through the hot afternoon and into the evening, the oratory rolled forth like the thunder of the twenty-four-gun salutes that periodically marked the progress of the day. Each speech was accompanied by a toast, and there were fifty-one toasts by actual count ranging from down with the Whigs, the Bank and the monied aristocracy to up with Old Hickory and the Democrats, the fishermen and the Fourth of July.

As for Jim Pattillo, he was a Jacksonian by principle and a son of Gloucester by adoption from that day on.

Introducing Jim to Georges Bank and Some of Its Denizens

ALONG IN THE FALL of the year 1834, Jim and his older brother met on Long Wharf in Boston, where Tom's schooner *Rival Packet* lay after a coasting trip from down home in Liverpool. Tom had family news.

Their mother was seventy-two now, still robust, but she'd been persuaded to move to Liverpool where the Roberts side was; Tom had found her a cottage near the Mersey bridge on the Brooklyn road. Jim's wife Anne remained in Chester, so poorly in her mind she couldn't take proper care of Alex, turning six, and they had packed the shaver off to live with his Grandma Pattillo. Tom was struggling with their father's estate, so weighted down with debts he'd have to sell the homestead to cover them.

These tidings and family reminders from his brother, who never failed to needle his conscience, dampened momentarily Jim's carefree view of life. He remembered, with some squirming, that he was a husband and father. Tom urged him to bring Annie and the boy to Gloucester when she was well enough, as she surely would be in a few more months. Jim hastily agreed and sent food, clothes and money back to mother and wife by the *Rival Packet.*

After that soul of propriety and pillar of temperance, brother

Tom, had sailed away and left him alone, Jim set about finding a likely berth out of Boston, as most of the Gloucester fleet was laid up for the winter. He shipped before the mast in the *Thorn,* a small brig of 132 tons, Captain George Ryder, a Cape Codder from Chatham. When they had returned to Boston, Jim signed to ship with Ryder in his new brig of 177 tons, the *Oak,* just launched and fitting out for her maiden voyage.

There were times, praise be, when it appeared that all was not hopeless with our man, when there came to the surface a certain canniness derived no doubt from Scotland. It began to dawn on him that he need not *necessarily* settle every dispute with his fists, that other means might on occasion be employed, with a saving of knuckles and noses.

One such opportunity arose while they were winding up their voyage in the *Oak.* It was in January of 1835. Head winds had frustrated every effort to drive the squat square-rigger up the Delaware River to Philadelphia and had pushed her back, at last, to the shelter of New York Harbor.

Among the forecastle gang was an old Portuguese sailor who had the only looking glass; it was in a pasteboard frame with a little pasteboard drawer under it in which he kept his comb and his money, notably twenty-five cents. All the men before the mast (there were five besides the old fellow, including Pattillo), along with the second mate who was in and out, had often used the glass and the comb during the voyage and of course had seen the old man's nest egg. Two days after their arrival at New York the coin was reported missing, and its owner swore up and down he'd been robbed.

Jim took it on himself to handle the matter, and considering his size and the force of his personality, the others readily agreed. When each in turn had protested his innocence (no one questioned *his*), Jim nodded and with a mysterious look informed them that he had a stratagem that would find out the guilty one, to which they acceded.

He went aft to the cabin, picking up a shingle on the way, and with the chief mate as witness split it into six pieces all of a length.

Shutting them up tight in his hands with the ends just showing, he returned to the forecastle and solemnly instructed each man to draw a lot; the one who took the longest would be the one who'd stolen the old timer's twenty-five cents.

They all drew, one after the other, leaving the last for Pattillo, and when they compared their lots, one was fully half an inch shorter than the rest.

"You vagabond!" Jim turned triumphantly on the astounded Jack whose stick stuck out so guiltily. "You stole it! All the lots were the same, but you were bound not to have the longest, weren't you, so you snapped off the end of it behind your back!"

The red-faced thief owned up and handed over the coin.

Jim left the *Oak* with a promise to Captain Ryder to ship with him again in the fall, God willing, and returned to Gloucester along around March. March is the New England purgatory, an endless month of suspended life, past the dead of winter but sterile of spring. We have five seasons here, folks say: spring, summer, fall, winter—and March. And March is the longest of all.

The Giles and Wonson fleet was fitting out, and Captain Addison Wonson, a son of the partner, signed Pattillo in *Mount Vernon,* a spanking new square-stern schooner of sixty-eight tons, launched in Essex only last year. If she wasn't the prettiest thing afloat, still she was put together in the fashion of the day, bluff-bowed, stout and sturdy. In one unusual respect, however, she departed from the mode, being a smack, the second one to slide down the Essex ways for the Gloucester fishery. Watertight bulkheads were built into her midsection between the masts, and three hundred holes were bored clean through her outside planking in this well, as they called it. The idea of this sea-going aquarium was to throw the fish in it as quick as they were caught and bring 'em back alive to market. In truth it was the beginning of the commercial fresh fish business.

The Wonsons were great for making their ingenuity (and courage) pay off in these early days of Gloucester fishing, always on the lookout for new grounds, new fish and new markets, and ready to try out new methods.

Back in 1827 another of Sam Wonson's boys, Add's brother John Fletcher, was returning to Gloucester in the same *Augusta* that brought Jim to Cape Ann. They were hove to on Georges Bank, a hundred and twenty-five miles southeast of home. Captain Wonson dropped a hook and line over the side to try his luck and soon had aboard two big halibut, the first ever known to have been caught on the Georges.

Thus began the exploitation of the most important, bountiful—and hazardous—fishing ground off the whole Atlantic coast of the United States, one which for decades would be reserved to Gloucester and her gritty "Georgesmen" and which would raise her to be the fishing capital of the world.

Georges Bank lay to the eastward of Cape Cod, shaped something like a halibut swimming off from Nantucket Shoals, covering eighty-five hundred square miles under depths from two to fifty fathoms. It included several extra-shallow spots such as Cultivator, Southwest and Georges shoals where the cod and halibut schooled at certain times of the year in great quantities. The tides ripped fierce around these places, rarely ebbing and flowing in a predictable cycle as nature intended, but swirling and rushing in every direction around the compass, meeting themselves head-on here, falling precipitously over an underwater waterfall there, making tremendous seas and breakers where the wind was contrary.

The Georges in wintertime was only for men who could stare down Death.

The first vessels recorded going there to fish were three pinkeys from Gloucester that ventured to the Bank after cod in 1821, Captain Sam Wonson's *Three Sisters,* Robert Marston's *Two Friends,* and the *Eight Brothers* under Elisha Oakes. They had all heard the old story about how the tidal current around the shoals would run any vessel under that attempted to anchor. But one fine day in June the three skippers resolved to try it at all hazards. So they doubled the crew of one by borrowing from the other two and let her anchor go. When the fluke bit up on the bottom and they checked the cable on the windlass, the schooner suddenly appeared to be tearing through the water at about three knots,

Captain Samuel Wonson, John Fletcher Wonson's brother. (Carolyn W. Pattillo)

nose down. As might be expected, the other two were drifting off with the current. The alarmed crew hove up their anchor, which took all of an hour and a half. The three pinkeys managed to find each other before nightfall and sailed for Gloucester posthaste with nary a fish between them, so relieved were they to get off that place alive.

Not until John Fletcher Wonson gave it a try in *Augusta* did anyone again brave Georges fishing. Catching those halibut had been like taking candy from a baby, and he kept them in the back of his mind until March of 1830 when he fitted out the *Nautilus* for the first halibut trip to the Bank in history.

Now, *Hippoglossus hippoglossus,* that King of Fishes, whose clear, white, firm and exquisitely flavored flesh is one of the delicacies from all the seven seas, deserves a word here, and he shall have it.

Old halibut is the greatest of the flatfishes, a veritable giant among flounders. He is quite as eccentric as his smaller cousins in that he, too, swims upright as every fish should when he is very young, whereupon, through some obscure biological thaumaturgy, his left eye migrates around his head and comes to rest beside the right. How inconvenient, thinks the victim of this ocular oddity. So he tips over on his left side, which being his new belly, turns white. His former right side, now his back, remains dark brown. His mouth twists disdainfully, and to complete this transfiguration, his fins shift around to conform to these goings-on in the same unsettling way.

Most of his life (and he may reach the age of thirty if he stays clear of the frying pan) the halibut spends near or on the bottom of the sea. He is a savage eater of fishes smaller than he, hence his habit of hanging around the banks where his dinner, such as the cod, comes in enormous numbers to spawn. He averages from twenty to a hundred pounds (although in 1827 two men picked up a halibut on the Maine coast that weighed 637 pounds *after* it had been gutted and was nearly ten feet long!).

There was a time when such hordes of halibut hung out in Massachusetts Bay that the men considered them as pesty as the little sharks called dogfish. But when their numbers declined on the inshore grounds, a popular demand for halibut steak arose (pity the poor fisherman, ever at the mercy of the market), and that was what led John Fletcher Wonson to make his famous trip in the *Nautilus,* catching twenty halibut and thereby opening Georges Bank for business as a commercial fishery.

John Fletcher came within an ace of losing Ben Marble on this pioneering voyage, and the incident for years after raised many a guffaw along the Gloucester waterfront at the expense of all hands involved. It seems that *Nautilus* was lying to on the drift, the men handlining over the rail, when Marble took a notion to have a try from the schooner's boat, which was slung in davits from over the stern, as was customary. He jumped in, was lowered away and cast off, dropped his anchor, baited up and went to work. The weather was moderate, all were absorbed in their fishing, and the vessel moved off with the current.

Dusk brought signs of a storm but none of Ben. Good Lord, there he was, nearly out of sight! Why the devil didn't he row back? A man was sent aloft to point the way, and Captain Wonson sailed after the solitary figure in the dory with the frantically waving arms. They reached him none too soon, between the weather and the darkness, and it was only then that someone noticed the oars laying on deck in plain sight where Ben had forgotten them in his haste to get going.

The firm of Giles and Wonson for the next four years cultivated the new fishery, sending out a few more trips a few weeks earlier each season. They instructed their skippers to roam the

Fresh halibuting on Georges Bank, three Gloucester schooners of the 1840s lie at anchor under double-reefed mainsails. Handlines are out, and it takes two men to gaff aboard the giant halibut thrashing at the quarter rail. (Goode's Fisheries*)*

Georges and feel their way around with the lead, exploring for the favorite gathering places of the fish.

There was rarely any problem getting a full fare; the hard part was trying to keep the halibut in prime condition for the Boston and New York markets, which were a day to two or three's sail from the grounds. "Fish fast and get in fast" was the word; but as the practice was to clean and dump them in the hold on the round beach stones of the ballast, they were taken out bruised and discolored The men also tried nailing them to the overhead by their tails, which improved their appearance but not their freshness, for the vessels were burdensome and slow.

So first *Forest* and then, hot on her stern, *Mount Vernon* were built as well smacks and sailed out to Georges that early spring of 835 by John Fletcher Wonson and his brother Add.

One of the three skippers who had first visited the Bank fourteen years before, Robert Marston, was on the *Mount Vernon* this trip as crew. Jim heard stories from him about the tide like the millrace when they anchored that time, sluicing by so hard the sea poured through the hawse holes, and he scoffed. Nor would he believe it when they told of days the halibut struck in on the south shoals, came onto the ground so thick they would haul the codfish clean off the hooks and follow the line to the surface, crowding so tight you might walk on them in any direction as far as the eye could see; and how they would jam up around the vessel as if they wanted to be taken, keeping two or three men busy all day, gaffing and hauling them aboard.

Was it possible? Was it really so that this great fish that belonged at the very bottom of the ocean as deep as a hundred fathoms down in the darkness would come up in such abundance that the sea literally disgorged him into the laps of the fishermen?

It was–and on that trip and others during the season Jim saw for himself the truth of these stories about the incredible Georges; the crazy tides and every-which-way currents, and the breakers in the middle of the ocean over the shoals, and storms with the violence of all hell turned loose that came up out of nowhere.

And there were the halibut, just as the men had said. Week after week they filled the well, drove their sluggish schooners to market, ran to Gloucester for food and fresh water and bait ('twas old haddock, *Melanogrammus aeglefinus,* caught by the dory load every day off Ten Pound Island right in the Harbor) and pushed on back to the Bank. If the weather was bitter, eighteen thousand pounds of halibut would stay alive in the well until market; if mild, only half that amount. But *Mount Vernon* and *Forest,* carrying seven men each, managed a round trip a week during the height of the halibut, with twelve thousand pounds of live fish a trip. One smack set the standing record for a day's catch when the boys hauled over the rail fourteen thousand thrashing pounds of halibut, on a handline every one, between ten in the morning and sundown.

Jim, as usual, rarely sailed on a sea of equanimity, and this spring was no exception. After a few trips on the *Mount Vernon,* a dispute arose between him and another fisherman named

Bridges, who happened to be Marston's son-in-law. While they were taking out in Boston, Bridges indicated to some people who came on board that he could flog that Pattillo or do about as he had a mind to with him. This boast reached Jim's ears, and after they had settled the trip he invited Bridges to step up forward of the windlass with him for a little talk. He asked the fellow what he meant by saying such derogatory things about a shipmate, especially in front of strangers, advised him to look out for himself and knocked him down on the deck by the heel of the bowsprit.

This summary action raised a rumpus with Captain Add Wonson and Marston. Jim offered to walk off the *Mount Vernon* then and there, but they persuaded him to stay with her to Gloucester, as they were short of hands; Bridges wasn't feeling too pert. When they arrived back at Cape Ann Jim left her and finished out the season in the pinkey *Lucinda* with John Fletcher's cousin John Wonson.

His second autumn in the States he made a freighting trip back to Nova Scotia with Captain Bill Brophy in the *Only Son*. The five tons of butter they carried they sold at a handsome profit in Boston, and that winter, as he had promised, he went to sea again with Captain Ryder in the brig *Oak*.

Two years had passed since our big friend was run out of the Provinces (or sailed off to seek his fortune in the Rogues' Hole, as he would put it). It was the spring of 1836, and the time was long overdue for a reunion with his family. Trusting that the Chester constabulary was short on memory and long on charity, he shipped with Bill Brophy in the ancient schooner *Manchester* on a trip to the Magdalen Islands in the Bay of St. Lawrence after herring. Brophy agreed to touch at Chester on the way.

The *Manchester* should have been rotting on a beach somewhere but instead was as strong as the day she was launched out of Duxbury fifty-two years earlier in 1784. Built big and heavy she was, for the offshore fisheries; they must have charmed her timbers for she would live to push a hundred and be the oldest working schooner in the United States. Good old *Manchester*! She saw generations of fishermen buried–and not all at sea, either. One of the stories she carried with her was of the day back around 1822 when an old cannon blew up on deck and killed a crewman with a Fourth of July salute going out Gloucester Harbor.

Chester was the same. Hot heads had cooled, bumps and bruises had subsided, and the wild Pattillo kept his fists in his pockets. But it wasn't the same either. The old father was up in the churchyard. The old mother was off down the line in Liverpool. And the old homestead on the water up the Front Harbor inlet, with the wharf where Alexander had kept his shallop and loaded his lime, all had been sold.

Jim and Annie met gravely after the long separation, and it seemed that she was well enough now to make the move to Cape Ann. He sent word to his mother to ship Alex to Chester by the packet and instructed his wife to be ready with their son to go on board of the *Manchester* when they called again on their return from the Bay of St. Lawrence.

Then Jim and his mates continued on for the Magdalens and the herring.

So exuberantly superabundant as almost to constipate Mother Nature's cornucopia in their rush to the shallows around the Magdalens, *Clupea harengus,* the herring, invaded the waters of the Bay with the regularity of a calendar. They came during the last week in April in schools so dense that spotters were posted on the island hills to direct the fishermen by signals where to set their nets from the boats or from the shore itself. Times were recorded with wonder when five thousand barrels of herring were pulled into the beach in one haul of the seine! By the end of May, spawn deposited, they were gone as miraculously as they came.

It was common practice among the American vessels to purchase their entire fare from the Bay fishermen, pickling the herring on board in the round, in their own barrels with their own salt, and this is what they did in the *Manchester.* In June, her aged frames working under the load, the old schooner sailed back through the Gut of Canso and down around the coast to Chester, where Anne Pattillo and her young son were waiting.

The boy was seasick most of the way to Cape Ann, and as the weather was warm, Captain Brophy allowed him to sleep out on deck under the stars. When they arrived at Eastern Point Jim rented rooms in the farmhouse of Isaac Patch. Mrs. Pattillo took up her housekeeping again, and Alex was entered in the district school to begin the education his father never had.

In Which Jim is Initiated Into the Occult Art of Mackereling

DIRECTLY AFTER the Fourth of July of 1836, having settled wife and child at Eastern Point, Jim returned to the employ of Giles and Wonson and signed with Captain Steve Rich for his second trip of the season to the Gulf of St. Lawrence, this time after mackerel.

Good Hope was a year old, the newest addition to the owners' fleet and at seventy-three tons the biggest, measuring sixty-six feet from apple stem to box stern. Like the rest, she had left off fishing for cod and halibut and was fitting out as a mackerel hooker so as to be there and waiting for the schools when they rose to the bait in the North Bay.

Rich had doubled his crew to twelve men. They cleared the schooner's deck of the fish pens and measured off the starboard rail in fishing berths every three feet or so—the best men to get the midships positions, the skipper taking the site just ahead of the main rigging, cook way forward to be near his galley, and one or two boys, still wet behind the ears, assigned farthest aft. Cleats, as many as a dozen of them for the highliner's lines, and jig bait boards were nailed to the rail at each berth. Two of the chum boxes were located inside the rail at the extreme fore and aft berths; the third and largest was made fast on the outside, amidships. When they got to fishing, the bait barrels would stand handy to the starboard rail, nearby to the half-hogshead strike tubs. The bait mill was always kept out of the way on the port side. Down below, the bulkheads were taken out, leaving the fish hold a dark cave floored with a loose dumping of cold pebbles; some of this ballast was carried in barrels, to be jettisoned as the containers filled with fish. Other barrels were packed with fine Liverpool salt, others with pickled menhaden slivers, others still with clams.

All this, along with various associated equipment such as a mile of cotton line, jig molds, bait heavers, gaffs, splitting knives, gib keelers and plows, comprised the mystic armamentarium with which the fishermen of Massachusetts practiced the occult art of mackereling. These tangible paraphernalia were as nothing, of course, unless one acknowledged faith in a Greater Power and sought His, Her or Its blessings. Therefore one did not begin a trip on a Friday or drive nails on Sunday; one most certainly did not turn a hatch bottom up or, God forbid, let it drop in the hold. It was the gravest sacrilege to permit the splices of the cable to come to a stop in the hawse pipe when anchoring . . . and to allow hawks, owls or crows to light in the rigging was virtually to invite disaster aboard.

All of these preparations and precautions combined, plus a dash of wizardry and a lifetime of experience, would without any doubt whatsoever guarantee a successful trip and a full fare . . . if the fish were right hungry, in the right place and at the right time. Otherwise, the smartest skipper in the fleet was just as likely to come home with a broker. Fisherman's luck? The phrase was invented for the mackerel killer; he was the greatest gambler of them all, and for the highest stakes.

So, while *Good Hope* and the other jiggers of Gloucester are running east on a fair southwest wind to join the growing fleet of hunters, let us examine further into the habits and habitats of the prey, that elusive rascal, *Scomber scombrus.*

He streams a liquid bullet from his nose's point to the delicate flair of his tail. The cloud waves of the sky streak the turquoise iridescence of his back, which glisters down each side into the supple silver of his belly. A flash of fins . . . he darts through the water, quick as a moonlit ripple.

Good gregarious mackerel, he loves the company of his kind, and they travel through life together by the thousands and the hundreds of thousands whither the temperature of the sea, food, fancy, instinct or the Great Mysterious beckons them. They sort themselves by size, in graded schools, for the protection of the species against an unfortunate tendency to cannibalism. Thus the year-old fry up to seven or eight inches congregate—tacks, or spikes, the fishermen call them. Then the two-year-olds—the tinkers—up to ten or eleven inches. They graduate into adulthood the third summer, ranging thirteen or fourteen inches, and thereafter Mister Mackerel grows very slowly, eventually perhaps up to eighteen inches.

Reproduction is the primal urge that gives the mackerel (and not alone the mackerel) its mystery, no doubt of it, but the wherebys are rather more evasive than the whys.

In the late autumn the schools disappear from the coastal waters without a trace. They simply sink out of sight—giving rise, as it were, to a body of lore concerning their winter hibernation, such as the once seriously proposed hypothesis of a naval man of rank that they spend it along the subarctic coasts with their heads and bodies stuck in the mud, only their tails protruding.

When spring comes they appear again, first in great numbers off Cape Hatteras in early April, next off Delaware Bay, then off southern New England in the first blush of May and on up the Gulf of Maine, finally in the Gulf of St. Lawrence during June, moving ever farther to the northward and inshore as spring progresses and renews the ocean's life with warmth and light.

They are thin and sorry-looking, the females ripe and hard with spawn . . . leatherbellies, as the fishermen indelicately describe them. They have not enough fat to grease the eyebrow of a mosquito, in the parlance of the day, and the whole breed fasts until the spawn has dropped, a happy event which occurs likewise in a northward progression that has much to do with the temperature of the nursery. Now the joyful parents eat greedily, roaming at times in seemingly infinite schools that have been said to cover miles and miles of the ocean's surface, pursuing the small fish or wee copepods of the sea such as the red feed, minute crustaceans so profuse as to turn the water scarlet . . . or themselves in flight from cod, shark, tuna or *homo sapiens.* By day a surfacing school gives itself away with a feather of ripples, at night by the unforgettably beautiful firing of the water as each flitting fish leaves a comet tail of bluish light momentarily generated by the phosphorescent organisms it disturbs.

Summer fattens the full-grown mackerel of a pound by a quarter of his weight. On his appetite and the fluctuations of his sexual capacity and the strength of his progeny and a dozen other will-o'-the-wisp things no one knows anything about, on these depend the fortunes of the fleet.

For ten years the mackerel had been striking in along the North Atlantic coast in unprecedented numbers. This invasion reached its climax in 1831, when the Massachusetts pack alone was more than three hundred and eighty thousand barrels—seventy-six million pounds—nearly every one caught by hook and line, and but the merest fraction of the schools. Why, they camc in so thick, as one old-timer put it, that an Indian on snowshoes could travel on them. But the catch dropped by a hundred and sixty thousand barrels the next year and steadily fell off until 1840, when it struck the bottom at a mere fifty thousand, scarcely a seventh of the 1831 pack. After that, the quantity climbed again as persistently as it had before declined.

Number Ones (the biggest and the best) fetched five dollars a barrel in 1830, the year that Captain Charley Wood, exploring the Provincial grounds in the schooner *Mariner,* made the first trip to the Gulf of St. Lawrence where the great river empties out in the broad bowl bounded by Labrador, Quebec, New Brunswick, Nova Scotia and Newfoundland. In only four weeks he brought back to Gloucester his vessel full of the finest kind of mackerel. Excitement along the wharves was high, and the following season—the grand year of 1831—the new fishery was embarked on in earnest. The fleet expanded by leaps and bounds thereafter. For forty years, until the purse seine replaced the hook, the North Bay, as Gloucestermen called the Gulf, was the summer mecca for that famous swarm of two or three hundred schooners known to the world as the mackerel jiggers.

Thus *Good Hope* pursued her course ever eastward off the coast of Maine, across the Bay of Fundy and by the familiar south shore of Jim's homeland. The days were warm and long, the nights were cool, the sea was calm, the wind was fair, the ship strong, the crew stout and the chances good. Altogether the voyage was for all the world a summer holiday, full of jest and youthful jollity as they fell in with small flotillas of schooners from Cape Cod, Boston, Marblehead and Beverly, from Sandy Bay on the other side of Cape Ann, from Newburyport and Maine. And there was much calling back and forth across the water and many the shouted jest when rival skippers spoke and pressed on canvas to be first on the grounds. All were bound for the North Bay, all seeking their fortune with the jig, each yearning for the high line, each coveting the first full fare, to be first home for the best price.

'Twas the jig that did it–danced a jig, it did, before the greedy eyes of *Scomber scombrus.* Transfixed him till he fell for the fatal fascination, and snapped at the bit of bait dangling from the jig like a gay tail (his last snap). And if he were beside himself with hunger and spellbound by the jig of the jig, he would take the bare denuded hook, poor deluded *Scomber scombrus.*

A Cape Ann fisherman had invented the jig not so many years before. He poured a sinker of lead in the shape of a cigar around the shank of a fishhook and bored a hole in the other end to bend the line through. It worked like a charm, as a charm it was in the hands of a skillful mackereler.

Aboard *Good Hope* and all the other jiggers ballooning their canvas to the breeze, the crews off watch poured their supply of charms, some in soapstone molds, others in a scoop of ashes or bucket of sand. Most used lead, but one man might prefer pewter, another tin, and each veteran fashioned his own peculiar shape and size which ran from a quarter of an ounce to two or three in weight, to be fished as wind, wave, drift, fancy and the ardor of the mackerel should dictate.

On board a Gloucester mackerel hooker in the Bay of St. Lawrence a crewman takes his trick at the bait mill mashing up slivered menhaden.

Working three handlines, the skipper tolls the mackerel toward his bait with scoops of stosh.

Jigging, slatting off the catch into their strike tubs and chumming them close alongside, the Gloucestermen fish intently to keep with the school amidst the fleet of mackerel schooners on the move.

The run of mackerel over for the moment, the men split, clean and wash the catch.

Pitching, salting and "plowing" for the trip home, this trio will drop everything and scramble for their lines at the galvanizing cry of "mackerel! mackerel!" (Goode's Fisheries*)*

A hurried stopover at Canso on the extreme eastern tip of the Nova Scotian mainland for fresh water and firewood–and then the long reach through the wind-whipped twenty miles of the Gut of Canso, wild Cape Breton Island rising like a bluff Scotch headland on the starboard hand. Emerging into George Bay a man could follow the Breton shore with his eye on a clear day as far as Port Hood till it bent out of sight, and likewise to Cape George to larboard.

Good Hope dropped the soft green rises and red sands of Prince Edward Island and pointed to the nor'ard for the Magdalens and the mackerel. The waters round about the islands were among their favored haunts; according to Captain Rich's calculations the leatherbellies were spawning right now and would commence biting like fury most any time. Nor was he alone in his figuring; a hefty portion of the armada was tearing along for the same objective under a press of sail.

Now the night watch was put to work grinding chum. Chum was the elixir, cast upon the waters, that tolled the schools to the surface and the hook. In the old days they boiled a haddock and slapped it to pieces against the topsides. Or the men ground it under their boots on the deck. As time went by they pounded it with mallets; then someone got the bright idea of chopping it on a block with a hatchet. Finally around 1820 a Cape Anner invented the ultimate refinement–the bait mill, a hand-cranked drum in a box, studded first with nails, later with knives. Filleted slivers of pickled pogies (menhaden) were dropped in this infernal machine, oozing therefrom as a yellow, oily, quite revolting mash. The bait mill soon was such a fixture aboard every mackerel hooker that the good wife of one old fisherman had to sit up half the night cranking one in the bedroom to get him to sleep between trips.

Rounding the rocks and pastures and sand spits of the scraggly Magdalens, *Good Hope* worked eight or ten miles north into the shoal water where the schools were likely to be lurking. At last comes the action, all no doubt of intense interest to Jim.

First Skipper Steve orders jib and foresail doused, and the schooner is hove to under mainsail, helm down to make a near square drift to leeward. A bucket of ground-up goo from the mill is slopped into the midships bait box at the rail; sea water is added, and the captain stirs this mess with his bait heaver, a long-handled tin dipper, until the consistency of the chum, or stosh, satisfies him. He takes a stand at his berth forward of the main shrouds, bait heaver in hand, and ladles a scoop or two over the side. The smooth eddies made by the drifting vessel and its own oiliness disperse the chum widely over her wake. He quickly baits two of his jigs with scraps of pork rind and drops the lines over.

All hands, Jim among them, lounge around the deck, tense and expectant, all eyes on the skipper and his lines. As often as not this can go on for an hour or more without a bite, before giving it up. Is there a school around? Will it come to the chum? Rich tends his lines with intense concentration, every few moments dipping over another scoop of stosh.

Suddenly he sings out!

"Here they are!"

With a jerk of his arm he pulls a fat mackerel out of the water clear up over his head in a skittering, glittering arc and right round behind into his strike tub, so perfect his aim he hardly turns, slatting it off with a counterjerk that yanks the jig from its cheek, all in one motion. Up comes the second line as fast as skip can grab it, up and over in a flurry of spray.

The two mackerel beat their tails in a frantic tattoo on the bottom of the tub. The men run for their berths at the rail with yells of excitement. That hysterical drumming of the first fish inside the first hollow barrel tingles the nerve endings of the fisherman, sets him all on edge for the kill. It is a mystic message from mackerel to man, of despair for the one and hope for the other.

Eagerly the men seize and kill the first-caught fish. With shaking hands they cut silvery strips from the belly back by the anal fin, scrape off the flesh and bait their jigs with the tough white skin, which will last on the hook for an hour of hard use, even when they're striking in thick–and how they are!

Rich has tolled up a spurt for sure. The school is rising to the surface alongside, pressing against the vessel. The shimmering fish are avid for the chum, all in a turmoil. The men are at the rail, some leaning way over the side as if pulled there by the lines they play like puppeteers, two or three in each hand. Hardly a word is spoken, so intent are they. Now and again someone pauses to pick up his bait heaver, dip stosh, and toll them closer in. The air is alive with mackerel slatting back into the strike tubs, sprinkling with fine spray from them. The tubs are filling unbelievably fast. The deck itself vibrates under foot with the resonant death beat of the caught ones. A highliner can pack a barrel of a hundred and fifty or two hundred mackerel in fifteen or twenty minutes, as many as fifteen barrels in a day's work; that's a ton and a half of mackerel for one man at the rate of one every six seconds of steady fishing, every one slatted off by hand!

After two or three hours the spurt shows signs of petering out. Though still up in the water, the school has left off biting and is picking. They nibble at the jig, but few will take it, and some of the men break out their broom-handled mackerel gaffs with the double hooks, impaling a few hundred more with brisk recoils of their weapons.

At length, enigmatically, and as suddenly as it rose to the chum, the school sinks and is gone. No amount of cruising about, heaving to, drifting and tolling will avail, and that's the end of the catch for the *Good Hope* off the Magdalens: thirty-five barrels in one brief strike.

The elation of the fishing has departed with the fish, but there remains the job of dressing and salting down this deckload, and it will stretch into the weary night under lanterns strung from the rigging.

Captain Rich orders his schooner hove to and divides the crew into dress gangs of pairs, a splitter and a gibber. Bone-tired already, they pull on their newfangled oilskin pants to keep the gurry off their duds. Splitter lays a board across a barrel head, with the deftness of a surgeon knives each shining mackerel down the back from snout to tail and tosses it into his mate's gib keeler, a wood tray athwart another barrel. Wearing gloves or mittens to protect his hands from the needly bones, gibber sweeps out the viscera with a quick motion of the thumb and fingers and throws them aside to be dumped overboard later.

And now the moment of deception. The cunning gibber seizes his mackerel plow, spreads the split sides of his victim and flicks this notorious instrument down each abdominal wall. Lo, the smooth lean flesh of an early season number three is transformed into the fine, cracked, fatty meat of a number two—at the gain, when culled on the dock, of three dollars a barrel. The inspectors may denunciate, and the state legislate, but the fishermen have been counterfeiting their catch thus—first with thumbnail, then with the back of the knife, and now with their peculiar plow—and will continue so until what began as a trick to fool the dealers (and of course the public) comes to be demanded by both for the sake of appearances.

Split, gibbed and plowed, much-abused Mister Mackerel lands in another barrel along with his brothers and sisters and a few buckets of sea water. When a backlog of these wash barrels has accumulated, a brace of dress gangs is sent below to start salting. Fish from the wash barrels on deck are flipped down through the hatch into trays of salt. Salter grabs a mackerel in each hand, rubs them vigorously in the salt until every part is covered, slaps them back to flesh and stows the pairs in layers in his butt, flesh side down (the fine Liverpool salt is preferred for mackerel; the coarser stuff from Spain "rucks up" the tender flesh). It takes a barrel of salt to pickle five wash barrels of mackerel and pack a butt. The packed fish are henceforth measured in sea barrels, of which a butt contains about four. When a butt has been filled, the salters place a round flat stone over the fish to keep them immersed in the brine.

Late that night the catch had been packed at last. The decks were washed, and the tuckered-out crew—all but the watch, which was assigned to the bait mill for the wee hours—tumbled into their bunks.

Leaving the Magdalens, *Good Hope* beat down across the azure waters of the North Bay to test the run of the mackerel off the northern arc of Prince Edward Island—the Bend of the Island, as the Americans dubbed that lovely shore. Fortune grinned for the second time, and there was one hectic day when they hauled in forty wash barrels twenty miles broad off St. Peters Bay. That was the end of it. Steve Rich ran up the flag to the main topmasthead and sailed for home.

And wouldn't it be the luck of the hooker, though? After chasing two thousand miles to the North Bay and back for seventy-five barrels of mackerel, they bumped into a regular swarm right off Cape Ann and caught two hundred more without winking!

Thus did Big Jim arrive back in Gloucester for his thirtieth birthday that September, and then he shipped again with Steve Rich in the *Good Hope* on a salt fish freighting voyage. They sailed down off the Atlantic coast, round Florida and across the Gulf of Mexico to Mobile, Alabama, with six hundred barrels of herring Rich had caught in the Magdalens that spring. Pickled herring was cheap slave food in the South and quantities of it were sold to plantation owners by abolitionist New Englanders.

They returned to Cape Ann in February of 1837 after a twenty-seven-day passage, and Pattillo was assigned back in the *Mount Vernon,* this time under Captain Bill Forbes. She was fitting out to go to the Georges halibutting in company with John Fletcher Wonson and the *Forest.* The owners had bargained with a dealer in East Boston to buy all the fresh halibut the two smacks caught at monthly prices agreed on in advance for the season.

Mount Vernon sold her first trip, but when she returned from the Bank with her second, at the end of March, the dealer swore the market had failed and broke his contract. So they sailed across the Harbor from East Boston to Long Wharf and disposed of their fare for what it would fetch.

Next day was the first of April, chill and overcast. The schooner wanted only wind for the run of a few hours down to Cape Ann. Forbes and the rest of the crew walked up into Boston for a look, leaving Jim in charge of the vessel. He waved them goodby, settled down on board and got out his pipe.

A few blocks away in the North End, a crowd was gathering, some coming on the run through the narrow streets, and making considerable commotion up against a building on which had just been posted this notice:

> April 1st–Picked up at sea by the brig Caravan, on the 22nd March, latitude 36 41, longitude 61 25, a large living male Elephant, supposed to be the same that escaped from the wreck of the steamer Royal Tar, in October last. It may be seen this day and tomorrow (gratis) at the end of Battery Wharf.

Everybody remembered the *Royal Tar* debacle. She burst her boiler and burned in Penobscot Bay while carrying a circus from St. John, New Brunswick, to Portland, Maine.

Down at the end of Battery Wharf it was starting to rain. A throng of about six hundred huddled in the developing downpour in the square before a warehouse. A simple announcement had been tacked on the locked door:

> The Elephant is in this building–the keeper will be here in a few minutes.

The curious of Boston hunched in the drenching rain for more than an hour, shivering, waiting to inspect the elephant that had survived a five-months' swim of seven hundred and fifty miles in the mid-Atlantic. Late in the morning, with still no sign of the keeper, the crowd mostly dispersed. There was some muttering.

While this scene was unfolding, back aboard the *Mount Vernon* Jim's reverie was disturbed by a broguish hail from Long Wharf. He stuck his head out of the companionway into the rain, looking for the source of the greeting.

It was a stocky Irishman, one of those who were emigrating to America as the freshet before the flood, driven from the Old Country by the hard times getting harder, eager for any kind of employment. He had been looking the smack over.

Sure, and what would captain give a man to have her pumped out, dry and tidy? he inquired cheerfully.

Jim took his pipe from his mouth, grinned and started to say something but changed his mind. His eyes narrowed, and he looked as solemn as a codfish.

"Paddy, it's nothing to me if she's pumped out or not, one way or the other–what would you do it for?"

A dollar an' a bottle o' rum.

They settled on half a dollar and the bottle, and the Irishman hustled off for a chum. In a jiffy they were back and aboard. One seized pump, the other pail, and they pumped and bailed the well in the rain for three hours or so, and the water inside didn't drop by the width of a hair.

Jim broke out the rum and handed it over to the perspiring and rain-soaked pair to refresh themselves for the redoubling of their efforts, and he went below to unstraighten his face.

The two pumped and bailed and cursed the size of the hold. They emptied the bottle and pumped and bailed some more until Captain Forbes and the rest of the crew came back on board in the afternoon. They were still hard at it.

"Who the devil are you men and what the devil are you doing?" bellowed Forbes with a look of astonishment.

Sure, cap, there was a big fellow around somewheres, he hired them in the morning to bail out the ship for half a dollar and a bottle of rum, but sweet Jaysus they'd pumped enough to float the Spanish Armada and the water was as high as ever.

"Do you lads know what day of the month this is?" asked the skipper, trying to keep control of himself.

Why the first of April.

"All Fools' Day, that's it! This vessel is a smack, my boys, and her well there has three hundred holes through the bottom, every one big around enough for you to stick your finger through. You'll never bail her out unless you empty the whole Western Ocean. Here's your fifty cents. Now get ashore!"

The air around them ringing to the haw-haws of the crew, bailer and pumper pulled on their jackets and stumbled onto Long Wharf with some hard words for that big one.

Jim remained in the forecastle until *Mount Vernon* got under way, preferring not to have a controversy with them.

The Pearl of Great Price

> The kingdom of heaven is like unto a merchant man, seeking goodly pearls: who, when he had found one pearl of great price, went and sold all that he had and bought it.
>
> –MATTHEW 13: 45, 46

WITH A LITTLE LUCK, so commented the newspaper disgustedly during what passed for spring in 1837, the ice will be gone out of Gloucester Harbor by August. Winter certainly was hanging on . . . and on, and on–cold, raw and plumb downright miserable.

But thirty fathoms down on Georges it was dinnertime, and the halibut were waiting to take the hook. The largest fleet yet had fitted out for Gloucester's newest grounds, sailed earlier and made more trips.

Familiarity had bred a measure of contempt for the tempestuous and treacherous shoals, and the master mariners now carried extra-heavy anchors and cable, paid out plenty of scope and hove their hooks in the sand with less fear of the tides. Why drift and jog all over Georges Bank when the fleet could anchor over a good fishy shoal and work it at leisure in company?

Mount Vernon ran from Boston back to Eastern Point for stores, water and bait. The waterfront chuckled over Jimmy Pattillo hiring the Irishmen to pump out the Atlantic Ocean. And then as quick as she came in she weighed anchor and stood out the

Harbor for the Georges, where she rejoined the fleet toward the end of April.

At precisely the same time, Jim's old winter berth, the good brig *Oak,* was crossing the southwest shoals of the Bank, homebound for Boston from a voyage through the Straits to Smyrna. That night, it came on to blow. Captain Ryder ordered her snugged down. One of the crew described what happened:

> We ran into the fleet of fishermen at anchor, just at daybreak. Spoke schooner *Fair American,* John Wonson, master, wind blowing heavy from south southwest, with snow. Captain Wonson informed us, in language peculiar to himself, that he would not heave up his anchor, but would sink her first. It was generally supposed that he did go down, as he was never known to be spoken afterwards.
>
> We ran in company with the smack *Ben Franklin,* Ben Norwood, master, which went down in the same gale. She and the schooner *Canton* came out new that spring and were rivals; they both left the Bank at the same time, and both carried sail heavily; but as both captains were much censured at the time for carrying sail so heavily, I will only say we saw the *Franklin* come up in the wind, evidently to shake the snow from her sails in a heavy snow squall, after which we saw no more of her. After it cleared somewhat, we saw the *Canton* under snug sail.

Nor was there any trace either, after it stopped snowing and blowing, of the schooner *Vesta,* Captain Josiah Fears.

The fleet came in, rounded the Point and leaned on past Ten Pound Island into the anchorage. The men went ashore with heavy hearts, full of dread. No one had actually seen any of the three take the plunge, the air had been that thick with snow and spray, so some hope was offered those at home that the missing three had been blown off the grounds and were on their way in. A fortnight passed, and the Gloucester papers carried a despairing paragraph under *Shipping Intelligence:*

A black squall streaks across Gloucester Harbor, in this old-time painting by an anonymous artist. The vessel at left rounds to while crews aboard the schooner and the sloop upwind of her hustle to take in sail. (Boston Public Library)

> Considerable anxiety is felt as to the fate of the fishing schooners *Fair American,* Wonson, about 50 tons, *Benjamin Franklin,* Norwood, about 70 tons, and *Vesta,* Fears, of Gloucester. Any information respecting them will be thankfully received by the owners, and the families and friends of the crews. They have been anxiously looked for about two weeks.

There was no information. The three doomed schooners carried twenty-one good men beneath the waves without a trace. It was the first catastrophe on Georges Bank, the first in a death roster of disaster.

How much blame belonged to cussed, stubborn skippers—one who would sink before he'd heave up anchor to gain sea room, another sworn to carry every stitch of canvas for the sport of it? And Fears—what had he done to bring down such a fate on himself and his men and the *Vesta*? Or was he in the clear and they the victims of a cruel destiny?

The Georges was no place for inward-thinking men; but the ones who had been to hell and back that April, gripping their lives, asked themselves in spite of themselves: Better him than me . . . but what about the next trip?

Among them James William Pattillo, the strongest man in the Gloucester fleet, drinker, brawler, cocksure, cussed, stubborn–invincible and indestructible.

It was the night of June sixteenth. How many times had he relived it? It was burned in his mind. Six weeks had gone, and with them all hope for the missing schooners. *Mount Vernon* had been back on Georges for several days and was racing in for Boston with a full fare of halibut in the well.

Although the wind was fair, the night was black and thick o' fog besides. Thunderstorms were about, and in the flashes of lightning the fog glowed so that for an instant a man could see from stern to stem. Jim was on the eight-to-eleven watch with Ned Wonson; he had held to the helm the whole trick rather than relax the lookout for the matter of seconds it would have taken them to switch places.

When their three hours were up he stomped on the quarter-deck to turn out the relief below in the cabin. Ben Wonson took over the tiller and Charlie Steward the lookout. Jim was on edge about their situation, the more so because they were crossing the ship lanes. When they had descended into the cabin he urged on Captain Forbes the proposition that they stand half and half, three in a watch, instead of by twos, to insure a constant lookout.

His skipper gave him a searching look.

"There was no trouble while you and Ned were up, was there Jim?"

No indeed.

"And do you consider Ben and Charlie as good as the two of you?"

No doubt better in every way.

"In that case, Jimmy, I don't spose there'll be any trouble while they're up, either." As much as to say he thought the big man was being just a mite too cautious for a Gloucester fisherman.

"All right," Pattillo shot back angrily. "I guess I have as many friends in hell as anybody!" And he tumbled into his berth . . . boots, oilskins and sou'wester all on, just as he came from the deck.

He lay in the bunk thinking about this exchange, and his parting shot at Forbes kept recoiling through his head . . . I guess I have as many friends in hell as anybody . . . friends in hell . . . Was he scared?

The water rushed and gurgled past the planks a few inches away; that and the creaking and working of the vessel were the only sounds in the dark. Outside, up beyond the hatch, a black night, a deep sea and the unknown.

And then, a cry of hysteria from the lookout:

"Hard up, Ben, hard up for God's sake! There's a ship coming right over us!"

Four men below leapt from their bunks, made for the companionway in a rush and jammed all at once so that none could get through for a moment. As they were sorting themselves out, Jim heard Ben Wonson scream from the quarterdeck:

"Oh my God! They're going to run us down!"

The four broke out topsides. Ben had thrown the tiller to windward and the schooner was bearing away. At that instant the lightning revealed a great full-rigged ship, coming right at them and so close off their bow that it towered high above and magnetized Jim's gaze, with magnificent irrelevance up and up the spread of canvas to the topsails, which he could dimly see were reefed.

The sighing crash of its massive hull through the seas and the rumple of the wind in its sails were hypnotic; the six fishermen on their little schooner, which was still slowly, so slowly, bearing away, froze before it as if their boots were nailed to the deck.

The two vessels passed. The sheer wall of the ship crescendoed by, perhaps three feet away. Had the schooner borne off another fraction of a point she would have jibed her main boom into the rigging of the ship, broached to and collided. Not a word was spoken, and as the length of the thing hissed past, Jim saw a dog standing by the mizzen shrouds, his eyes shining in the dark.

It was gone.

That was enough for Captain Forbes. Shaken to his boots, he wanted to heave to for the rest of the night.

"Have no fear now," muttered Jim. "There'll be lookout enough."

So they decided to continue on for Boston, the six of them straining their eyes into the blackness. There was no more sleep for that night, and no more talk than needed.

These were men with a strong grip on a perilous life. They put their faith where they reckoned it would do the most good . . . in themselves, in one another, in their boats.

Yet all in one stroke, but six weeks since, Death on the Georges had taken a score of their friends, men just like the six of them, with the same chances good and bad . . . and tonight Death was rolling the dice again.

Jim could not doubt it nor deny it to himself: if his mates were jolted by what had just happened (as they were; a spell of silence had fallen over all), he was the more terrified the more it came back on him. He tried to swallow away the waves of a fear, like nausea, that he had never known before and the sinister words he had spat out at Forbes rushed up in him . . . *I have as many friends in hell as anybody.* He clenched his fists and bit his lip till the blood ran. The sweat was streaming off his face and he wiped it away with a clammy hand. His mouth was dry and sticky.

My God, I am damned! he thought. If I die with my next breath I am damned to all the fires of hell forever for the wickedness of my life and my blasphemy and cursing and the things I have done and the drinking and all the neglect of my dear old mother and my poor wife and the little boy that needs me. Oh God, I am damned!

His guilt and his pity for himself beyond understanding flooded up and engulfed him, and there in the black of the foul night he stared out over the tossing ocean that he knew better than his own self and swore to God that if he ever got home he would not go to sea again until he had found the pearl of great price. If there was a reality in religion, he would have it.

Mount Vernon went two more trips to Georges Bank without Pattillo. Toward the end of July Captain Forbes called at his home (they had moved into the abandoned Proprietors' Schoolhouse over in the town) to find the man still distraught after almost a month ashore.

The best medicine would be to get back to sea, Forbes urged. They were fitting out for mackereling in the North Bay—come along, they needed him.

Jim shook his head. He was not in a fit state to sail, he told his visitor. His mind was disturbed about his soul's salvation. He had promised God he would remain ashore until he had found peace, and he had striven in every way he knew, but it would not come to him.

But his wife had had enough of this brooding. She persuaded her drinking, self-damning husband to agree to go over to Eastern Point the next day and to lend a hand at least with fitting out the *Mount Vernon,* even if he didn't sail in her.

In the morning Jim was assigned aloft. He went up in the bosun's chair and slapped a coat of white paint on the foremast-head. After lunch he tackled the maintop, unseated the topmast, set it down and followed it to the deck, painted it and went aloft again to set it up. He secured the topmast rigging. His buckets and brushes were sent up, and he commenced painting mast-head, blocks and other woodwork white, hardware black, absent-mindedly, automatically, drowsy from the heat of the July sun, his thoughts disturbed and far away.

Then—his foot slipped . . . and he dropped into thin air. It was forty-five feet to the deck. The paintbrush flew from his hand. He reached out and grabbed a shroud and hung on by one arm, his body swinging with the gentle rocking of the schooner.

And at that moment, right before his eyes, appeared the image of Christ, arms outstretched.

Praises be to God!

Whooping and shouting, Jim hauled himself back to the spreader and roared out a round of hallelujahs that caused the men on deck to look skyward, for no one had witnessed his near fall, so sudden and noiseless had it been.

More hollering from aloft:

"Oh, I have found peace at last! Oh, what a load has fallen off me! Praise God for what He has done! He has sent His Son into the world to seek and save the lost! Oh praise God He found me, guilty me!"

Jim let himself down to the deck so fast the gantline fairly sang through the block and smoked in his hands. He was a wild man when he landed in the middle of the astonished crew, laughing and chortling and waving his arms and clapping them on their backs, chattering incoherently all the while of his happiness and his salvation.

"Oh, I have found the pearl of great price!" he bellowed, and he exhorted his mates to cast off their evil ways and join him in the faith of Christianity.

And then, as abruptly and vigorously as he had arrived on deck from on high, Jim vaulted the rail to the wharf and strode off toward home to inform Annie of the miracle that had taken place. Nor did he appear to pay the slightest heed to the waterfront idler who had witnessed this remarkable performance and was foolhardy enough to comment quite audibly that Pattillo had gone crazy and they will have to put him in a strait jacket and cart him off to the madhouse.

Anne Pattillo was a devout woman and they rejoiced together and praised God for what He had done. They had a happy time and great closeness. Jim felt that the pearl of great price was in his hands. He thought he knew what he must do to keep it. He vowed that he would never again touch liquor.

When *Mount Vernon* two days later sailed for the North Bay in company with *Good Hope* and the others, that great Pattillo was back in his old berth, to all appearances a new man, radiating good cheer and a certain righteousness which his shipmates found a trifle wearying after several days at sea.

During these soul-trying weeks, the remembrance of his mother had recurred to Jim, each time causing a wince of guilt. Off Nova Scotia he persuaded Forbes to put into Liverpool overnight.

The Widow Pattillo was not in her neat cottage when the

prodigal son burst through the door and called out for her. He crossed the street to his Aunt Roberts, but she was not there either. As he was talking with Aunt in the parlor, Betsy came hurrying in; someone had told her Jim was home.

Mother and son embraced in tearful reunion. The toil-worn old lady still carried the strength of her prime in its form; only the substance had drained away. She was wearing the dress and shoes she was so proud of, the ones he had sent her by John Anderson's packet from Boston last February for her seventy-fifth birthday. He had not forgotten; he had always wanted to please her, poor Jim. How often she had prayed for him, how sadly she had stood him and his wayward ways against his brother Tom, the comfort of her old age, a good Baptist and a strong temperance man, looked up to by everybody.

They walked to her little house, and Betsy cooked the last supper she ever would for her boy. Jim fervently related his experience, how he had found the pearl of great price, and Jesus was his all in all. Oh, the salvation of him! Was it possible? She thanked the Lord that her prayers for this son had been answered. They wept together and rejoiced, and when he had to leave to get back to his vessel at nearly midnight, it seemed to him that he parted from his mother at the throne of Grace.

It was the last time he saw her on the shores of time.

All through August and September the fleet of two hundred American sail cruised hither and yon over the blue, fogless waters of the North Bay, tolling all the likely haunts but having hard luck wetting their salt. The mackerel were slack.

They were off the west coast of Cape Breton on the third of October when a gale sprang up from the eastward. Several of the fleet, including *Mount Vernon* and *Good Hope,* ran for Cheticamp, coming to anchor under the low and verdant meadow of Cheticamp Island. The island was only half a mile offshore, and it was this quite long reach between isle and mainland that made the pretty little Acadian village a fishing port and harbor of refuge. During the storm the anchorage was flat and gray as slate, being in the lee. Sheets of rain moved across, fanlike. But the wind hustled over it something fierce and by slow degrees pushed *Good Hope* and a down-East schooner clear up against the low-lying bank of the island, their anchors bouncing uselessly along the bottom. They were run up so high and dry that at the height of the storm the men simply jumped off their decks onto the field of grass.

Before the gale had blown itself out the crews of both vessels were taking off stores, ballast, fish and everything that had weight and piling them in the pasture. The down-Easter was got off this way, but *Good Hope* would not float. Steve Rich and his boys spent all of four days at it; they carried three anchors and cable into the channel by their yawl boat trying to kedge her off, but the flukes would not hold in the bottom and dragged back to the schooner with every turn of the windlass.

Captain Rich was on the point of giving her up at last when Jim, who had been observing these futile operations from the deck of the *Mount Vernon* with singular forbearance, offered nonchalantly to carry the anchors out and place them where they would hold against any purchase whatsoever. The two skippers readily agreed, whereupon Pattillo hired twenty-five Frenchmen from Cheticamp; after four more days of sweat and strain–moving anchors around, erecting derricks and digging trenches in the mud–they kedged her off on a high course tide in the middle of the night.

Good Hope was hardly the worse for it, but Jim had been in the water shifting the derricks; he was wet to the skin, shivering cold, and his teeth were chattering. Now Joe McClennan knew Jim was trying to live a better life and that alcohol was his greatest enemy, but he could not stand by and see a pal take a chill, so he got him to take a drink. One followed another, from medication to celebration. They rowed out to the *Mount Vernon,* where they climbed aboard and made a noisy and unsteady entrance into the cabin.

While big Jim was shifting into dry clothes, some of the crew who had been in on the first unsuccessful attempt at salvage joshed him about his feat, and Jonathan Douglass had the poor judgment to snicker, with a wink at the others, that as the job was the kind that called for more back than brains, it had naturally fallen to a Novie.

This shaft hit the mark. Jim was dog-tired and mad at himself and McClennan over breaking the pledge, half-drunk and pricked by these thorns in his laurels. He gave an oath, up with his fists and hammered the two of them, McClennan and Douglass, stretching them cold on the cabin floor before the rest jumped in and pulled him off.

Everything was put back on board of *Good Hope,* and she sailed directly for Cape Ann. *Mount Vernon* paused on the way to try around Margaree Island, twenty miles down and a league off the Cape Breton shore. They were in luck; something had drawn an enormous school of mackerel there. They hooked two hundred barrels so close under the land that they had to anchor and bend a spring line from the cable back to the port quarter, which held the schooner near square to the tide; the current carried the chum and their lines away to starboard, and in this way they came near to filling up. They topped off with another spurt of a hundred barrels fifteen miles offshore and labored into Gloucester a week later, having the only full fare out of two hundred hookers in the Bay that season.

Jim walked ashore into a wall of reproof. One of his victims had talked around about his drunken behavior at Cheticamp. Men wanted no trouble with Pattillo. He was bad news when in liquor, and it seemed to him that they avoided him. Since he was not the kind who took easily to a word of friendly advice or encouragement, none was offered. And so he fell back on the bottle and soon was his old self. The pearl of great price had slipped through his fingers.

The Adventure of the Tiger: Going Up

> If heaven in the creation gave a right, it is ours at least as much as yours. If occupation, use, and possession give a right, we have it as clearly as you. If war, and blood, and treasure give a right, ours is as good as yours. We have been constantly fighting in Canada, Cape Breton, and Nova Scotia, for the defence of this fishery, and have expended beyond all proportion more than you. If, then, the right cannot be denied, why should it not be acknowledged and put out of dispute? Why should we leave room for illiterate fishermen to wrangle and chicane?
>
> –JOHN ADAMS TO THE BRITISH, PARIS, 1782

CAPTAIN SAM GILES, vice president of the Gloucester Temperance Society, town father, church pillar and partner in the fishing firm of Giles and Wonson, pondered what to do about that great Pattillo from Nova Scotia. He was the bull in their shop, all right, this moody brawling brute, this fugitive from Her Majesty's justice who was preaching to his mates one day and cracking their skulls the next.

What could they do indeed with one who in the four years since he landed on Cape Ann had proved the best of sailors, a highliner, courageous, ingenious, universally feared, true as the needle to the pole and a born leader, drunk or sober?

So in the spring of 1838, when Jim came back in the *Forest* from New York with the Wonson boys after taking the first load of frozen fish ever to land there, the partners had made up their minds to do the only thing left for them. They called him into their office and addressed him as Captain Pattillo, with the information that they were giving him command of the *Good Hope* which he had saved from ruin in the North Bay; and they told him he would damn well keep his rum and his work separated if he wished to hold on to it.

Here was a turn for the better. With unconcealed joy the recipient of this promotion assured his employers that their confidence had not been misplaced.

All that remained was to get around the matter of collecting the Federal bounty on codfish, which would be $280 at the end of the year provided *Good Hope* was commanded by a citizen. Having no cradle to rock Jim in, Giles and Wonson merely entered the name of William Rowe, an American crew member, as the nominal master in her papers.

Captain Pattillo's first trips in charge of a Yankee vessel were unexceptional except for the placid nature of their course. Besides Rowe and a couple of others, he had along his youngest brother-in-law, Jack Gorman, going on seventeen and fresh from Chester on consignment to Jim for a quick lesson in growing up; and another young Chesterman, Josiah Lovett, whom Annie and he had nursed through a serious illness that winter. When Lovett turned up sick in Gloucester on one of Ben Parsons's schooners, Jim found some satisfaction in taking him home and playing the Good Samaritan, for he remembered all the dirty names Lovett had called him when he left Chester in some haste.

They took *Good Hope* codding and halibutting to the Georges through the spring; in July they refitted for mackereling to the North Bay.

It would not do at all for Jim to revisit his old home waters in triumphant and vindicative command of a Yankee vessel without spitting in the Queen's eye, to put it crudely. Therefore, one fine day up in the Bay he ran *Good Hope* along under the Cape Breton coast, and they hooked fifty barrels of fat mackerel so close on shore they could have packed 'em out on the beach.

Which was illegal.

The fact is that Americans were prohibited by international agreement from fishing within three marine miles of the whole tortuous coast of the British North American Provinces except for Labrador, the Magdalen Islands and certain parts of Newfoundland. This disagreeable state of affairs was created by the Convention of 1818, which tied up the loose ends of controversy left dangling from the Treaty of Ghent that ended the War of 1812. Father and son, the New Englanders had fished freely in these waters as far back as the oldest timer could recollect. John Adams was the hero of the fishermen for securing their traditional rights of free access to Canadian territorial waters when he bargained them into the treaty that wrapped up the American Revolution in 1783. Then along came the peace negotiations in 1818, and the United States renounced forever these rights as they applied within three miles of the Provincial shore.

The New England fishermen swore bitterly that their government had sold them down the river, and treaty or no treaty they would fish where they had a mind to, as they always had. This was mostly guff until the Cape Anners found mackerel in such abundance ten years later, and greater fleets each summer pointed for the Gulf of St. Lawrence. The fish knew nothing of imaginary lines at sea when food or fancy drew them into shoal waters, and the temptation to toll up a school within the confines of a marine league from some cozy shore was often irresistible.

Though still a British subject (and legitimately entitled to fish along his native shore–on his own hook), Pattillo was a fractious and troublesome individual, and he embraced enthusiastically the American view of the matter . . . and the vast new vista of opportunities it spread before him to have at it with his old enemies, the officialdom of the Crown.

And so they poached their fifty barrels of the Queen's mackerel, filled out the balance of their fare–some two hundred and twenty more–quite legally here and there, and hove in by the Eastern Point lighthouse for home around the end of October.

It was a first-rate trip of mackerel, and Messrs. Giles and Wonson were not going to let any grass grow under the boots of their junior skipper at this rate. They promptly put him in command of the pinkey *Tiger,* to leave as quick as possible on a trial trip to Newfoundland after a load of salt herring for bait. Though many of the south coast bays of that rugged island were reported to be alive with immeasurable armies of these fish in the spring, the first American vessel had yet to make a trip after them. It would be a hard chance on a desolate shore beset by barricades of ice, but the partners were anxious to give it a try, and Pattillo was just their man.

Tiger was a small, able schooner of fifty-two feet and as many tons, launched in Essex in 1830. Nothing fancy–the full bluff bow carried no figurehead, and she was rigged simple and easy with three lower sails and main topmast staysail. The rising arc of the rails and bulwarks where they joined at the narrow arch board of the stern was called the pink, swept so high by the sheer that it was able to crutch the main boom when sail was down. Up forward was the dark cabin; during the day it was dimly lit from the companionway and two deck deadlights of thick glass, at night by tallow dip or the brick and plaster fireplace, and all was black with soot. *Tiger*'s deck was free and clear and sixteen feet wide amidships. She carried her spars at a saucy rake, and with a good breeze of wind working for her, she could hull-down most challengers. This smallest of the Giles and Wonson fleet was fast and weatherly, and she would go anywhere; she rode the seas like a gull.

A man would have to love punishment, just the same, to leave Cape Ann at the start of winter and sail to the eastward for Newfoundland, where the winds howl down from the Arctic like a thousand devils, and sea and shore become one waste of ice and snow. Yet for a Gloucesterman no hardship could be worse than a handlining trip to the Georges or Grand Bank in January. This voyage offered a chance for something away from the rough routine of the winter fishery, a pioneering trip poking along the Newfie coast for herring with a promise of excursions ashore, and fresh venison and bear for the shooting, they said, which is why five muskets and a brace of powder kegs were stowed aboard *Tiger* along with the usual provisions, some trading items and of course the gill nets to catch the fish.

This time the papers were taken out in the name of fisherman Joe Caine as master for the record. Besides Caine, Jim shipped Jack Gorman again, Ned Cavener, another man and a boy–six of them altogether. On the twenty-eighth of November, 1838, capped, jacketed, mufflered, mittened, booted and still shivering under the gray overcast, they waved to the farewell group huddled on the wharf across Smith Cove from the end of Rocky Neck, swayed up sail and were off.

Louisburg was the last port of call before dropping Cape Breton for the passage to Newfoundland, a run of two hundred miles across the open Atlantic to the south of Cabot Strait which separated the two islands. Hoping to hunt up a pilot familiar with the coast for which they were bound, Captain Pattillo worked *Tiger* round the mean reef of rocks that guarded the entrance and anchored in the southwest harbor.

Above them on the crown of Blackrock Point were the bleak and overgrown ruins of the once greatest fortress in America, the bastion of French power on the Western Ocean, so finally and forever crushed by Sir Jeffrey Amberst and his Redcoats exactly eighty years before. The fulcrum that balanced the fate of a continent and two empires was now but a fishing village, bracing itself against winter's siege.

No one in Louisburg was about to hazard a long freeze-up in the Newfoundland ice pack for the chance of a few barrels of herring, so Jim and his men concluded to go it alone. They upped anchor and beat over into the northeast harbor, where the holding ground was better, in case it should come on to blow, as it looked. They were heeling by four Nova Scotia vessels at anchor, when the bunch idling at the rail of one (she was in from Newfoundland with twenty-five passengers) threw them a broadside of catcalls and smart remarks to the effect that the Yanks must be scared to spend the night in sou'west harbor, just because a hatful of wind might come along. Jim growled at his crew to pay them no mind.

About midnight a fierce squall burst across the harbor from the northwest, and at dawn who should be seen on the reef off

Blackrock Point but the boatful of wiseacres; they had dragged their anchor and fetched up hard on the bar, with the drift ice blowing in all around to make it worse. Their skipper managed to get his boat overboard and rowed over to the other Novie vessels in turn, begging the loan of their boat to carry out a kedge, but none would risk it, so he oared away upwind to the *Tiger* in her snug anchorage, to eat crow.

Surprise of surprises, Jim recognized the man who boosted himself over his rail as Bill Caton, from their boyhood when Caton's folks would visit the Pattillos, coming from Blandford across Chester Bay, and many was the night he shared his bed with him. But he kept his counsel and said to himself he'd teach the dog a lesson in civility before he was through with him.

Sure he would get him off, he told Captain Caton. But he would not give him the borrow of his boat. No, he would do it himself with his own men and in his own way; he wanted no strangers harming it, because it was the main dependence of his voyage. And he sent Caton back to his stranded vessel.

The crew of the *Tiger* hoisted their dory over the side and threw in two sixty-fathom warps which they had tied together. They bent one end to the pinkey's main boom horse, and then they rowed and drifted downwind to their objective, paying out the line. Holding under Caton's bow, they took on his anchor . . . and lucky not to upset, too, for the weight of it near put them down to their gunwales. Slow and careful, Jim and his boys hauled back along their warp, hand over hand against the whipping wind and choppy waves, while Caton's gang paid out their cable. When a shout from Caton signaled that they were approaching the bitter end, they pushed the anchor over with a soaking splash. The Novie crew turned to at the windlass; the cable came up taut; their grounded schooner groaned, budged, crunched and was off.

The Bluenoses kedged alongside the *Tiger,* all grins and gratitude, and Captain Caton invited Jim below for a victory drink. Not until now did he learn, to his amazement and redoubled chagrin, the identity of his benefactor. When he had recovered his wits, Caton vowed that the pal of his youth should have any compensation he asked, as Jim had saved his vessel for him, him abandoned by his own countrymen. But the expatriate would have none of it

"Billy Caton," said he in a firm and upright voice, "that's not the errand I came on. I came to do you a kindness for all the abuse you and your gang gave us when we went by you. Now if you ever run into someone in a like situation, I advise you to do the same as I have done with you and make your crew treat every other man as you'd have 'em treat you as long as you're master. By God, you never know when you're going to have to call for help, or who on, and that's all I've got to say to you!"

Having delivered himself of this lesson on the uses of the Golden Rule, Captain Pattillo turned on his heel, marched aboard of the *Tiger* and stood out Louisburg Harbor for Newfoundland.

Christmas was only ten days off when the Gloucester pinkey turned to the nor'ard from the fogs and chills of her offing along the Newfoundland south coast and entered Fortune Bay. The Bay had a reputation as one of the hardest places on a hard shore, and it was well named, the fortune being good or bad according to a man's luck getting in or out in one piece. It dished up unexpected and furious snow squalls and gales, and anchorage was limited to a handful of small harbors. Fortune Bay was by reputation the best herring ground anywhere off Newfoundland. Burin Peninsula separated it from Placentia Bay to the eastward. The French islands of St. Pierre and Miquelon lay out in the sea from Burin. They were lumps on the horizon to the men of the *Tiger* coming in, dropping bold Brunette Island and its Little Brunettes to starboard; before them the coast stood up, and they were at once put off and fascinated by its look of wildness. Along the north shore of the Bay, ocean and land pierced each other with gashed fjords and fingers of scrub-topped rock that dove into the sea; it was in these chasms of water that the herring were said to strike as early as January, to remain right through the summer spawning and feeding.

Tiger worked around cautiously off places with the names left

Ruins of the Louisburg fortress as they appeared in Pattillo's day. A re-creation has since been built on the site. (Beaton Institute, Cape Breton)

by the clash of empires . . . Deadman Bight, Great Bay de l'Eau, Wreck Cove, Boxey Point, English Cove, Blue Pinion . . . and put in at St. Jacques, one of the scattered fishing settlements with a safe anchorage, guarded by a double-humped island at the entrance. They lit in a covey of home-hewn shallops. It was discouraging to look up at the place from the water–a desolate cluster of miserable, weather-tortured shacks that the people there called home, which clung to the steep slopes of rock and grout, interspersed with flake frames for drying codfish, like a desperate colony of lichens.

Jim and his men spent Christmas here. The fare was thin but the cheer was from the heart. Somebody got up a dance in one of the wretched abodes; the girls were all there, and the flimsy floor shook to the clumsy capers of the Gloucestermen and the *live-heres,* as the Newfies quaintly called themselves, shuffling through the squares and jigs in their heavy boots to the *chin music* of the "orchestra" (that is, a young fellow said to have a bent for music who whined out his tunes in a tumble of nasal grunts). However, rum has been the bringing of the Old Harry to many a party, and in a while the men were roaring and winking, the girls blushing and giggling, and the oldsters all a-cackle and tapping their feet. Then, in the early hours, it was back to the *Tiger* and, for those still sober enough, lying in the bunk in the dark with thoughts of Christmas and of home so far away.

They set their nets—but caught nothing. Then, toward the end of January, word came down that the herring were striking in up around Bay du Nord, some twenty miles deeper into Fortune Bay at the point of its most northwest penetration. So they hove up anchor and sailed along past the fishing stage and tongue of a beach of Belleoram, all dominated by Iron Head rising straight up from the sea, past the heights of Chapel Island, and through Corbin Bay, dropping Lord and Lady Island, Dog Island and Bell Island, into the Bay of Cinq Isles, smaller yet, under the tall white bluff of Lally Cove Head and at last into the canyon waters of Bay du Nord. What a God-forsaken place to arrive on a bitter cold first of February!

But they were in the middle of the herring, whose bubbles gave them away, rising to the surface all around the schooner. Out went the nets that first night, moored with weights and buoyed with floats in the deep water, and *Tiger* was moved to the cove where they anchored.

It was the coldest kind of cold that night—a still and quiet and crackling cold, and not a stir of wind—and in the morning the Gloucestermen stamped out on deck, slapping their sides, breaths white, frozen in, the ice as smooth as glass. That day and the following night were like the first, and on the second day they all walked a mile over the ice with axes, to where the buoys and markers led them to the nets. They chopped holes, pulled the nets up through and picked out the gilled herring. They hauled the fish to the schooner and the gear to the shore to dry.

This is too much like work, thought Jim. So they fetched the nets from shore and set them through holes they had cut in the ice right alongside the *Tiger*. This was more like it. After every set

St. Jacques, Newfoundland, date unknown. (Provincial Archives of Newfoundland and Labrador)

they hove the catch up on the deck, sprinkled the fish with a good dousing of salt and rolled them in it thoroughly, sea-packed them in barrels in the round and threw in a few more scoops of salt. When the herring had been properly struck, the barrels were headed up and stowed below.

Thus the month passed. There was sport, too. Hunting through the snow-drifted scrub up behind the banks of the Bay du Nord River brought venison and fowl, and there was all the wood a man could cut to keep the fireplace ablaze and the cabin choking with smoke.

By the first week in March the flour and molasses were giving out, and Jim sent Gorman and Cavener to St. Jacques for provisions. The whole crew hauled the dory three miles across the ice to the open water, where Jack and Ned bent on the spritsail and pushed off on their twenty-mile voyage for vittles. Three days later they were back with the bread, molasses, tea and whatnot they had bought from William McCoe, the storekeeper, along with an indigestible item he had thrown in for free. Boat and supplies were dragged across the ice again to the *Tiger.* The bonus consisted of a morsel of news, and it was not good.

Word had reached McCoe from Harbour Breton, farther on to the westward, that Thomas Gaden, the Provincial Customs Officer there, was planning to surprise the American schooner with an armed force, seize the vessel and arrest the crew, all for fishing inside the three-mile limit.

Pattillo and his men had often discussed this possibility; the chance that any of Her Majesty's Collectors would stir himself over a few barrels of poached herring seemed about as remote as Bay du Nord itself. But Jim had gambled and lost . . . and to twist the *Tiger*'s tail, they were frozen in with the goods.

To tell the truth, the convention of 1818 had left half of the south coast of Newfoundland west of the Ramea Islands open to American fishermen; *Tiger,* unfortunately, was trapped by the ice along the banned eastern stretch which included Fortune Bay. To add to the flagrancy of the violation, the British drew the three-mile limit from their own peculiar point of view called the headland theory–that is, commencing it from a series of straight lines connecting cape to cape, excluding all the waters inside, however extensive. The Americans, as expected, insisted that it merely paralleled the shore wherever the shore chose to go. To the British way of thinking, then, the *Tiger* had no business in Fortune Bay at all, except for the purpose of getting shelter, making repairs or taking on fresh water and firewood.

So there they were, frozen in till spring, filling up with the Queen's herring. Jim plunked his hands on his hips, stuck out his jaw and faced his crew, four men and a boy.

"Some whoreson Judas must have gone all the way to Harbour Breton to inform against us, and here we are. Now lads, I suppose Gaden is coming after us with his army to take the *Tiger* and salt us away, and there's one of two things we must do, as I see it. Either we plead ignorance and give up . . . or we stand our hand and defend ourselves the best we can. What'll it be?"

He looked them up and down. Four men and a boy, they declared they would do as he wished them to do.

"All right. For my part, I would sooner die right here on the ice of Bay du Nord than to lose the *Tiger* without a fight and be lugged up to Harbour Breton to jail for the sake of a load of herring. I have always said and I will to my dying breath that God put fish in the sea for men to catch, and we shall follow the fish where Providence sends them, and not the Treaty."

He looked them over again.

"So I say we stand our hand."

Jim dug out his Bible, and each one of them swore on it that he would stick by him and the *Tiger* to the end. And what else could they do? He could wallop them all separately or together as he pleased.

This was all on a Friday.

They walked ashore with their axes, felled spruces the thickness of a man's leg and rassled the logs aboard the *Tiger*. These were fitted and joined under their captain's direction into four batteries–one way aft by the pink, the second right around the mainmast, third around the foremast and the fourth up forward of the windlass–and each had a slit for a port to give a marksman some swing for his musket.

With the *Tiger* thus fortified, Captain Pattillo hustled his men to work sharpening her teeth. They collected every mackerel jig aboard and stoked up a bed of red coals in the fireplace, melted the whole lot in a pot and ran the lead into balls in their old bullet mold. Made cartridges next, twenty-five to a man, and stacked flintlocks, ammunition and all at readiness in the batteries on deck.

It was now Sunday. Every castle needs a moat. The men of the *Tiger* attacked the ice with axe and club and cleared one all around their floating fortress. Still no sign of Gaden and his army.

At dawn on Monday, the eleventh of March, Jim took his spyglass and rowed across his moat to the edge of the ice, where he left the dory. Continuing on foot to shore, he tramped up through the snow to the crest of a hill that commanded a grand view out over the miles of ice to the blue of Corbin Bay and beyond. Away below lay his vessel in her patch of water, a toy boat in a tub. The eastern sky was alive where the sun was lurking behind the black horizon. The big man stood up there on high, alone with himself, and watched the disc of fire climb over the stark face of Newfoundland, giving an ember glow to the snow on the opposite slopes.

Morning wore on, and he kept his vigil. The time was at hand. If the story was straight and Gaden was coming, he must surely be close, and he would take the long way round by sea, because the interior from Harbour Breton was for all practical purposes impassable.

And there they were. He caught the glint of their sails through the glass, five small boats in a small flotilla crossing the bay toward the edge of the ice from the direction of Corbin, the place where they doubtless passed the night.

He watched. They worked in and dropped sail at the ice not far beyond the steep face of Lally Cove Head, no more than three miles off. They left their boats, and like ants following their trail marched over the ice to shore. From here it was a hard trek through the snow, and he had an excellent view of their maneuvers, until they came to a point that hid the *Tiger* from them. Now they were close enough for him to see that there were thirty in the band, all armed. One, apparently sent ahead to scout the situation, climbed up and peeked over the ridge, scanned their objective for a moment and ducked back.

The unseen observer of this expeditionary force left his vantage with a leap and bounded down to shore through the deep snow, sprinted across the ice, jumped into his boat and pulled for the *Tiger.*

Jim vaulted the rail with a shout to get ready, for the war would soon be on.

"I trust you lads are all of the same mind as when we started this on Friday, because they're coming–a regular invasion, thirty of them armed to the teeth!"

Catching the youngest of his crew by the arm (the boy was white with terror), he hustled him below. Then to the consternation of the rest, he seized one of the kegs of gunpowder, sprinkled a train to the fireplace hearth and roared at the lad:

Icebound on the snowbound coast of Newfoundland. (Provincial Archives of Newfoundland and Labrador)

"Now sonny, you stand down here and tend the fire, away from the flying bullets. Keep your ears open, and if you hear me sing out *Touch her off!* you grab a brand from your fire and light that train. Don't fail, mind you! If you fail me, I'll come down and knock your head off, and then I'll fire her off myself!

"I tell you, boys, I'm bound to blow us all to kingdom come before they take the *Tiger*!"

The Adventure of the Tiger: Going Back

TOMMY GADEN was the bigwig of Harbour Breton in the Province of Newfoundland and the great politician around Fortune Bay. He started being important where other men were content to leave off, for besides his post as Sub-Collector of Colonial Revenue, he was Stipendiary Magistrate, Coroner, Registrar of Deeds, a member of the Board of Education and Road Commissioner. He was notably a man of pacific inclination, preferring to row toward his modest objectives–as they said of Mr. Van Buren, the American President–with muffled oars.

This functionary was understandably intrigued, then, when a member of his wider constituency by the name of John Cluett accosted him one day in an animated fashion. With a bellicose slant to his chin, Cluett informed him that he had sailed all the way around from Belleoram carrying the news that a fishing vessel from the Boston States was frozen in, up Bay du Nord, taking herring through the ice . . . and what was he going to do about it? The vessel was a sitting duck–only five men and a boy on board–and it would be child's play to go seize her and clap the lot in jail. If the Yanks are fixing to come to Fortune Bay after our fish and our livelihood, he declared with bitterness, now's the time to choke 'em off.

Cluett was gill-netting for herring himself, and it rancored him to see the Gloucestermen ensconced comfortably in the Newfoundland ice, salting down Newfoundland herring, shooting Newfoundland deer and burning Newfoundland woods in the fireplace, arrogant as you please in defiance of the Treaty. Then, too, he may have run afoul of them while they were lying nearby at St. Jacques, but if so he kept his counsel on that end of it.

Whatever his motives, Cluett's arrival at Harbour Breton agitated the people there, and some of the men contrived to push Gaden toward taking a gang up to Bay du Nord to seize the schooner. The multi-officeholder was at first reluctant, but the muster of thirty of his townsmen—all with their firearms—turned his diffidence to enthusiasm for the projected expedition against five men and a boy stuck in the ice; he was sure to return with a prize, and his initiative and courage in defending the interests of the Crown would be looked on with favor by his superiors at St. John's. Gathering up his official papers and the trappings of office in his particular capacity as Her Majesty's Sub-Collector of Colonial Revenue, Tommy Gaden commandeered five boats, embraced his wife and little daughter and embarked with his task force.

Over the ridge and into plain view they marched in single file, no more than half a mile off, and as they approached the shore through the snow and then stepped out on the ice, the waiting crew of the *Tiger*—throats dry and butterflies in their stomachs—could see the gleam of the guns up and down the column when the sun struck the barrels at the right angle.

"Take your stations, boys," directed Captain Pattillo, in a low and easy voice. The four men scattered to their barricades, while he took a stand at the rail, arms folded across his chest.

The enemy advanced to the edge of the ice at the other side of the moat some hundred feet from *Tiger* and there bunched up. A ragtag and bobtail bunch they were, too, and they regarded the objective of their campaign with curiosity and some uneasiness. This was not what they had expected at all; the Gloucester pinkey had a nasty look there with its four batteries of logs set up on deck, nothing stirring aboard save for that big bruiser eyeballing them from the rail as cool as could be . . . he was a bad one, you could see.

Gaden was nudged up to the front ranks, gave a hail and asked who was in command.

"Joe Caine!" called back Pattillo, giving the name on the documents.

"Come over here in the Queen's name and bring your papers!" Gaden shouted.

"I'll do no such business," was the reply. "But if you're a-minded to pick out three of your best men and let the rest go away, I'll meet you any way you like, one by one or all together!"

"No, no!" protested Mister Gaden. "We're not here for a fight. I only want to talk to you about some matters."

Without a word, Jim wheeled around from the rail and disappeared below. In a minute he was back, papers in hand and stripped to the waist, wearing only shoes, stockings and duck pants. At the windlass he caught up a handspike three feet long and summoned Jack Gorman to leave his post and row him across their moat to the ice. With nothing on above the belt, he told his brother-in-law, they'd find him slippery as a flounder if they tried to grapple with him. Get back aboard and all hands keep me covered, he instructed, as the boat grated against the ice.

Pattillo swaggered over to the Customs man, swinging his rounder with one hand, papers clenched in the other.

"All right, Caine, let me see your papers."

"For what? Who the hell are you and what's your warrant?"

"I'm Thomas Gaden, Sub-Collector of Colonial Revenue at Harbour Breton, and I have the authority to board and take your vessel in the Queen's name for fishing inside of three marine miles of the coast in violation of the Treaty." The official dug inside his coat and pulled out a parchment certifying to his office and stamped with the fine wax seal of the Empire, lion, unicorn and all, encasing a bit of ribbon . . . and along with it a miniature oar of silver which he displayed as his commission to board any vessel.

One grizzled Newfoundlander stood awkwardly behind Gaden with a pistol cocked at the Yankee captain, and he was flanked by two others holding their muskets at the ready.

Fitz Hugh Lane's 1834 lithograph looks across Smith Cove, the tip of Rocky Neck at left and the inner harbor to Gloucester. Giles and Wonson's fishery is on the point to the right of the beach now occupied by the North Shore Arts Association. The tide is out, and the pinkey beached at the wharf is none other than Tiger. *(Carolyn W. Pattillo)*

Jim glanced at Gaden's commission; he thrust it back to him carelessly and handed over the *Tiger*'s papers. This was the move Gaden was waiting for, the signal for the interrogation to commence.

"What are you doing here, Captain Caine?"

"It's a good place for hunting, there's plenty of deer and game, and there's plenty of wood besides for to keep warm, and plenty of herring."

"How many herring have you on board?"

"How many? How the devil should I know? I ain't counted 'em. But we have a good store, I can tell you–we eat herring three times a day."

"Why didn't you stay at St. Jacques when you were there?"

"Well now, Mister Gaden, wood was scarce for one thing, and for another there was no game."

"And for another there was no herring, ain't that so, Captain

Caine?" Gaden's solemn face broke into a smirk of triumph, for all the world like the Queen's Attorney pricking the defense's balloon.

"So you Yanks came here to carry home a load of fish from Bay du Nord which you know as well as your own name is the best place for herring in the whole of Newfoundland, and all in violation of the Treaty! And now, Captain Caine, step aside if you please. I am going to take your vessel!"

Jim gripped his handspike in a most menacing fashion, and he seemed to swell up until he looked ten feet tall. He was an awesome figure, his massive muscles all working as if to keep the wildness under control, and the fire blazing from his eyes. He advanced a step, and his adversary backed off.

"My friend," quoth the giant in even tones, "the first man attempts to cross the rail of that vessel will never know what hit him. Do you see those guns sticking out through the ports? They're aimed at your heart. And there's a boy down below with a hot fire and a keg of black powder, ready to blow us all to hell when I say the word. So what d'ye think o' that? I advise you to go back to Harbour Breton where you came from and leave us be, unless you like the smell of brimstone."

The muzzles of the muskets were most plainly protruding from the log bastions, now that this madman had drawn attention to them, and the discovery caused some dismay and a murmur of discord in the ranks. The mouse had turned on the cat, or the tiger on the hunter.

Gaden shifted uneasily, not knowing what to do or how far the man was bluffing, when his mind was made up for him by an oath and an outburst of recognition from his aide-de-camp, Constable Stewart.

"I know this fellow! His name ain't Caine, it's Pattillo, and he killed a man in Halifax!"

"That's a lie, a damn dirty lie!" Jim turned and glared at his accuser, raising his club as if to swing on him. He thought better of it, however, lowered the weapon and growled, "When I'm through talking with your master here, if you have something to say I'll talk with you."

Model of Captain Pattillo's floating fortress, the pinkey Tiger. *(Peabody Essex Museum)*

This exchange sealed Gaden's decision to call it a day and retire from the field. For sure, this half-naked brute was a desperado who would not hesitate for a second to carry out his threats. He ran up the white flag:

"Well, Captain Caine, Pattillo or whoever, I would order you out of here, but it's no use. You can't leave the ice."

"Don't bother yourself over it, friend," was the affable reply. "Whenever it breaks up we'll be heading for home on our own account."

At this, the Customs Officer about-faced and retreated to the shore, his army following. He had with him one significant souvenir of his ignominy . . . *Tiger*'s papers, the return of which, in the flush of victory, her master had forgotten to demand.

One of the army hung back, John Cluett by name. He wanted to sympathize with Jim in his plight—yes, he was a poor fisherman himself and sorry to be on such an expedition; it was the last thing in his thoughts to injure the Yanks, but Gaden had forced him to come.

Pattillo smelled a rat, however, which put him in a rage.

"You're a Judas, Cluett!" he bellowed. "You traveled the whole way from Belleoram to Harbour Breton to inform against us, I knew it, and you put Gaden up to bringing this gang up here!"

Quick as thought, he drew back and gave the man a clip under the ear that sprawled him on the ice, then followed with a couple of kicks to send him and his gun sliding on their way.

"Go about your business and steer clear of me, you vagabond!" he grunted. He stepped into his dory and rowed back to the *Tiger.* As he crooked a leg over the rail he could see Cluett high-tailing to catch up with Gaden's army, disappearing by twos and threes over the same ridge they had invaded from less than an hour before.

Thus put to rout, the Newfies split up for the night. Half trudged across to the place of a man who lived over beyond Lally Cove, and he gave them bed and board of a sort. The rest hiked a couple of miles to the fishing stage of John Scott, who would not spare them a mouthful to eat and said curtly they could fetch their own wood, build a fire and sleep on the floor, but he was damned if they would get anything further from him for they were fools to be after the Yankees, who could do them all a sight more of good than harm in the long run, considering the pocketful of fish they took.

In the morning the two crowds held council in the snow. A few were all for going back and calling the Yankee captain's bluff. But the heft of them told Gaden, with some disdain and much to his relief, that if he would not grab the great rascal when he was alone and within reach, they would never take him in his fort. So they went down to their boats at the edge of the ice and sailed back to Harbour Breton. The rest of the populace received some pretty short and sharp answers when they inquired about the expedition and the whereabouts of the prize.

Tiger was icebound and unmolested for five more weeks, when a long thaw broke winter's back; the ice cracked, and offshore winds carried it drifting out the Bay. It was time to get moving again. Early in the morning of the seventeenth of April, having been frozen in on the Newfoundland coast for two and a half months, Jim and his boys took in their nets, bent on sail, weighed anchor and scudded out of Bay du Nord—glad to see the last of it.

At St. Jacques their captain rowed ashore and collected what his friend McCoe the storekeeper owed him for two cases of smuggled boots, and then they got under way again, standing off to the southwest in the hope of spending the night under the lee of Brunette Island, a twenty-five-mile run. Within an hour they overtook and passed at some distance on their port hand a small jack schooner with distinctive red sails which they recognized as John Cluett's. He appeared to be headed for the island of St. Pierre, probably with a load of herring for the dealer there. No doubt he recognized the *Tiger,* too.

When they found they would not be able to make Brunette by nightfall, Pattillo swung off to the westward and beat into Great Bay de l'Eau, where they anchored in the snug harbor at Little Bay West.

The loss of his papers to Gaden had been a bone in Jim's throat, and he was mighty reluctant to sail for Cape Ann without them. Lying so near the Crown official's headquarters this afternoon (it was only a walk of a couple miles across the cape they were on to Jersey Harbor and then a short row to Harbour Breton), he made up his mind to send Joe Caine after them. Caine would pass himself off as Pattillo and would have three hours to get there and back. If he had not returned in that time, Jim would know something had gone awry and would move *Tiger* to another den.

Herring were all around them, so as soon as Joe had been put ashore they set their nets and caught a deckload. While the rest were salting and packing, Jim was growing uneasy; the three hours were up already, and no sign of his man. He rowed ashore himself.

There was that little fishing boat at its mooring as he oared by; they had noticed it in the afternoon off Breton Head when they tacked across. He inquired and found it belonged to a man who worked for old Mrs. Kettle up the hill. He walked to her house, banged on the door and told the good woman he would have a word with her hired man if she would be so kind.

The fellow was at supper.

That vessel with the red sails–Cluett's–the same that passed him while he was fishing earlier . . . did it go on to St. Pierre, or did it head up and make for Harbour Breton?

Straight into Harbour Breton, was the reply between mouthfuls.

Jim hurried down the hill to his dory. This explained why Caine wasn't back. Gaden must have kept him there on some pretext so he could get up a gang to take the *Tiger* by surprise, probably after Cluett gave him the word that they were putting into Little Bay West right around the corner.

There was still enough light to get clear of the anchorage as he swung aboard his schooner. They made sail in a hurry and snuck across Great Bay de l'Eau into St. John Harbor, an hour to the southeast–and none too soon, for the Collector and his crowd came puffing into Little Bay that very evening to find the elusive *Tiger* gone.

At the break of dawn the Americans were under way, and by noon they had dropped their hook in the pocket-sized harbor on the east shore of Brunette Island which they had passed coming into Fortune Bay four months earlier. It was more like four years, and they all ached to get home, but first their skipper wanted to top off his fare of herring, regain his papers if he could and rescue Joe Caine.

It happened that John Scott, who had slept the half of Gaden's army on the floor like dogs for persecuting the Yanks, had moved from his winter quarters at Bay du Nord to his summer fishing station on Brunette. On Sunday he planned to sail the fifteen miles across to Jersey Harbor for supplies. *Tiger* in the meanwhile had filled out her fare, and her master determined that the time had arrived to face Gaden down on his home ground. Leaving the vessel in charge of the rest, he and Ned Cavener put over the dory and took a tow behind Scott as far as the entrance to Harbour Breton, where their friend cast them off with a wish of good luck and continued on his way.

The two bent to the oars, and when they glided through the anchorage the cry went up amongst the fishermen in the boats– "Here comes the Yankee captain!"

Before they had reached the wharf the word was spreading through the town as if on wings, and when the dory bumped against the piles, its occupants climbed out to find themselves confronted by a crowd of two or three score curious folk, arrived on the run to see the famous giant from the Boston States who had made a fool of Tom Gaden up at Bay du Nord.

Jim sent Cavener off to look for Caine and inquired of a young fellow where Gaden lived. He was directed a short distance up the street from the wharf. Thanking his informant, he climbed the hill, the crowd at his heels and growing by the minute, strode up onto the porch of the house and knocked on the door.

A servant girl answered.

"Lass, I want to see Mister Gaden if he is in." The booming voice of the man who filled the doorway resounded through the rooms like a command from the quarterdeck.

The frightened girl shrank back into the hall, for she had heard of the Yankee captain and saw the crowd gathering. What name should she say?

Joe Caine . . . and would her master come to the door as he wished an interview with him.

The fateful name near finished the poor thing off. She retreated past the parlor, where she blurted out this message with a squeak and fled to the kitchen.

The visitor waited some moments, when instead of Gaden a little girl of about seven next appeared, apparently out of curiosity but probably sent to reconnoiter the situation and report back. The visitor asked her name gruffly. She broke into tears and ran for the kitchen, too.

"Well, well, young lady, are all the folks in Harbour Breton like you in this house with no tongues in their heads?" he flung after her with a laugh.

The third member of the household to come to the door was Mrs. Gaden.

"How do you do, Sir?"

"Good day, Marm!"

"Do you want to see Mister Gaden?"

"I do, Marm."

"Could I not serve as well as my husband, Sir?"

"My business is with him, Marm."

The Sub-Collector's lady went back into the parlor, and after some lengthy talk which Jim couldn't make out and a deal of commotion, the master of the house proceeded haltingly down the hall, carrying a pistol. He was shaking so that he couldn't have hit the side of a mountain with it. Keeping his distance from his visitor, he addressed him by his proper name, Captain Pattillo, and asked him what he wanted.

Jim beamed affably.

"I came to see if you might be well pleased enough to give me back my papers as the ice has broken and I am on my way home."

My God, the brass in this man! thought Gaden.

"What a shame–I already sent them up to St. John's to the government."

The Yankee captain reddened.

"What! Well, in that case I can't get 'em. But you, Sir, can write me out something or other to satisfy any party that might ask about the *Tiger* or try to stop me, to say that I'm not a pirate and haven't run off with another man's vessel."

Oh, the brass, the brass! thought Gaden.

"But Captain, I don't think I have the right to do that for you."

"You don't have a right to make me out a piece of paper?" Jim tightened his fists, and his voice shook the rafters. "By thunder, you thought you had the right to take my vessel when you brought your army up to Bay du Nord! Why didn't you take her?"

Gaden was getting his goat.

"Captain, you told me I should not take her."

"Then why did you go off with my papers? I suppose you took 'em expecting to get the *Tiger,* too—but you don't have her, so the papers are no good to you. I say you're no gentleman for all your grand airs and silver oars. I handed back your documents and you weren't man enough to return me mine, and I say you stole 'em!"

Jimmy had now worked up a good head of steam, with Gaden stoking the fire, and lucky the Sub-Collector was that they were interrupted by a familiar bray from the porch.

"Haw, haw! Listen to the great blower! He was going to blow up his vessel and all hands if we boarded her!"

Pattillo spun on his heel, face to face with Constable Stewart, the one who called him a murderer out on the ice. The policeman had arrived on the porch to protect Gaden from his visitor and delivered this taunt for the benefit of the crowd that filled the street in front, waiting to catch a glimpse of the Yankee captain and straining to hear every word of the debate through the open door. Jim turned the fullness of his wrath on this new enemy:

"Look who's talking! They came, thirty of them and him with them, up to Bay du Nord, and they stood within three feet of me and never laid a hand on me and went back just as they came!"

"Ah, we hear geese gabble!"

"That's enough—look out for yourself!" and Jim jumped for the constable, hauled back and knocked him flying clean over five steps and into the bosom of his audience.

Our friend could not help but think to himself (now that he had this out of his system) that geese might gabble or not, but his was surely cooked, and he braced himself for the onslaught of an angry mob.

Instead, an old man piped up from behind him, where he had taken a stand to hear the talk better:

"You served him just right, Cap, just right . . . he was wrong to insult you in that manner, for you had not said a word to him!"

Evidently this oldster had some influence with the people, because they cheered lustily (they had been waiting, if truth be known, for somebody with the pluck to give Constable Stewart a good clip, for he was a bully).

Tommy Gaden–a personage, as noted, who lived by his wits–observed to himself that the fancies of fate had chosen the Yankee captain the man, if not of the day, at least of the hour in Harbour Breton. He laid aside his pistol and winked at the old gent who had come to Jim's defense and who was, in fact, his fellow magistrate from over to Grand Bank across the Bay, here on business. Each grabbed an arm of the surprised Gloucesterman and marched him down the steps, through the applauding crowd and up the street–not to jail, but to the public house where they treated him and Ned Cavener and Joe Caine (whom Ned had found safe and sound), all three to a fine dinner.

Somewhere between soup and succotash their hosts opened a conversational tacking duel intended to get to the windward of the Yankees and learn the whereabouts of the *Tiger.* Gaining the distinct impression from Captain Pattillo that his schooner was way down at French St. Pierre, the disappointed but now gallant Gaden hailed an acquaintance at another table who was embarking that night in his little vessel homebound for Lamaline, around the bend of Burin. The man readily agreed to give them a ride and their dory a tow, as the island was not so very far off his course.

At eleven in the evening the wind hauled round to the northward, and they got under way. Not until they had cleared the coast did Jim let on to the skipper that the *Tiger* was in reality laying under Brunette, less than a third of the way to St. Pierre, and could they trouble him to let them off there. He was only too glad. It was a fast passage through the Bay, and they were cast off by the southeast end of the island. Hugging the black bulk of the shore, under a skyful of stars, they rowed the two miles around the bluffs to the *Tiger* where she lay so quietly at anchor in the southwest harbor, stout and steady, the wavelets lapping her sides.

Gaden had not given up the game, however. Hardly had his dinner guests departed that evening when he was laying plans for another and quite different party in their honor. Word reached him in short order that his quarry was not skulking under the

Big Jim and his Tiger *crew outbluff Collector Gaden on the Newfoundland ice in 1839, as the fanciful illustrator for the* Youth's Companion *conceived the encounter, with undue regard for Victorian sensibilities; our hero had stripped to the waist.* (Youth's Companion, *November 1883)*

French flag at St. Pierre, as he had supposed, but hiding right under his nose behind Brunette.

Immediately Her Majesty's Sub-Collector alerted the commander of the Provincial revenue cutter and issued a call for volunteers to fall in on board, ready for a fight if need be. They set sail in the afternoon and just before dusk rounded the southeast point of the island, intending to take the *Tiger* by surprise. And right then the wind pooped out, leaving them adrift on a flat sea with sails a-flap, blocks creaking idly and nothing of interest to be seen to the westward except the setting sun, which they had all seen before.

But the cutter was observed and recognized by the lookout on the Gloucesterman, and it did not take the crafty Captain Pattillo and his rogues long to conclude what she was doing there . . . less than a league away on the other side of the intervening headland so that only her topsail was visible. Nor did Jim have to open his mouth. With one thought they jumped to it, yanked stops off sails, made for the halyards, throat and peak, and hustled up canvas–first the main, then foresail and jib, and finally up with the drooping maintop staysail.

Nightfall and a stark calm. The moon rose cold-bright in the cloudless starry heaven, scattering her train of diamonds on the sea, cloaking the harsh humpback of the island with a gossamer veil of white.

At midnight a stir and flutter of sail, a quiver of rigging, a bit of a breeze from off the land to the nor'ard.

Quick to the windlass, lads . . . heave-ho, over and down. In comes the dripping cable . . . where the devil is the anchor, what takes it so long? . . . ah, here it breaks the surface, hard up helm, we swing off to port. Let the sails fill, start all sheets, boys, give our wings a breath of air–and we're off, silently except for the swish and spray, reaching out the harbor and away.

Tiger slipped off, close under the lee of Brunette to keep from standing up against the moon where the cutter could see her. And it worked. She cleared the harbor while her pursuer fetched into it not more than a half a mile to leeward. Jim reached on a league to the western cape of the island until he lost sight of the cutter, wore around out of curiosity and reached back. This time Gaden spotted the Yankee and gave chase. Pattillo wore around again. With a toss of her head and a lash of her tail in the freshening breeze, *Tiger* laid into the sea–and did she move!

They ran five miles to the westward of the island over the moonlit bay, out past the Little Brunettes, but it was no race. The swift pinkey showed the cumbersome Canadian the stuff she was made of, and when the cutter seemed to give it up and bear away in the direction of St. Pierre, Jim wore around for the third time, coasted back into the harbor and hove to, just to catch his breath.

Not for long.

A skiff approached from the shore, a young fellow making the oars fly like windmills. It was George, the son of their friend John Scott. He gave a hail and called up that they were the luckiest men in the Bay that night—at least till now—because Gaden was in the cutter, after them again, this time with an army of sixty. His father had just come down from the hill where he was watching and saw the cutter coming right back and had him row out and give them the word.

"Thank you kindly!" shouted Jim. They could make her out now, working in closehauled, the moonlight catching the white spume dancing off her bow. "I think I'll just hit 'round and try her on the other tack for a change. Hell, the *Tiger* can jump one way as well as another!"

He sprang to the helm and pushed over the big tiller. The pinkey fell off the wind on a broad and fast reach out the harbor that headed her dead for the oncoming cutter. He figured to keep right on if they opened fire, and at their exact point of meeting to wear around suddenly and ram the end of their main boom; it was now blowing so fresh, and the *Tiger* was making such time, that the impact would tear sail, boom and mast right out of the enemy.

The two vessels passed within a cable's length. The Canadian was so taken aback that he never altered course until it was too late, and not a shot was fired by the astonished army that crowded her deck.

Tiger kept right on for home, and it was the last they ever saw of the persistent Sub-Collector.

On the fourteenth of May, 1839, five and a half months out, *Tiger* beat into Gloucester Harbor by the familiar spring-green shores, hauled around Rocky Neck and shot right up on the mud flat a hundred feet from the Giles and Wonson wharf. The men all ran down and stood there staring at her as if she'd fallen out of the sky.

"Hey, what the devil's the matter?" Jim yelled over at John Fletcher Wonson, who was in the crowd, dumbfounded like the rest, for they all were glued to the ground, with not a word of greeting.

Wonson found a shaky voice:

"Great God, where did ye come from? We gave you up for lost three months ago!"

The Yankee captain roared with laughter, and his lads with him.

"Here we are!" he shouted cheerfully–"and all well!"

Jim Becomes a Whitewashed Yankee

TIGER'S FORBIDDEN FARE of herring was the first ever brought back to the States from Newfoundland, and they sold it in Boston for $7.50 a barrel. July saw them set out for the North Bay as usual, except that Pattillo thought to take the long way around and try the Georges first. There were no mackerel, but they struck cod, caught fifty quintals and swung across the Gulf of Maine to Canso, where they left their catch with Peter Publicover for him to dry and have ready for the pinkey to pick up on her way back from the North Bay.

They had dropped Little Canso, as the jiggers called the Cape, far astern and were just coming into Sand Point at Big Canso where the Gut begins, when a boat rowed out hell-bent for the *Tiger,* four men at the oars and an officer in the stern-sheets, Union Jack flying.

Jim told the helmsman to hold his course. Next thing, there was a puff of smoke from the boat, and a musket ball zinged across their bow and choonked into the water some distance beyond.

Keep your course, growled the skipper.

But the wind was not with him this time. It died, and they were overtaken. The oarsmen pulled alongside, and the officer, who was fair livid with rage at this show of contempt, leaped aboard, greeted Pattillo with an oath and demanded to know why he didn't heave to when fired on.

"Heave to for what and who the devil are you?" inquired Jim blandly.

"For what! Why, for light money! I'm McMullen, the Customs at Canso, that's who I am!"

"Lemme see your authority," said Jim, thrusting out his jaw.

McMullen drew his sword and shook it in the face of the surprised captain with another oath.

"*That's* my authority!"

Pattillo lunged for him, grabbed the cutlass by the hilt, broke it in two across his knee and tossed the pieces overboard. He caught the officer by the collar and the slack of his britches, hightailed him to the rail, raised him up above his head and dumped him over the side into the laps of his oarsmen.

"That's *my* authority!" he leaned over and roared down at them.

On the twelfth of November of that year 1839 James William Pattillo, age thirty-three, went up to Boston, renounced roundly his fidelity to Her Majesty Queen Victoria and all things Britannic and solemnly took the oath of allegiance to the United States of America.

After nearly six years, the fugitive was finally the patriot, and the Rogues' Hole the land of the free and home of the brave . . . so much depends on the point of view. Besides securing to himself all the usual rights and privileges, Jim was from here on eligible to command American vessels without resorting to the subterfuge of false papers taken in another man's name (a risky business for himself and the owners); indeed he might now be an owner himself. No doubt of it, citizenship was a practical necessity for an ambitious Gloucesterman who wished to make his way in this tariff, treaty and bounty-bound industry of fishing.

There was another thing about it. By traveling up to Boston for a coat of "whitewash," as the Nova Scotians scorned it, Jim at once covered his checkered past and clad himself in the armor of moral consistency against any future skirmishes with the Crown. There was a certain covert irony, that he disliked when he thought about it, to being the ghost skipper of a Gloucester schooner, sailing into his native waters which were forbidden to his vessel and his men but not to him, and taking the fish of his former countrymen . . . well . . . Jim had his scruples, and he felt like the boy who ran away from home and snuck back every night to raid the pantry. When it came to championing American rights to fish the Provinces, how much less vulnerable to be an American than a Provincial!

So Jim became a whitewashed Yankee.

That winter he went to sea for the third time with his friend Captain Ryder in the brig *Oak,* and a terrible winter it was, serving up a series of gales that struck devastation against the coast. The men of the sea took the brunt of it, and the worst came at Gloucester.

It was on the night of the fourteenth of December, 1839, a Saturday. The storm screamed in from the Atlantic out of the southeast. Tempestuous winds brought sheets of rain and squalls of snow all mixed together, gigantic rolling swells and upwards of sixty sail from aroundabout that lurched in, all reefed and hatches battened down, past Eastern Point to anchor.

By daybreak, when the gale had blown itself out, twenty-two vessels had smashed up on the western ledges and were totally wrecked. Thirty more still rode at their anchors, decks swept clean, and dismasted either by the force of the storm or by their crews with axes to save them from dragging ashore. Another two or three had drifted clear out of the Harbor and off to sea, no one knew where. Twelve corpses were found on the rocks, but at least twenty were known to be dead, about all of them sailors swept overboard and drowned–how many more, who could tell? Perhaps up to forty in all. A number were taken off their ships and rowed to safety in small boats by heroic Gloucestermen who pushed out through the surf to their rescue at the height of it.

The storm was the most destructive since the settlement of Cape Ann. Gloucester was still picking up the pieces on land and sea when the second one smashed in, twelve days later. As luck would have it, this time there were only eight sail caught in the Outer Harbor. Four of the five that were blown ashore were smashed on the rocks. The crew of the sixth cut away her masts, and she held her ground. The remaining two rode it out unscathed.

The *Oak* came through these storms at sea, and along about fitting-out time for the Georges Jim returned to Gloucester. It was the middle of February of 1840, the dregs of the New England winter. Giles and Wonson had no vessel available for him, so Jim shipped with James Mansfield and Sons, a respected fishing firm over town on the other side of the Inner Harbor and only a quick walk from his new home on Prospect Street. Old Mr. Mansfield, seventy-five and retired, kept a stern eye on his business, but the running of it had fallen to his sons, Alfred and Junior. The Mansfield wharf was among the longest on the waterfront, extending way over the mud flats at the head of Harbor Cove to provide their vessels berths at low water. They owned a fleet of about ten schooners and engaged Pattillo as captain of the *Abigail*, an Essex-built pinkey a trifle bigger and five years younger than the *Tiger*.

While they were off on their second trip to Georges Bank in March, a gale of wind struck the fleet. When it cleared they counted noses and were one short; the old *Ida* was gone, straight to the bottom with five good friends and Captain Job Rowe, the best chowdermaker on Cape Ann, who had conspired to pit Jim against the cocky fellow from the next wharf that first Fourth of July. And so the fleet sailed in, flags half-mast high, with the sad word. They took out and returned to Georges, came to anchor and resumed fishing.

On the twenty-ninth of April another gale blew up. At the height of it Jim climbed aloft to the main topmasthead to secure the rigging, a chance he would ask no other man to take. *Abigail* lay to her anchor in a welter of sharp, broken seas, pitching and rolling erratically, flailing her spars with a willful kind of whip as if she were trying to shake the man loose from his crazy perch.

She did. His foot went out from under. So sudden was the lash it broke his grip. There was nothing to grab but air . . . no shroud in reach . . . no vision of salvation. He fell like a rag doll, down, down through the screech of the gale and the spray toward the patch of deck, fifty-seven feet below . . . .

He was lying on the cabin floor when he came to, and his men were strapping a board on his leg for a splint. When they finished and wedged him in with blankets and odds and ends to keep from rolling, they made sail in the teeth of the gale, weighed anchor and drove her for home.

It was three days and nights of agony. But then it was all over, and *Abigail* was coming into Gloucester quiet and steady, and they brought her into Mansfield's. They carried their captain up to his house and his anxious wife. Someone had run ahead and told her to get the bed ready for him and then gone on to call the doctor.

They came, not one but two to set the leg of this big man–jolly John Moriarty ("Dr. Moriart" everybody called him) and Joseph Reynolds to help, a crusty sawbones with old-fashioned notions and very liberal with his prescriptions, as he also ran a pharmacy. The two examined him and pronounced his thigh broken in three pieces. They rolled up their sleeves and with their combined might and main, which was considerable as Dr. Moriart was known as the heaviest man on Cape Ann, they set the fracture while their patient mercifully lost consciousness. Both marveled that he was alive at all after such a prodigious fall; he was a lucky dog, they told him, that the bone splinters hadn't broken through that tough Novie hide, because a compound fracture doomed the limb to gangrene and the saw.

For nine weeks Jim was laid up. During his convalescence he got an earful of Dr. Moriart's troubles during the visits that abdomenous gentleman was able to squeeze into his political schedule. They were the same age. The patient had first seen his fat friend (how could he miss . . . at 350 pounds?) the day of the famous chowder of the Democrats on Eastern Point six years ago. His jovial energy as a loyal Jacksonian had been rewarded with the job of Port Surveyor. Doctor Moriart was riding high.

Now all that had changed. The cheery doctor was in a political stew, a mess . . . and worse, his ample back was to the wall, his own party was raising a hue and cry against him, the Whigs were gloating, and his beloved fishermen–the unkindest cut of all–were hanging him in effigy up and down the coast!

The bounty on codfish was the cause of the whole thing. It began with a letter Dr. Moriarty wrote Thomas Hart Benton of Missouri, President Van Buren's leader in the Senate, who was arguing for lower tariffs, including outright abolition of the duty on salt and hence of the bounty on cod, the former being a rationale for the latter. Dr. Moriart disclosed his discovery that Add Wonson, Jim's old Eastern Point shipmate, had unlawfully collected the bounty on Giles and Wonson's schooner *Eagle* in 1837. Add was under the impression that he was entitled to it if he discredited the time he spent taking mackerel while on a codding trip; he went to Customs Collector William Beach with this admission two years later, in 1839, and Beach–Moriarty charged–had falsified a voucher for the bounty.

Senator Benton read all this on the floor of the Senate in behalf of his contention that fraud and abuse were the handmaidens of the bounty. He was right. They had slick tricks, especially down East, where one man would let another take a spent old vessel for nothing to earn what he could with her in return for the bounty, a maritime pursuit called bounty-catching; sometimes these hulks never left the remote coves in which they dozed out their last days but were represented as great cod-catchers anyway. There was the "customs house oath" and a spurious log of the trip to prove that a mackerel catcher had been really after cod. The bounty was paid at so much per ton, and displacement was a factor of length; some observers of the passing scene down along the wharves swore that the measuring tape was made of rubber.

No great surprise, then, that when the news of Dr. Moriarty's letter and Senator Benton's use of it reached Gloucester, there was hell to pay. Henry Tilden, the Whig publisher of the *Gloucester Telegraph,* danced with joy and poured it onto the Democrats. This was an election year, and the Whigs were aching to turn the rascals out of office. The unfortunate physician and his party were accused of libeling the honest fisherman and snatching bread from the mouths of their babes. His friends called him a traitor. A mob gathered before his house, broke his windows, and threatened him with a beating; and his rotund effigy was strung up in every fishing town on the coast where the bounty was paid and the story found its way.

In August, when Jim had recovered enough to rejoin the *Abigail* fishing, the Democratic chowder boiled over. A number of party stalwarts (it was supposed) including John Fletcher Wonson and Sam Giles (Add's brother and brother-in-law) announced to the public that they were switching their support from Van Buren, the Red Fox of Kinderhook, to the Whig candidate, old William Henry Harrison, hero of Tippecanoe, running with John Tyler of Virginia.

Simultaneously Dr. Moriarty resigned as Surveyor for the Port, harassed and crucified, and moved out of town. Life had been made too miserable to bear for a man simpleminded enough to tell a truth nobody wanted to hear.

But though the washer departed, the dirty linen remained. A promising young painter of Gloucester scenes named Fitz Hugh Lane got up a great streamer for the Whigs showing a sea serpent rearing its head out of the water with the inscription: *The Deep has Felt the Attack Upon her Interests and Sends Her Champion to the Rescue.* (This was a reference to the famous "monster" that frolicked in the harbor for several days in 1817 before the eyes of nearly everyone on Cape Ann and even a pair of out-of-towners, Colonel Thomas Handasyd Perkins and Daniel Webster, who coached up from Boston to see it.) There were mass meetings and torchlight processions, Whig floats bearing log cabins draped with coonskins in honor of General Harrison's humble beginning and barrels of hard cider (in honor of an honest vote) and chanted songs of "Tippecanoe and Tyler Too!"

It was Jim's first chance to cast his ballot as an American, and of course he went down the line for Van Buren, because he was a Democrat and a Jacksonian before he was ever a citizen. Rum and hard cider flowed like sin, and great was the temptation. But he had sworn off liquor during the long days of his invalidism. Hard as it was, he had survived those two months, and not a taste of spirits had wet his lips. He was never again to touch a drop. He had grappled with the Demon and finally won.

Sandy Bay had just been created a separate town from Gloucester, but the men there still marched across the Cape, as they had always, to vote in the church at the Green. Up front was the rousing scream of fife and beat of drum, and tagging along behind in the dust were all the boys. From far and near the voters crowded into Haskell's Tavern, two blocks up from the wharves, for a pandemonium of good cheer before they cast their ballots, getting plenty of crusty advice from that thinning legion of Gloucester's veterans of the Revolution, the ancients who hunched on their benches in the sun with their clay pipes, still clinging to the knee britches and cocked hats of their heyday.

The Whigs carried the day, and the outs were the ins, not without the moral support of a trio of spinsters who lived uptown and displayed an elegantly ambiguous transparency from their porch proclaiming *Hope On, Hope Ever.*

That winter Captain Pattillo stayed home and enrolled in the navigation classes of Master Moore. This venerable gentleman was seventy-seven, spry as a lobster and conducted his school from his house on the hill above Freshwater Cove two miles from town on the west shore. His father William had built the place with a grand, sweeping view of Gloucester Harbor in 1752, and Joseph Moore had been teaching the principles of navigation for eight dollars a quarter to any mariner with the brains and patience to learn his system . . . and doing it for more than half a century. Smooth-pated over a fringe of flowing white locks, and smooth-shaven under, the stern old schoolmaster stared down his rough crew of seafaring pupils with eyes that bored them through; but always he gave himself away when the wide mouth between the long nose and the long jaw cracked into the most sardonic of smiles. Respected by all as "a man of simple tastes and habits and of many excellent traits of character," he had a story to tell, and here it is:

Master Moore was a raw lad of twelve at the beginning of the

Revolution, but he remembered the Gloucester companies of fishermen marching off to the fight at Bunker Hill. It was a few weeks later in that hot summer, while the Redcoats were still consolidating their occupation of Boston, that His Majesty's Sloop of War *Falcon,* Captain John Linzee, sailed into Cape Ann waters on a mission of blockade and harassment. On the fifth of August, 1775, *Falcon* stood off Coffin's Beach across from Annisquam in Ipswich Bay and sent in a barge with fifty men to forage for sheep. But Major Coffin wouldn't have it; he drummed up a half a dozen of his neighbors and led them out on the baking hot sand of the dunes, where they concealed themselves and put up such a brisk fire the invaders thought they were faced with a company and rowed back in a hurry to the haven of their ship.

Master Joseph Moore, Gloucester's navigational wizard. (Author collection)

Three days later Captain Linzee, smarting from this infamous defeat at the hands of the Yankee knaves, fell in with two schooners bound for Salem from the West Indies; he made a prize of one and chased the other into Gloucester Harbor, where her crew ran her up on the flats by Five Pound Island.

Under a white flag the British commander dickered with the Committee of Safety to get possession of his stranded prey, but the citizens gave answer instead with ball and shot from two antique swivels and all the muskets they could muster. When the smoke cleared from the brief, hot fight that followed, the Gloucestermen had retained the beached vessel in their hands, captured the other schooner that Linzee had armed and sent into battle, a British cutter, two barges and thirty-four men. The enraged master of the *Falcon* sent a party to burn the town, but they, too, were taken. In a delirium of frustration, he poured a couple of broadsides into Gloucester, weighed anchor and retired.

It happened that the Moores, father and son, were in their small boat nonchalantly fishing off Freshwater Cove during this excitement, when the British sloop of war, determined to take a prize however modest, ranged alongside and ordered them aboard. Captain Linzee was persuaded to let young Joseph go. The boy was put in his boat and rowed himself ashore at Kettle Cove a mile away. He never saw his father again; they said that after he refused to pilot *Falcon* on further coastal raids, he was shipped down to New York Harbor and died in a prison hulk.

Time passed. The boy had a strong talent for mathematics and an original mind. As a young man he taught in the district school and so thoroughly soaked up the principles of navigation that he was persuaded to inaugurate his classes for mariners. These were the days of the private schools of navigation, and many seaports had one.

In 1815, Master Moore published the fruit of his life work: *Navigation Improved; with a Number of Requisite Tables to Ascertain the Latitude and Longitude at Sea: together with Proper Rules and Examples for Illustrating the Same.* The author remarked in his preface that his was a "wholly original" method for getting a fix at sea without recourse to any books or instruments other than the quadrant. It required merely that the student memorize two basic (and very long) tables of figures of the writer's own devising, a formidable assignment for most of his pupils but surely nothing for Pattillo, who had the memory of an elephant. The good pedant finished off his introduction with this homely quatrain:

> Large ships, that are well rigg'd and found,
> May reach the ocean's farthest bound;
> But little boats, with feeble oars,
> Must never leave their native shores.

Thus did Master Moore, with humor and endurance, pound his tables into the groggy heads of the rough and unschooled Gloucestermen, fathers unto sons.

Big Jim took over the *Abigail* again in the spring, informing the Mansfields that he intended to try for another load of Newfoundland herring–and off he sailed. (His reputation was building as one skipper who fished where he had a mind to, and the owner, Crown official or whoever who offered to tell him where to go would be told himself in plain words.)

Rounding Cape Sable in a little puff of wind, they sprung their foremast and put in to Halifax for a new one. While revisiting the scene of old jolly times and minor crimes, the whitewashed Yankee paid his light duties for the year, as he wished no renewal of conflict with the Haligonian authorities, and they resumed their voyage.

Britain had long since tossed the bone of fishing rights on the Newfoundland west coast to her arch enemy. France clung bitterly to this last shadow of her New World empire, with St. Pierre and Miquelon, and she attempted to drive off all foreign fishermen from the French Shore, as they called it, with the dubious claim that it was hers exclusively.

Now this was a challenge to any man who believed that the fish in the sea are free.

Having eluded Sub-Collector Gaden and Her Majesty's cutter two years earlier on the south coast, the Yankee captain thought he would try the mettle of the patrols of Louis Phillippe. So he fetched *Abigail* into St. George's Bay on the French Shore, just as bold as brass, and had netted ninety barrels of herring when he was spoken by the French cutter from St. Pierre, whose captain courteously ordered him out.

Pattillo complied this time and slipped to the nor'ard by the harsh cliffs of Cape St. George and the rosy bluffs of Red Island, around the reefs of Long Point and back to the south'ard through Port au Port Bay into East Bay, only to find that the herring had spawned and left. The cutter, however, had not. The Frenchman–still in St. George's Bay–was seventy-five miles away from the Gloucester boat by sea but could observe her spars piercing the sky where she lay at the head of East Bay on the other side of the sandy isthmus connecting Port au Port Peninsula (that *Abigail* had sailed around) with the mainland.

The captain of the cutter ordered his boat over the side and was rowed into the beach; they dragged it the quarter-mile across the neck, embarked again and came alongside the *Abigail.*

Perhaps the Americans would be so kind as to inform him what they were doing there?

Came looking for herring but found none.

Ah, but they had been requested to evacuate St. George's Bay because they had no right to fish there, and it was no more permitted to fish here!

Well, there were no herring, so they couldn't fish for them in any event, thus whimsically replied the great giant at the rail. Would the captain of the cutter enjoy to come on board and join him for dinner–some nice fried fish, perhaps?

The officer thought it prudent to decline this compromising invitation. Jim bid him goodby with the cheery challenge that he was bound to catch a load of herring on the French Shore before he sailed for home, to which the Gallic commander politely responded that he was bound to seize his vessel if he did.

They parted, and while the cutter's boat was being dragged back across the sand spit to St. George's Bay, the *Abigail* hauled anchor and stood out East Bay for up the coast.

Since the whole of Port au Port Peninsula came between them, *Abigail* had a fifty-mile start on the cutter. The Americans moseyed along until they found a cove called Shallow Bay, nestled in a half moon of wilderness, fairly bubbling with fish. They filled out their fare of French herring and made off for Cape Ann, leaving their gallant adversary no less knowing, to be sure, but none the wiser.

Damn You! Won't You Heave To?

WE FOLLOW *the fish, not the treaty.*

This was the motto of the New England skippers in the quest for mackerel that attracted more of them every year to the Gulf of St. Lawrence and up to the very shores of Nova Scotia. As for the owners, they were equally contemptuous of international convention and only slightly more circumspect, as became men of business. . . . *Where Providence sends the fish, we will send the fishermen.*

Each July an armada of jiggers invaded the North Bay, cruising to and fro and hither and yon over its azure waters in squadrons, and scouting every bay and cove by ones and twos. When mackerel struck, the news flew from rail to rail, and the fleet came pounding in like gulls on gurry, piling canvas to the topmast trucks, racing for the run while it lasted.

If the mackerel chanced to school in some shore fisherman's back yard, worse luck for him. Out of the swelling ranks of those who had slight esteem for the three-mile limit there was usually some captain ready to sail within a jig's throw of the overhanging spruces, heave chum by the barrelful and toll the school to the fleet from under the noses of the Bluenoses.

There were other pebbles, too, in Novie boots.

First, resentment ran high against the bounty, which gave the American fishermen an edge in the market for cod and then, by gum, turned around and subsidized their theft of Canadian mackerel. Next, any man with eyes in his head could see that the Gloucester schooners were bigger, better, newer and more thoroughly and less dearly outfitted than the Provincial fleet. Next, when the Yanks ran out of bait and couldn't catch enough or didn't want to be bothered, they ducked in just like that and bought all they needed from the fishermen along the coast either at prices the Nova Scotian mackerelers couldn't afford to meet or for inducements they couldn't match–like smuggled gin, tobacco and all that. But the dirtiest trick of all was the exodus of high liners to Gloucester, lured away by these myriad attractions, many of them to settle permanently under a coat of whitewash like Jim Pattillo.

So finally these waves of bitterness lapped at the walls of Government House in Halifax. Protection was the cry, and in 1836 the Provincial Legislature passed the "Hovering Act" that was supposed to put some muscle into the Convention of 1818. It empowered customs, impost and excise officers, sheriffs, magistrates and others holding Crown commissions to board and search foreign vessels within bays and harbors or "hovering" inside the three-mile limit from headland to headland; they were authorized to confiscate contraband and to seize any foreign vessel, and its cargo, found fishing or preparing to fish inside the limit; the Customs was directed to hold a seized vessel, and if condemned in Admiralty, to sell it off at auction.

The Hovering Act was an embarrassment to the British, who lacked enthusiasm at the moment for an incident with the United States over a mess of mackerel. They carefully avoided any commitment of Her Majesty's Royal Navy to the execution of these rash Provincial threats, and three years were to pass ere the dog had a bite to match his bark.

The three years passed, and by 1840 three Provincial cutters had been fitted out, armed and commissioned to Captains J. W. E. Darby (who was only twenty-three), James Marshall and Andrew Stephens. That summer they seized twenty-eight vessels, of which eleven were condemned and sold, along with a quantity of contraband. It began to look as if the Canadians meant business.

His trouble-seeking (drinking) days now behind him, Captain Pattillo on his first trip to Bay St. Lawrence in two years took care during the summer of 1841 to keep off the Nova Scotian coast; the crew of the *Abigail* hooked their entire fare of mackerel on Orphan and Bradelle banks between Prince Edward Island and the Gaspé Peninsula.

They returned to Cape Ann about the first of September and were readying for another run up to the North Bay when a young lady was introduced to Jim, seeking passage to Canso. He refused her out of hand. *Abigail* was no vessel for a female, first off, and in the second place he was not licensed for passengers and could be seized by his old enemies for smuggling, the more the risk with the new cutters so active up that way. And in the third place they had a grudge against him at Canso for chucking Collector McMullen overboard.

But Eliza Cantrell was a pretty lass and she pleaded with him so prettily. She had come to Gloucester from Lowell, where she worked in the mill, after getting the sad word that her father, Dr. William Cantrell, the Health Officer at Canso, was dead. Her widowed mother needed Liza back home.

The big captain still hesitated. Then Liza got his wife's sympathetic ear, and Anne pressed him to take the chance for the poor thing, because everyone knew he could do whatever he set his mind to. In the end he gave in, with some misgivings, and advised Miss Cantrell to have her things ready to go on board, as *Abigail* would sail on the first fair breeze.

Next day the wind turned favoring. They warped the pinkey through the press of the fleet in Harbor Cove to the edge of the stream off Duncan's Point. While his crew made sail, Jim rowed ashore for his passenger. In an hour Liza was aboard–trunk, bandbox and all. They weighed anchor and were off.

In due course the bold contours of Canso presented themselves. As Jim had no especial desire to tarry at this stronghold of offended authority, he merely hove his vessel to in the harbor and put the dory over, followed by Liza and her effects, for him to deliver ashore at Whalen's and then hightail back so they could all get out of there and on to the North Bay.

Jim saw his grateful charge to her destination; he would take no money in payment but hurriedly bid her goodby and rowed for the *Abigail.* Stroking up to her, he was surprised and not a little suspicious to see a boat alongside and his crew gathered around three strangers by the mainmast, all engaged in heated argument. He gave a hail as he coasted up, tossed the painter to one of his men and swung aboard. The apparent leader of the trio, a burly, red-faced fellow in the uniform of a Crown official, stepped over and asked him if he was the master.

He was, said Jim, for lack of a better.

His visitor pointed over at the mainmast about shoulder high, whereon was scrawled what looked like a crude arrowhead in red chalk, and announced importantly:

"I have seized this vessel for smuggling. I know you have just landed a girl and her things, and your men tell me you came from Gloucester. That, sir, is smuggling, and the broad arrow says this vessel belongs to the Queen. Now let me see your papers."

They had been too quick for him, that was all. Jim did not know what to do, so he said all right and directed his men to hook the tackle in the beckets and hoist his dory aboard. Seeing the ship's work going on as usual somehow irritated the Queen's man, and he impatiently repeated his demand to see *Abigail*'s papers.

"Mister," grunted her master, "I'll attend to my own job first and then I'll wait on you, so hold your water." Old John Parsons was at the helm; Jim told him to look sharp and bear out the harbor. Then he motioned his "captor" to come with him below. *Abigail*'s papers were in a canister on the shelf above his berth. He took the tin down, and when he opened it the receipt for the light dues he had paid in Halifax in April fluttered to the cabin floor. The official in his overbearing way picked up the slip, glanced at it and took the papers, which he rifled through, searching for something. Jim was burning anyway and asked him what the devil he was after in his documents.

Without looking up, the unwelcome guest growled in a peremptory manner that he wanted the *Abigail*'s tonnage so as to figure up the light dues owed, and then if he could have quill and ink he would give him a receipt for it.

"What! The light dues! Why, I've paid them already in Halifax–you just read the receipt! Am I to pay them over again–and after you've seized my vessel? Say . . . who are you anyway?" Jim's temper rose with his conviction that there was no justice in losing *Abigail* as his reward for a Christian act on behalf of a poor girl in distress; and on top of it all, this foolishness about light dues.

The official identified himself as William Bigelow, Collector of Light Duties. (He had held the job for only a year since his retirement at thirty-nine as a sea captain in the West Indies trade, which accounted for his quarterdeck manners.)

"And where's your authority?" demanded the Gloucesterman.

Captain Bigelow had to admit that in his haste to board the American schooner he had left his papers behind.

What luck! Jim could hardly believe his ears.

"Why, you're nothing but an impostor!" he roared triumphantly. "Here you have come trespassing, trying to rob me of my vessel and rob me of light money, and you have no papers, no authority at all, you vagabond! Go ashore! You have no business here! Get out!"

The red face of the beefy Collector flushed redder still; the wind had momentarily left his sails.

"You won't pay me then?"

"Certainly I won't pay–not a cent, not a bloody cent! You're an impostor–out with you, out before I throw you out!"

Captain Bigelow was not accustomed to having the tables turned on him and was possessed of a temper to equal Jim's. He jumped for the companionway, climbed on deck and bellowed out to John Parsons to put the helm hard down. Old John was so flustered by all the excitement that he obeyed, and the pinkey started to come into the wind.

But the master of the *Abigail* was right behind. He exploded up through the hatch with fire in his eye, just in time to see the sails luff and her head swing in toward a reef of rocks.

"Hard up the helm!" he thundered–"Hard up, I say! By God when Bigelow is master of this vessel, Uncle John, he will furnish his own crew, but as long as I am aboard of her I will look out for her!" This time old John knew whom to follow. Her canvas filled again, she fell back off the wind, and they passed to leeward of the rocks.

Once more the Yankee captain and Her Majesty's Collector confronted one another, and for this round they squared off by the mainmast, with their followers gathered about. This last performance had almost convinced Bigelow that he knew the identity of the giant smuggler who stood glowering before him.

"What's your name, Captain?" he clipped out, his eyes narrowing.

"J. W. Pattillo."

"Pattillo!" The name aroused him all anew. "You villain, I know the Pattillos!" And indeed he did, for his predecessor McMullen had told him about being thrown overboard by a great brute of a whitewashed Yankee named Pattillo from Cape Ann who they said was one of the strongest men alive.

"You know the Pattillos, do you?" grinned Jim in a sudden change of temper. "Then you must know me because there are only two of us, my brother and I!"

Although Bigelow and his two men were outnumbered by the captain and crew of the *Abigail*, a cul-de-sac which led him to suspect that he was a captive aboard his own prize and headed out to sea at that, he was a man of exceptional choler and (it must be conceded) courage.

"You damn sneaking Yankee smuggler, this vessel is the Queen's, and by thunder you will sail it across to Big Canso!" he shouted, stamping his feet. "There will be a man-o'-war there to take you, I swear, and if there is not a man-o'-war, there will be a cutter, and if there is not a cutter I will raise the militia, I swear I will! I am bound to take you, you damn pirate, and you and all your Yankee gang will have the fun of walking home to Gloucester–a nice little trudge for the bunch of you between now and winter!"

This tirade was cut short by a cry from the helmsman that a cutter was indeed bearing down on them at that very moment . . . and there it was, still some distance off, beating in toward the harbor.

"Ha!" yelled Bigelow with a shake of his fist at Pattillo. "Here comes the cutter–now I will take you, right into Great Canso!"

"Go where you like, get man-o'-war, cutter or what you want," Jim was trying to control himself. "But this vessel is not big enough to carry the two of us together, I warn you. You will have to get your own conveyance, and quick!"

This was too much for Bigelow. In all the years he had been to sea (since he was eighteen and the master of a vessel) he had never been crossed so. He off with his jacket and put up his fists.

"We'll settle this right now!" he stormed, "I tell you, you rogue, it takes a man to handle me!"

But Jim thought to himself that the fellow had got into the wrong shop for that kind of work, and as cool as he could be he proposed a compromise, for he had no wish to hurt the man if it could be avoided.

"All right, Mister Bigelow, I will tell you what I will do. If you are the Light Collector and will return ashore for your document to prove it, I will heave to right here and now until you come back–that is, if you are what you say you are and will forget about seizing, I will pay the dues though I have paid them once already, to show you that I am a good fellow and want to make no trouble. Now how does that sound to you?"

The answer to this proposition was a string of invective from the port officer, who looked to be on the verge of apoplexy.

At last Jim surrendered to the gods of Wrath and Offended Virtue. He spat in his hands, cocked back and threw such a swing at Bigelow it would have taken his head off had he not ducked in the nick of time.

Pattillo came back at him, quick as a cat for such a big man, fended off his blows as if they were a child's and seized him by his favored articles of clothing for handling Crown Officials–his collar and the slack of his trousers. With one heave he lifted the struggling Collector clear over his head, crossed to the rail and flung him overboard into his dory with such violence that his body shattered the main thwart–the board was wide and close to an inch thick–and lucky for him it broke his fall.

The unfortunate Bigelow lay in the bottom of his boat, moaning and crying, "My God, don't kill me!"

"You're a bag of feathers instead of a man," grunted Captain

Pattillo, looking around to see if the other two wanted to be passed on in the same style, but they hastened to leave ship under their own power.

The crew of the *Abigail* had been enjoying each scene of this little drama as it unfolded. By way of ringing down the curtain, they cast off the painter of the Queen's dory and watched the Collector's men row off toward the town, their battered chief still resting in the bottom.

"All right, lads, snap to it!" cried the Yankee captain, and they proceeded on their way.

Passing through the Gut of Canso and into the North Bay, Skipper Jim and his jolly lads chummed up a school of mackerel off the Bend of Prince Edward Island and hooked seventy-five barrels. While they were salting, *Abigail* was spoken by other Gloucester jiggers carrying the news that Pattillo might be the hero of the fleet for the bouncing of Bigelow, but Darby, Marshall and Stephens in their cutters were after his hide for it.

"In that case, never allow yourself to be unprepared," declared the captain to his crew. So while they were down along the Cape Breton shore looking for the mackerel to strike in, *Abigail* slipped into the western harbor of Cheticamp and dropped anchor behind the island where Jim had kedged off the *Good Hope* the time she stranded during the gale. He went on shore in the dory, picked out two good rocks of about a hundred and fifty pounds apiece, carried them back and swung them up on deck. This done, he lashed fish barrels to the main chains under the shrouds at both rails to hold them from starting and placed a rock in each.

"That should do it, lads," said Jim, brushing his hands. "Let's get under way. If the enemy tries to board us, why we'll dump a nice little rock right through their bottom and then they'll all be knocked into the water like drowned rats."

The air had an autumn bite to it as the fleet of some fifty American sail followed the Cape Breton coast down toward the north entrance to the Gut of Canso, homeward bound with all the mackerel the Lord intended them to hook that year. On the third of October the wind backed around in the morning and by afternoon freshened from the east until first one vessel, then another and finally the whole fleet followed suit, hove to and shortened sail.

Since there was every sign of a double-reefed gale by nightfall, the skippers concluded with one accord, as if through some private telegraph of their own, to make for Port Hood, the seaside coal mine town that was a familiar haven against an easterly, just around Cape Linzee where the coast bent to the southward. In short order they fetched Port Hood Island a mile offshore, straggled around it on a beat and beam-reached into the spacious harbor, each vessel picking her particular place of refuge.

Up went the cries of "Hard down your helm! Stand by your jib and your windlass!" and the schooners turned deliberately into the chill of the wind, sails whipping and cracking like pistol shots. Down collapsed headsails, heaped in the bows. When the hookers had drifted into irons, the wind regained control and pushed them into sternway, and then all across the water could be heard the sturdy sound of chain rasping through hawse pipes, releasing the huge anchors to plosh into the depths. Not until each captain had judged there was scope enough of cable did the windlass gang snub up to test the feel of it, to be sure the fluke had dug itself solid in the bottom before making fast. "Jump to your halyards, boys!" Down fell foresail and then the big main in clatters of hoops and rumples of canvas, and the job of securing for the night was under way, with time for a smoke or two and a gam between vessels before dark.

Smack in the middle of the fleet was the *Abigail.*

In an hour a shout was flung from berth to berth, and all eyes scanned to the southward where three sail had come into view, beating up the coast toward the harbor. Ten more minutes and they were recognized as the revenue cutters of Commanders Darby, Marshall and Stevens. Two of these distasteful companions for the night, Darby and Stephens, anchored off at some distance under the mainland shore, but Marshall hove to at the very edge of the Yankee fleet, as if with some object in mind.

The arrival of the Provincial patrols provoked some mighty

stir, both in the harbor and on the shore, where the people could be seen gathering. Among the vessels there was much calling back and forth above the wind, and a number of the Gloucestermen were putting over their dories and rowing to the *Abigail.*

In no time she had a crowd of visiting fishermen aboard, and it was the opinion of all that the cutters thought they had Pattillo trapped and meant to move against him at any moment. Several repeated the persistent and rather unpleasant rumor that his pursuers had orders to capture him, dead or alive, for his treatment of Collector Bigelow.

Even as these friends in their oilskins were milling around *Abigail's* deck and offering her master advice, a boat manned by eight armed men and two officers pushed out from Captain Marshall's cutter and was rowed through the fleet to an English brig anchored upwind and separated from the *Abigail* by two other schooners. The officers climbed aboard the brig, and Jim could see them through his spyglass, talking to her captain and all gesturing in his direction. Doubtless the master of the brig had identified that great Pattillo's vessel for them.

He snapped his glass shut and sprang into action.

"Come on men, jump quick, let's get under way! We're moving out of here. You other fellows, if you want to lend a hand, good for you–otherwise clear off if you please and get back aboard of your own vessels and watch the fun!"

His crew seized handspikes and made for the windlass, while the tail end of the visitors, before leaping into their boats, bounded for the halyards with a shout and ran up mainsail and foresail, still reefed as they were when furled . . . and a good thing, too, for the wind was flicking up whitecaps and dashes of spume, even there in the lee of the land.

It was a long pull on the windlass against the gathering strength of the gale, and they were still straining at the drumheads when the cutter's boat left the brig and half-rowed, half-drifted downwind toward them on the port side. Jim crossed the deck and stood by the barrel with its rock, his heavy artillery. Right abreast a couple of fathoms off, the rowers backed water and one of the

After warning off Commander Marshall with his rock in 1841, Captain Pattillo sails Abigail *out of Port Hood in a living gale and under fire from the Canadian cutter. When two articles appeared forty-two years later, about this encounter and that with Collector Gaden off Newfoundland, the old fishing skipper pronounced them "substantially correct."* (Youth's Companion, November 1883)

officers (it was Captain Marshall himself) called out:

"Ahoy! You're getting under way!"

The Yankee captain plucked the rock from the barrel as if it were a ball of cotton and balanced it on the rail:

"Now how did you guess that? Too bad you didn't save yourself the trouble–you could have seen from where you were!"

Captain Marshall made no answer; he regarded the man and

the rock from his tossing boat, silently. He then ordered his oarsmen to row for the cutter and put their backs into it. In no time he was aboard his own craft again and marking preparations to get under way himself.

The greatest dunce in ten counties could see that a grand show was about to open, and every fisherman in the fleet scrambled up the rigging of his vessel for a choice view, while the shore was dotted with spectators.

Up in the bow the windlass still clack-clacked and the dripping cable coiled aboard. Jim yelled over to Captains John Bayley and Ben Laroque in the next berths for the one to heave his vessel ahead and the other to pay out cable and drop astern so *Abigail* could pass between the two on her way out.

The anchor broke ground, finally. Up the forestay flew the jib; Jim hauled the tiller hard up; the furiously flapping sails filled and shivered smooth; her head swung off to starboard, and they were under way on the port tack, shouldering by the bow and stern of Bayley and Laroque, gaining speed from those powerful curves of canvas, the other crews waving their sou'westers and shouting encouragement as *Abigail* thundered by them, squalls of spray whiskering off her buxom bow.

She bore away until the wind came abeam. With deft touches of the tiller her master guided her through the maze of anchored vessels as a rider would his steed with flicks of his crop. Her course was calculated to carry her just close enough for him to thumb his nose at the cutter as they careened by.

The hell-bent Gloucester pinkey was fifty yards off Marshall's stern at that precise moment when he was getting under way and on the point of slipping off the wind. Jim was about to fire a few choice words across the tossing stretch of white water and spume that separated them when the cutter–still swinging round to take the wind on her beam and begin the chase–came broadside to them.

Suddenly, a ring of smoke spurted from her foredeck, followed instantly by a sharp rip overhead, a *ker-pow,* and the plunk of a cannonball in the water away off to starboard.

Marshall was dead serious, at that. He had his twelve-pounder in action. Was he trying to start a war? Jim glanced up at the hole in the mainsail six feet above his head. His first reaction was that of any sensible man in such a situation: he put the tiller hard down to heave to and surrender.

But with scarcely a second thought, the whitewashed Yankee captain changed his mind and followed the cross of his grain. He brought her off the wind again, back on her headlong, headstrong course. Henry Smith called nervously from the lookout to know if he intended heaving to.

"No!" his skipper roared back, waving an arm at the hatch. "All hands clear off the deck and get below!" This order was obeyed with a scurry of pounding feet. He looked astern. The cutter was right on his tail, hanging off *Abigail*'s port quarter.

Then came Captain Marshall's voice, carried downwind loud and clear:

"Damn you! Won't you heave to?"

Pattillo cupped a hand to his mouth and replied with a bellow to raise the dead:

"Not by a long shot! Not at present anyway!"

To get under cover of the bulwarks, he flopped down on his back. The steep sheer of *Abigail*'s afterdeck provided him with an awkward view of his course, which he steered by reaching up to the tiller overhead.

The cutter fired a second round. It came whistling across, smashed through the first plank under the port bends and bored to a stop in one of the main deck beams a foot from his body.

He kept her right on course, down the harbor through the fleet.

Ker-pow! The third shot struck the bulwarks abreast of him and wobbled across the deck, clanged into the starboard main chains under the sheer poles and rolled into the midships scuppers like a runaway bowling ball.

Abigail now was pounding along off Henry Island, almost two miles southwest of Port Hood Island and well clear of the fleet. Jim squared her off before the wind, and the fourth round screamed in; it knocked a piece off the forward edge of the mainmast, a few inches above the boom saddle, and passed on into the sea.

The pinkey was decidedly stretching her lead over the slower cutter, but the marksmanship of the Canadians was not to be denied. *Abigail* was rounding Justaucorps Point at Henry's southern tip and standing out to sea in rough water when the fifth ball from the twelve-pounder lobbed in and tore a chunk off one of the windlass pawl bitts.

Six more shots they unloaded, but their aim was spoiled by the heaving of the sea and the lengthening range, and all fell short, making geysers in the bubbling wake of the saucy little *Abigail.* Henry Smith and Dan Brown and old John Parsons and the rest reappeared from below after Jim stomped on the deck over their heads, and for five more miles they drove her out to sea in the rising gale until Marshall gave up the chase and fumed back.

That night the fleet held a gala in the harbor of Port Hood. The Americans put together a band with fife, drum, fiddle and kettle, pot and pan, foghorn and whatever else would make a noise. And then they took to their dories and by the light of their lanterns flickering in the storm, rowed round and round the anchored cutter, banging and tooting and whistling *Yankee Doodle.*

As for *Abigail,* she lay to at sea all night long, close-reefed in the teeth of the gale. In the due course of time she arrived home in Gloucester with her load of mackerel, a patch in her mainsail, an assortment of splinters and two Canadian cannonballs.

Whatsoever a Man Soweth

ABIGAIL CAME HOME to sad news. The same October gale that winged her out of the reach of Marshall and his twelve-pounder dashed Steve Rich and seven men of Gloucester to the bottom off Cape Cod in the schooner *Forest.* And so Steve followed Job Rowe to the same end. Many were the roaring good times his old skipper and Jim Pattillo had shared on board and ashore . . . and all the fellows with him, too, the finest kind every one . . . oh the sorrowful sea.

The time had come for a change. Pattillo and Abigail were too notorious together to risk again in the North Bay, and Jim was restless for a bigger, better, newer boat. He found her in the well smack Hosea Ballou, named for a famous Universalist preacher, which he took to the Georges in January of 1842 for the three owners, John Woodbury, Gus Wonson and Gloucester's leading Baptist, Deacon George Garland, the author's half great-uncle.

The lines of *Hosea Ballou* were considered shockingly swish when she swooshed off the greasy ways into the Essex River two years before, and the waterfront graybeards wagged their heads in disapproval every time she cleared; to their way of thinking she looked tricky and confounded unsafe. There was a hint in her, not to be denied, of changes bound to come, even to the fisheries (which people liked to look to, with a certain comfortable feeling, as one line of work immune to the vogue for frivolous experimentation). She was so much less chesty than her forebears that some called her a half-clipper; most surely she breasted the wave with more feminine grace than the stock from which she sprang, and most of the talkers had to admit she was more damsel than dowager. At all events, she served her master well, and he was cautious enough to avoid the Bay St. Lawrence for the three years he sailed her, and he saved up his earnings.

His last year in *Hosea Ballou* Jim fell in with the three Riggs brothers, all master mariners and vessel owners, and they proposed to go partners with him down the middle in the building of a new schooner. Fitz, Gorham and Nathaniel were the hard-working sons of Andrew Riggs, who died of wounds received while serving with the Gloucester privateer *Orlando* during the War of 1812. Their wharf was four removed from Mansfield's up at the head of Harbor Cove.

The first Gloucester vessel Jim could halfway call his own skidded over the Essex flats into the mother water during the fall of 1844 and was christened *William Wallace.* Like *Hosea Ballou, she* was a *she* in spite of her name, and a smack too, following the same model (if slightly larger). She registered sixty-seven tons and cost her owners about $3000 to build and outfit.

William Wallace was one of the staunchest sail carriers in Gloucester right from the start, and she proved herself during her second year on Georges Bank. Ten of the twenty-nine in the winter fleet departed for the Bank on the fifth of January, 1846, including *William Wallace, Hosea Ballou* and old *Mount Vernon.* Jim had top boat and top crew without any argument. His first two trips of halibut brought the biggest money in the fleet—$500 and $610—which was regarded as sensational and became the topic of every conversation around the stoves in the stores and on the snowy wharves and street corners. The Georgesmen averaged five trips that season, and at the end of it *William Wallace* was high-line with a stock of $2135, one half to the owners and the other shared by the crew.

These smacks served their purpose, sped to and from the grounds by the imprecations of the men who manned them. In the absence of refrigeration they kept most of the fish alive, if blearyeyed, for market, but the bulkhead hadn't been invented that would stop all that water in the well from leaking into the hold, and it was a rare Gloucesterman who could boast that he enjoyed spending half his watches out to the Georges and back at the pump.

Jim was generally conceded to be the man who came up with the solution, and a revolutionary one it was. He built an ice house in *William Wallace,* said to be the first ever constructed in a fishing vessel. It was in the spring of 1846. The ice hold had sets of double bulkheads separated by two or three inches and filled with tanbark for insulation. As a companion innovation he built a wooden platform over the ballast in the ice house to keep the catch from being bruised by the stones—a device he had used once before, and with singular success, to divert the prying eyes of the Provincial Customs from a cargo which was not fish.

For the first time in six years Jim ventured in 1847 to poke his nose into the North Bay (they said there was only one cutter on station). He put off in *William Wallace* at his usual time of departure, directly after the Fourth of July, and besides his crew of teetotallers (he would not sign on a drinking man since embracing temperance himself) there were two passengers, his wife and his son.

Anne was poorly, and one surmises that she was subject to spells. Perhaps a visit with her people in Chester would help. Alex went along with his mother, as much to watch over her as anything. He was now a small and neat young man of eighteen, with a keen head for figures and no fear of hard work so long as it was ashore. The sea had no charms for him; he had none of his great father's obsession with fish, vessels and the ways of the water. Dry land and dry goods for Alex . . . he would make his way from the lee of the counter, clerking in John Calef's store.

Jim landed wife and son at Chester and continued on to the Bay. In a month he was back with a fare of mackerel, but Anne was either not ready or in no condition to leave, so he proceeded on to Cape Ann and settled up his voyage.

On the first of November he sailed from Gloucester as a passenger, for once, in a vessel belonging to Chester to pick up his family, and for another interesting purpose. When he departed so informally from the place of his birth thirteen years before, Jim had to leave behind six hundred dollars—in debts. But he took his conscience with him and over the years had saved up to pay them off with interest, which he now proposed to do.

The whitewashed Yankee had not been long back amidst the beauties and memories of that lovely little haven of white cottages and green spruces set in the heavenly blue of Mahone Bay, when word of the nature of his errand was abroad. Among the first to hear was a certain sly fellow who thought he would turn the return of the prodigal to his own advantage. He happened to know that among Jim's creditors was a certain rich man across the Bay in Blandford, and he even knew how much was owed—forty pounds.

So when he heard that Jimmy Pattillo was in with a purse of gold to do right by old friends and neighbors, Mister Foxy jumped on his nag and spurred her along the dirt road around the shore to Blandford. When he came to the bend before the rich man's house he fetched her up short and they ambled casually along into the yard. The rogue tied her to the post and sauntered up, just to pass the time of day, being along that way on business, don't you know, and while in conversation with the creditor offered him fifteen pounds for that note from Jimmy Pattillo, as of course everybody knew the rascal didn't have the brass to show his face in Chester, and if he ever did he had too much of it to pay his debts to honest people.

However, this generous offer to buy up a worthless note was refused. The offer was doubled and again refused, the holder of the note vowing that he would not sell it for a ha'penny less than its worth—no, not for the whole of it under any circumstances whatever. If Jimmy Pattillo was still alive and had the money he would surely pay, sooner or later, and if he hadn't the money, then he needed all he had and was welcome to it.

The next day Jim turned up in Blandford and paid this man of faith, in gold. His creditor would accept no interest and tried to persuade him back to the Provinces; indeed he would go him as high as three thousand pounds or higher for the building of any

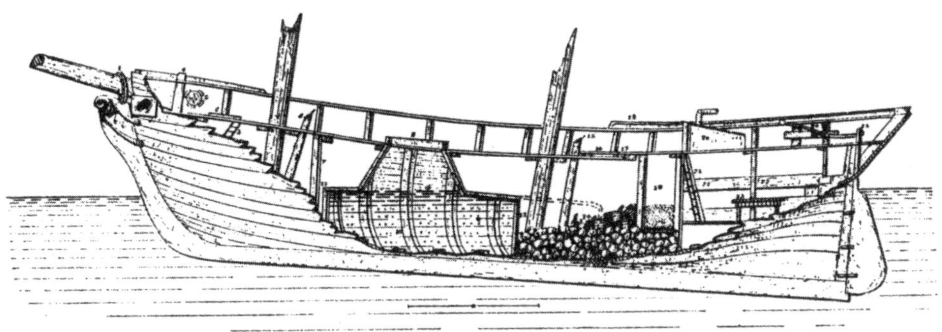

Layout of a Georges well smack such as Mount Vernon *and* William Wallace. *The water-filled well designed to keep the halibut alive is bulkheaded amidships, ahead of the stone ballast. Directly behind the masts the hollow-log pumps descend from deck to bilge. Foc's'le is in the bow, skipper's cabin in the stern. Note the carved billet head under the bowsprit; Gloucester schooners never carried figureheads. These smacks sailed with the Georges fleet from 1835 until Pattillo stowed ice aboard* William Wallace *in 1846. (Goode's* Fisheries*)*

size vessel he wanted if only he would return.

Captain Pattillo thanked him for his kindness and went on his way, around through the countryside, paying off his debts, large and small, principal and interest, until all was square.

Whatsoever a man soweth, that shall he also reap.

For every man he owed, there seemed to be another in his debt, and when the Pattillo family boarded the boat for Halifax, Jim took stock and discovered he had more than when he arrived. Yes, these were some of the happiest days of his life, he told his wife–being able to pay his honest debts.

It was along about the second week in November when the Pattillo party (they were four, including a niece making the trip with them) arrived in Halifax. They put up at the South Country Market Hotel to wait for the arrival of the steamship *Acadia*, expected any day from Liverpool, England, bound for Boston.

Jim scraped up an acquaintance with Deacon Shaffner, a farmer from Nictaux, inland from the Fundy coast, boarding at the same hotel on business. The old man had a long face full of worry, and he kept wanting to know if the weather was such that a vessel could come from the westward. Not a chance was the invariable reply—head winds all the way.

Every little while the Deacon would walk over to the window and peer out at the sky, and then he would turn back with a sigh and ask his seafaring companion if now the wind was right. And the answer was the same, until finally the comment was tacked on that Deacon was plainly anxious about some vessel or other.

He was, said the farmer—she had loaded at Annapolis Royal some days before with cider, apples, cheese, butter and such for the produce market, and he prayed nothing had befallen her.

"And what kind of a master does she have?" inquired the Captain offhandedly. "Is he a competent man? And what sort of a vessel; is she a good sailer and everything on board staunch and fast?"

"Yes—everything is of the best; yes, yes, the captain is the finest kind and boat new and well found and all in order."

"Well, well, Deacon . . . Tell me what day she sailed from Digby Gut, and I will tell you within an hour when she will reach Halifax."

The old gentleman gave him the day, with a look of disbelief, for the voyage was the better part of a week's work through a shuffle of wind and tide.

Captain Pattillo overhauled his memory and brought to mind how the wind was when the vessel started. He carried her down to Petite Passage the first day; the next day he got her down to Grand Passage and the day following to Barrington Passage inside Cape Sable—and there he knew she would have to remain until the wind was favorable to make the westward passage.

During the night the wind hauled around to the southwest, a fair wind, and so he mentioned to his nervous friend at breakfast—right casually—that if it held and her master tended to business she would be in Halifax at nine o'clock that evening.

After supper the old farmer and the giant fisherman walked over to the Granville Street Baptist Church to hear the Reverend Crawley. The prayer meeting was out a few minutes before nine, and the Captain suggested to the countryman that they take a turn down to Market Wharf to meet his vessel.

They walked along through the dark streets to the harbor, and just as they reached the wharf, the vessel shot right into the dock between Queen's and Market, and Jim took her fast.

Next morning Deacon Shaffner could hardly attend to selling his produce, he was that tickled at Captain Pattillo telling him the very hour his vessel would reach Halifax all the way round from Annapolis Gut, and he spread the story far and wide.

In Which Jim Pattillo Does Sam Cunard a Kindness

THE STEAMSHIP *Acadia* docked at Halifax Thursday evening, the eighteenth of November, 1847, with ninety saloon passengers from England (she had no steerage), fourteen days out of Liverpool.

It was a fast passage, considering the season, though three days off the record for the westward crossing *Acadia* herself had set on her maiden voyage in August of 1840, eleven days and four hours. They darn near blew her boiler that first trip, because she averaged 9.28 knots, which was as hard as the seven hundred and forty horses in her side level Napier steam engine would drive her massive paddle wheels . . . and that with the help of the wind in her sails.

Acadia was by all odds the fastest of the four sisters with which Sam Cunard had founded the British and North American Royal Mail Steam Packet Company, starting the first regular transatlantic steamship service (subsidized by a contract to carry Her Majesty's mails). The original Cunard liners, *Acadia, Britannia, Caledonia* and *Columbia,* were built in Glasgow on the Clyde along identical lines. Each was bark-rigged, for it was only by the combination of wind and steam that regular service could be maintained; an ugly high smokestack belched sparks and clouds of horrid fumes, to the utmost peril of sails and rigging. All of twenty-five feet across, the spanking paddles churned through the water under their housings, propelled with clanging throbs by the stately oscillation of the giant beams that were rocked up and down in the bottom of the ship, day and night, by the slow, hissing eight-foot stroke of the pistons.

Into the bowels of this hermaphroditic monster a steward escorted the Pattillo entourage to the staterooms which Charles Dickens had likened to a "profoundly preposterous box . . . no bigger than one of those hackney cabriolets which have the door behind, and shoot their fares out, like sacks of coals, upon the pavement."

After much hustle and running to and fro in the night, loading and unloading of freight and mail, and transfers of passengers and their baggage, whinnying, clatter of hooves and ring of wheels on the cobbles, shouting and hailing, taking on the coast pilot, banging of doors and a full chorus of shipboard noises, *Acadia* rent the darkness with a throaty blast on her whistle, the gangplank was pulled up, her fasts were loosed, bells jittered, the engine clanked into life, the paddles beat the water into foam and she moved majestically out into the stream, her lights twinkling at the town asleep under the mothering bulk of its Citadel, the billows of smoke from her stack all hellfire-red and spark-strewn against the black of the night.

At daybreak, long before the other members of his family were awake, Captain Pattillo hove himself out of his berth, dressed and went up on deck. The steamer was rolling sedately, not uncomfortably, just riding with the swells. The wind had backed around to the northeast, damp and cold, penetrating to the bone, and the dawn sky was a scudding gray overcast. The decks were deserted except for the watch–the lookout, the helmsman–and the pilot. Jim shaped a course for this important individual, strolled up with his widespread rolling gait and by way of making conversation allowed as how he supposed they were going along off Cape Sable. Right enough, replied the pilot, whose name was Lyle, from Shelburne.

They talked for several minutes, the two of them leaning against the rail of the pulsating ship, looking out over the tossing seas, and in the course of time Pilot Lyle dug from the hefty passenger that he was a seafaring man, brother of Tom Pattillo of Liverpool, and that while skipper out of Cape Ann he had sailed into Boston in every kind of weather, thick and thin, many's the time . . . and could again when called on to do so, he imagined.

Lyle mentioned, on his side, that the glass was falling and that he was unacquainted with Massachusetts Bay himself and furthermore had no responsibility for navigating it. And confidentially, this was the Captain's first trip with the *Acadia;* not only that, and just between the two of them, he was on trial with Mr. Cunard, having been suspended for nearly four years from any command after he had wrecked another vessel in a fog on the coast of Sable, luckily without loss of life. If he was referring to *Acadia*'s sister, *Columbia,* Pilot Lyle did not say (though no doubt he was). After imparting these disquieting scraps of information, he left to check their course, and Jim went below to the saloon for his breakfast.

All day the wind held from the northeast (as it nearly always does, three days running, in the stormy time of the year), increasing to gale force and blowing in some snow squalls that shut visibility right down to nothing. The steamer rolled and yawed wretchedly in the lap of the following seas, beset by the swift currents of the Bay of Fundy. While his family clung to their berths in sick misery, Jim downed a hearty dinner in the almost deserted saloon, after which he put on pea jacket and cap and turned out on deck to join some members of the ship's company in the bow round the capstan for a smoke.

Pilot Lyle was in the group, and so was the Captain, an amiable man who wore a look of preoccupation. When they had finished their smoke and knocked out their pipes, the master of the *Acadia* invited Captain Pattillo to visit with him for a few minutes in his quarters. Jim was quite agreeable and followed him below. His host shut the door.

"Now, Captain Pattillo, they tell me you are pretty well acquainted around Massachusetts Bay and Boston Harbor, thick or thin."

Paddlewheels churning, yards furled, the Cunarder Acadia, *fastest steamship in the Atlantic and perhaps the world, breasts the wave of the future. A wonder the sparks from her smokestack haven't set her canvas afire. (Peabody Essex Museum)*

"Why yes, Captain, I suppose I am."

"Now just as a matter of curiosity, you understand, how do you figure to ascertain your whereabouts down this way when it's thick?"

"How? Why with the lead, Captain, of course! We all just feel our way along with soundings." Jim was getting the drift of the conversation already.

"I see. Now, Sir, let me be frank with you. It's been some time since I've passed this way at this season of the year, and to tell God's truth it's my first voyage with *Acadia.* Now my pilot's no good away from his coast. I tell you, Captain, I would hold it a favor to have just a mite of advice, from one with your experience in these waters, on getting into Boston. Now what would you do right at this moment if you were in my place, with the weather making up so?"

His visitor suppressed an exclamation and stared at the master of this great ship surging through the Atlantic.

"If I was in charge of this vessel, Captain, why I'd heave to when I got to within thirty or forty miles of land and find out what kind of soundings I had. When you're crossing Fundy the current will deceive you if you don't understand it. One flood tide, d'ye mind, will set you farther in than two ebbs will ever set you out. So I'd take soundings."

The Captain thanked him. Nothing more was exchanged on the subject. After a few pleasantries of no consequence, Jim bid him good night, walked to his own stateroom and turned in.

At four o'clock in the morning he was awakened by a knock on the door. It was a sailor, sent down by the master with the request that Captain Pattillo meet him on the quarterdeck. Jim threw on his clothes in the dark and hurried topsides.

The night was black. The wind was howling in a full gale, with swirls of snow, a tipsy topple of seas, drunkenly sloping decks and reefed-down sails. First one and then the other paddle wheel would thrash like a windmill when it breached water with every roll, then shuddered most alarmingly as it dipped full into the sea. A shower of sparks and streak of smoke from the funnel swept off to port.

Two sailors wrestled with the wheel, trying to hold her on course. Abaft the helm the Captain waited impatiently, scarcely recognizable in sou'wester and oilskins. They had just sounded, he shouted to Jim over the roar of wind and waves, and marked off seventy-four fathoms of water. He showed him the lead, armed with tallow to sample the bottom, and yelled in his ear:

"Here's your sounding and here's your bottom! Now where the devil are we?"

"Hold this course another twenty miles and sound again!" directed Jim. No use going below now, so he stayed on deck. In two hours they hove the lead for the second time and marked forty-two fathoms. It was snowing thick.

"All right, where are we, where are we?" the Captain demanded to know. Jim asked to see the chart, and they banged and bumped their way below to the master's quarters. With the snow melting and dripping off them on the carpet, they stood over the chart and Jim inspected it close by the light of the lamp.

"How do you calculate Marshfield, or say Cohasset, bears from us now?" the big man mused. "You've kept the run of the ship, so you must have some little idea, and up to now all I've got to go on are these two soundings."

The Captain said he judged Cohasset, or perhaps Boston Light, bore west by north on the course he was running.

Jim slapped the chart table with the flat of his huge hand, straightened up and transfixed the man with a look that would have killed a haddock.

"West by north, eh? Well by God if you continue this course you'll run us ashore in the thick of it before we ever get past Cape Ann! Now if I were in your place and the course depended on me, from what I know of the soundings and the run so far, I would bear right off to west by south directly and without delay, for I tell you, Captain, I have as much at stake on board of this vessel as any other man–my wife, son and niece besides myself!"

With that he whirled around and stamped out, and before he had reached his own stateroom he could tell from the way she lurched that the steamer was changing course.

Dawn broke and Jim was back on deck. He glanced at the binnacle. The course was west by south, as he had advised. Just then a hole opened up in the weather and the lookout cried "Land ho!"

"What land is that?" inquired the Captain.

"Cape Ann," answered Jim coolly. "The line of Pigeon Hill up in back of Sandy Bay. We're not above two miles outside of Thacher's Island. If we had kept west by north we'd have gone ashore at Ipswich or maybe Newburyport. Just come up to southwest by west, and when you fetch Boston Light sing out and I'll take you in. Right now I believe I'll have a bite of breakfast."

Some three hours later *Acadia* nudged into her wharf at Boston, safe and sound. Jim rounded up the deathly pale members of his family and their luggage and herded them down the gangplank, muttering to himself and biting his lip.

Why, that fellow whose neck he'd saved, and his ship from piling up on shore, why he wasn't even man enough to refund their passage money!

Wherein is Buried a Sad Note

IF THE OLD DOGS down on the Gloucester wharves shook their grizzled heads when *Hosea Ballou* was brought around for fitting-out back in '39, their jaws dropped at what they saw gliding up to Giles and Wonson's slip one fine spring day eight years later.

She was the schooner *Romp,* handsome no doubt of it, even "yachty" you might say, and didn't she shine in her coat of black? Just like a hearse. Whatever in tunket possessed Andy Story to let such a thing in the water? They say he took some of the lines off a Baltimore clipper, trying to squeeze another knot or two out of the molds; she'd get another knot, all right, and it would take her plumb to the bottom. 'Twas a sea coffin. Cap'n Giles must have been crazy to buy her. He'd never get a crew except feet first out the back door of the barroom. Why, the first good breeze of wind on the Georges the damn thing will bury its nose and never come up.

With these and similar croakings was *Romp* greeted when she slipped round from Essex. The misgivings of the fishermen were easy to understand–when a man's vessel was lying to an anchor on the Bank, it gave him some comfort to feel the way her good bluff bow, bouncy as an empty barrel, rode up and over the big ones when they came along like living mountains. *Romp* looked all wrong, sharp and fine up front where she ought to be full, and a person could imagine how she'd nose down in every sea. The prejudice was so strong that Story had to build his radical new schooner on speculation in the early months of 1847. But Captain Sam Giles was a man of vision, and when he saw her he had to have her. He talked Fred Gerring into going master, dug up a crew somewhere and sent her on her way.

Romp was happily named. She came back at the head of the fleet, with a full fare of fish, to haunt the croakers. She was the sweetest, fastest, sleekest vessel ever to round Eastern Point . . . and as for taking the plunge, she rode to anchor as dry as the rest of 'em, maybe drier. A regular sharpshooter, somebody said admiringly—and that's what she and her line were called from that moment on.

Captain Jim Pattillo was among the first to appreciate *Romp*. Late in the same year she was launched, after he had returned from Halifax, he sold out his half of *William Wallace* and put down his quarter (three years to pay, as was the custom) on a new vessel of his own, a sharpshooter. They started framing her in Gloucester that winter, and before the snow was off the ground she splashed into Harbor Cove and was christened *Alexander* in memory of the auld Scot himself. *Alexander* displaced eighty tons, measuring sixty-six feet long inside the bowsprit and nearly nineteen feet in breadth. Standing on his toes on her keelson down in the hold, Jim could stretch up and brush the overhead beams with his fingertips . . . a big schooner she was, one of the dozen biggest in the entire Gloucester fleet of a hundred and fifty.

How different from *Lily of the Valley and Bear of the Sea*, the first boat his old man had helped him buy twenty-seven years ago! What a cockle shell that was compared to this fine, big, advanced vessel. If only old Alexander were alive to see her . . . was he looking on from wherever he was with some pride in that great wild son after all?

She wet her lee rail in January, off to the Georges after halibut, the earliest start of the season yet. The '47 catch, pushing three and a half million pounds, had been a record, and this year was off to a good beginning already with the arrival during the first week of January of *Centurion* with a hundred halibut and a mess o' codfish.

As January turned to February and February to March, schooner after schooner came in, bursting their bulkheads with halibut; they would take out in a lather of speed and race back to the grounds. It was the way it had been in the old days when they opened up the fishery, the halibut schooling so thick alongside that the men hung over the rail and gaffed them aboard as fast as they could strike. One vessel filled up with fifty thousand pounds out east of Cultivator Shoal in forty-eight hours; another took two hundred and forty enormous fish in one day.

Halibut was King, and eighteen hundred and forty-eight was going to be the big year for everybody. There was plenty of ice for all, following Jim Pattillo's lead, thousands of tons of it sawed last winter from the ponds and packed in sawdust to the ridgepoles of the ice houses, waiting to be taken on at Gloucester and Boston. And the market . . . why the market for fresh fish was unlimited, said the promoters; and indeed a case could be made that the entire eastern seaboard had been brought to dockside that long-awaited day last November when the first steam locomotive of the Eastern Railroad puffed into the depot of its new Gloucester Branch, pushed through at last along the North Shore from Boston.

To insure that infinite supply and unlimited demand should meet on terms most favorable to themselves, a group of dealers organized the Gloucester Halibut Company, contracting with the fishermen to purchase fish at such and such a price (a low one) each month during the season. As it had always been, and as the cynics said it ever would be, the price of fish was fixed by the dealer. But the new company added a new wrinkle to this old custom: having virtually cornered the fishermen's Gloucester outlet, it arbitrarily established a differential between white and gray halibut, claiming the former was superior to the latter (it wasn't—only smaller). The cullers determined which were gray and which were white, and they were employed by the company, which by this means was able to undercut its contract prices by as much as fifty per cent.

Sixty-five Georgesmen shuttled between the grounds and Gloucester all that early spring, groaning with the most prodigious fares ever seen. In April the market was glutted. The constipated channels of distribution backed up, and the whole system collapsed. There was one unbelievable day that month when twenty deeply laden schooners were tied up at the company's wharf, each with a fare of from forty to fifty thousand pounds–a million pounds of fresh halibut afloat in Gloucester Harbor . . . and not a buyer in sight. The supply suffocated the demand by a hundredfold. Most of the fish had to be taken outside Eastern Point and dumped.

The Gloucester Halibut Company failed to meet its contract prices for April and closed its doors after only four months of existence, strangled by its own greed.

As for the Georges halibut fishery, it never recovered. Within two or three years after the slaughter of 1848 the quantity fell off so sharply that a full fare could not be secured. Had the shoals literally been fished out, as some fishermen believed? Or had something else merely caused the fish to migrate to more distant grounds? Whatever the reason, King Halibut's realm was taken by the common cod, and the days of his reign on Georges Bank took their place in the lore of the port.

The *Alexander* did not join the fleet of hookers that left for the North Bay as usual after the Fourth of July. Jim confined his mackereling that summer to home waters. He was silent on the subject, but assuredly he dared not be away from Gloucester for any length of time.

Anne's mental condition was declining rapidly, with frequent and unpredictable periods when she was unable to carry on. Dr. Herman Davidson, a graduate of the Harvard Medical School and an excellent physician, was seeing her but he could do nothing. Mrs. Pattillo was on the road to madness, and he gently advised her husband and son to be prepared for the worst.

Then there was one stormy night that October when the *Alexander* stood out to sea to avoid the press of vessels in the Harbor, only to run into a schooner from Salisbury the next morning while beating in through. They cut down seven strakes from deck to waterline, and the *Alexander* was damaged some, too. But Jim assisted the other vessel to a wharf and arranged for temporary repairs. The owners and the insurance company still weren't satisfied, and the affair dragged on for some while before it was settled.

So this did not help matters at home.

A month later the news came down from Chester that old Pat Gorman had passed away. The death of her father struck poor Anne hard, and she went from bad to worse. Jim and his son of twenty did not know what to do. Trying to hold off the inevitable, they had many conferences with Dr. Davidson that winter. But it was not to be.

On the thirtieth of March, 1849, the distracted husband went before the Selectmen and took out the formal petition to the Essex County Probate Court in Salem, filling in the names and signing it: "Respectfully shows, James W. Pattillo of Gloucester in said County, Mariner, that Ann Pattillo, his wife, is so furiously mad as to render it manifestly dangerous to the peace and safety of the community, that she should be at large. He therefore prays that she may be duly committed to the State Lunatic Asylum at Worcester."

Young Alex swore in a second document that his mother "is insane and her malady increases daily on her so that she is incapable of taking care of herself or her family." In this he was joined by Dr. Davidson.

The next day Judge Daniel White ruled that Anne Pattillo was a lunatic. He ordered her committed to the Asylum at Worcester. The shattered woman was taken from her handsome clapboard home on the slope of Hancock Street, where she could look out from the second-story bedroom window over the wharves and the whole Harbor full of ships and beyond to sea, and that was the end of her.

In the spring of 1850 Captain Pattillo boarded the train for a short business trip to Providence, Rhode Island. His age was forty-three, his vigor undiminished, his reputation undisputed as a master mariner and fisherman supreme. Thirty-five years later he left an offhand portrait of himself, half in shadow but sketched with broad strokes from the palette of his memory:

> I put up at the Errol House, arriving there in time for dinner. After booking my name at the office, I walked into the spacious dining room. There were, I should think, two hundred guests sitting down at the different tables, all well-dressed people. I appeared on the scene, having on a regular sailor suit, blue pea pilot jacket, blue turn-down shirt, and I sailed into the room in true seaman fashion, but as the channel was somewhat new to me, my gait was a little awkward. However, a tall colored man piloted me to a seat with my back turned towards a number of carvers who were cutting up joints of meats and poultry at a long table, which I afterwards discovered.
>
> As I did not fee the waiter who attended on me with say twenty-five or fifty cents, he was very indifferent whether I had anything to eat or not, and although very hungry, I made a poor dinner. After going through the performance and still being hungry, I went to a neighboring saloon and disposed of some twenty-five cents' worth of oysters. I went through a similar proceeding at supper and had again to satisfy the inner man with some more oysters. I passed my evening in the smoking room and office, and being a stranger, no one took any notice of me.
>
> When it was time for retiring, along about ten o'clock, the gentlemen took their little lamps and went off to their different rooms, so I thought it about time for me to stow myself away for the night. I said to the clerk, if you have any place for me to tie up, I should like to have it, for I was weary. He said, certainly. He called a colored man about six feet in his boots to show me to a room. I followed him up five flights to the top of the house. He showed me a room and left.
>
> I looked round to see if there was any window to make one's escape in the event of fire, but I found there was none,

and all the light and air to be had was through a glass in the door leading from the passage. So I concluded that if there came a fire I could not make my escape very easily. All this came into my mind much quicker than it has taken to relate.

I caught hold of the bell rope and rang. My former guide soon made his appearance. He said, what do you want, sir? I told him, a hatchet. He was frightened and ran down stairs.

Soon the clerk came up to know what I wanted. I asked him if he thought I was a horse, that I supposed he thought a sailor was a horse. He asked me what I would like. I said, a hatchet. He inquired what I wanted to do with a hatchet. I told him that when my father came from Scotland he went into a wilderness, where were all woods, and when they went anywhere they blazed the trees with a hatchet, so that when they came that way afterwards they could find their way back by the blaze marks. I wanted the hatchet to chip my way down, so that I could find my way by the blaze marks in case of fire.

He then said, come along with me. I did so, and he gave me an elegantly furnished room on the first floor, nice spring mattress, and everything fitted up in the best shape. So I thought to myself that as I had secured a good bed, I would look out for a good breakfast in the morning.

I was up bright and early, took a little walk and was in the house when the first gong sounded at seven for the guests to rise. The next gong was half past seven for breakfast. I was the first one on hand.

I took the first chair at the head of the table, and the next man who came along said to me, you have my seat. I told him it was well filled at the present. He said nothing more and walked along.

I sang out for beefsteak and cup of tea. A darky soon came along with a piece about the size of two fingers. I told him, that was the kind, bring me another, and he followed this one till he had brought me seven helps. He brought a piece of butter, about an ounce in a glass dish, so I took half of it and said if it was grab game I could do my part. Four buns were placed on the table. I took two of them, then on came the tea.

While eating my breakfast, a number of guests who had come in in the meantime, some standing and others sitting, were looking on at me, enjoying the joke and seeing the waiter dance attendance on me. They knew I meant business. I said, if a man could eat glass, plates and waiters he might get something to eat. I sang out for another cup of tea and a piece of custard pie to top off with, and as I left the room it was amidst a merry peal of laughter.

On going to the office, I asked the clerk what kind of a house he called this. He said it was the Errol House. I told him that I was glad that a name had been found for it. I paid my bill and left and walking briskly I arrived at the station in time to take the eight o'clock train for Boston.

A Yankee, and a Baptist in the Bargain

The beautiful and innocent of all earth's living things
Drink nothing but the crystal wave that gushes from the springs.

—SONS OF TEMPERANCE

A WELL-WORN TOPIC of talk in the cabin of the Gloucester fishing schooner *Alexander* during those long evenings of the windy month of March in the Year of Grace 1850, as everywhere else on land and sea, was the approaching trial in Boston of Dr. John W. Webster, Professor of Chemistry at Harvard Medical School. This usually mild scientist was charged with clubbing to death his distinguished if irascible colleague, Dr. George Parkman, at the height of an argument over a debt, after which he took his victim apart with his jackknife and divided the remains between the furnace and the privy in his basement laboratory at the medical school.

When they arrived at Woodbury's wharf on the thirteenth, Captain Pattillo sent the *Alexander* back to the Georges under the command of his mate, for he was determined not to miss the trial the following week.

A press of carriages and citizens had blocked the streets

around the Courthouse by dawn of the nineteenth of March, and when the gallery doors swung out, the spectators surged in. Arrangements had been made for the seats to be cleared every ten minutes, out of fairness to all who had come from miles around to see justice done. Jim had no great trouble gaining a place; he politely shouldered a path for himself through the throng.

Ah . . . there was Dr. Webster himself, hunched forlornly at a table between two bailiffs, pale and downcast, jerkily slipping his fingers under his rectangular spectacles to rub his eyes. Plumb hard to believe that such an educated, famous professor could do such a horrible thing . . . how are the high and mighty fallen.

Twelve days later the jury delivered its inevitable verdict. The almost prostrate little scholar, having been viewed by sixty thousand of his peers from the gallery, was sentenced to be hanged.

Captain Pattillo rejoined his vessel, entertained his crew with an account of what he had seen and his opinion on the matter and finished out on the Georges the middle of June. They wound up the home season with a mackereling trip off Cape Cod, then back to Gloucester on the ninth of July. Almost immediately they swung off for the North Bay. Once through Canso Gut and into the Gulf of St. Lawrence, however, word from the other hookers was that mackerel were scarce; and so Jim decided to try the run of the fish up past the Gaspé Peninsula on the Labrador coast at Seven Islands Bay.

They dropped the red and the green of Prince Edward Island to larboard, and all went well while they reached across the Gulf until the second day, when one of the crew was taken ill—not seriously, but enough for doctoring if there was a doctor to be found. The Gaspé coast lay ahead, a streak on the horizon in the shimmering heat of July, and the *Alexander* made for it.

Before they fetched the land they could hear it, the cry of it above the sigh of the swells dying on the strand, a hundred thousand blended cries carried to their ears by the offshore wind. It was the ululation of the birds of Bonaventure, the gulls and gannets and their kin at nest in white undulating drifts on the sheer seaward cliffs of this island rookery of the North Atlantic. Strange how the great birds clung to the barren precipice, while the rest of Bonaventure sloped back in gentle green toward the harbor of Percé across a mile of water. The *Alexander* leaned around this shrieking swooping colony of feathered snow and rattled down her anchor in behind, close under the Rock . . . Percé Rock that lifted its flat backs, big and little, out of the sea as if cast there from the mold of a canyon. Percé—pierced through with its hole—was the most dramatic rock in all Creation, implacable, fickle, changing its hues in shadow and light under the open-and-shut parade of clouds past sun, a rock to be reckoned with.

This was the Gaspé, Quebec's seaside, a wild forest rimmed by water from the mighty mouth of the St. Lawrence around to Bay Chaleur. The French settlers of the Gaspé and pockets of Tories who fled the American Revolution worked their roots into the cracks where a stream came down to the sea, if there was a nearby lee for their boats. They slashed strips of green land up from the surf and out of the woods above the flakes of drying fish. They plowed behind their cottages, the shingles silvered by the weather, and kept patches of pasture for their animals that were as tough as they, these fishermen and sometime farmers.

Percé village was a sanctum smiling under the blunt front of its cliffs and its island and its rock, and it had a doctor. While he looked at the sick man, Jim walked over to the store for a tub of butter. It was shut because Bishop Mountain of Quebec was there confirming for the Church of England people, but the owner told him that after the folks were all in the church he would pass him a tub out the back door. He was as good as his word. They rowed back to the *Alexander* with their butter and their sick man and made sail for Labrador.

They had logged no more than twenty-five miles, having cleared the pronged capes of Gaspé Bay, when a cotton mountain of thunderheads billowed up in the northern sky. They were broad off Cap des Rosiers, the wickedly reefed Cape of the Wild Rosebushes which only three years before had stove in the *Carricks* and drowned her load of Irish immigrants. *Down all sail!* ordered Jim, and the black squall exploded like a barrelful of wildcats and drove her under bare masts the whole way back to

Cape Gaspé. They ducked inside and caught their breath in company with six other American schooners. Dressed in storm canvas, this makeshift fleet beat ten miles up the magnificent roadstead of Gaspé Basin (a mariner's haven since the Vikings pointed in their fierce-prowed boats) and dropped their anchors in the cozy inner harbor of Gaspé Village, amongst the shallops of the fishermen.

They were still furling sail when a skiff pushed off from the beach. The oarsman hitched over the rail of the *Alexander* and introduced himself as Mister Eaton, the village storekeeper. He looked around him up and down the deck with curiosity, explaining that this was his first time aboard a Yankee vessel. And had they heard the news? He had seen it in the papers from Canada: their President Zachary Taylor was dead, carried off on the ninth of July by an attack of bilious colic.

Jim and his crew had all figured Old Rough and Ready was too cussed to die in office. The rambunctious hero of the War with Mexico had been in the White House for only sixteen months, put there by the same kind of raucous Whig campaign that had carried the day for General Harrison. The other schooners were hailed, and the American fishermen in that far-off place struck their colors to half-mast out of respect for Old Zack.

At Eaton's invitation, all seventy of the Yankees embarked in their dories on a friendly invasion of the tranquil village that hugged the shore as if houses and land were one. When they ambled into his store Jim declined his offer to sell him a tub of butter with the explanation that he had stocked up on that very item in Percé in the morning, and it was like stealing, because they had to sneak it out the back way; everything was supposed to be shut down while the Bishop was confirming the children.

"The Bishop? Did you see him?"

"Well, I saw the one they called the Bishop. He was right tall and wore a big broad-brimmed hat, knee breeches, black stockings, shoes with great buckles and a broad-tailed coat."

"That's him—that's him!" And with some excitement Eaton packed off his boy to notify Parson Arnold, the rector, that Bishop Mountain was on the circuit and in Percé already and would surely be in Gaspé that very afternoon or next morning at the latest.

In a few minutes the Reverend himself entered the store, a pleasant-appearing, red-faced man with a Scotch look to him, dressed in the long cassock of the Anglican father.

"This is the Yankee captain that saw the Bishop in Percé," said the storekeeper.

After satisfying himself as to the truth of the report, Parson Arnold engaged Jim in conversation, evidently as interested in the visit of the Americans as in the impending descent of the Bishop from Montreal. Folding his arms and relaxing against the door, he observed with an air of innocence:

"I must say, Captain, you are droll folks in the States. You kill men and cut them up, and the North is at variance with the South, and the South is against the North. It sounds like a most dreadful place to live. Tell me, will they hang Dr. Webster, who killed Dr. Parkman?"

Jim responded respectfully that there was no doubt the professor would hang, the more certain as he had confessed the whole thing to his pastor after the trial. He had been there and seen him in the dock himself. He had the confession and accounts of the affair aboard of his vessel and would send them ashore to him if he liked, an offer that was eagerly accepted by the curious preacher.

"Now Reverend," said Jim in the stout tones of a man who knows what he's talking about, "as for the other, perhaps you are not aware of the cause of the difficulty between the North and South." He spread his hands before him, as if he were in the pulpit, and his listener below. "I think I can explain it to you in a nutshell."

"Let me have it!" encouraged Parson Arnold, intrigued.

"It's this way. Suppose you lived in Charleston, North Carolina, and owned a hundred slaves, and each was worth a thousand dollars; you would be good for a hundred thousand. So if I lived in Massachusetts and had a hundred thousand in real estate and what not, we then would stand equal as far as property is concerned. But here is the rub. You could have what amounted to sixty-one votes and I would have but one, and that's the big cause of the trouble with the slavery question and here's why . . . all because the Constitution says three-fifths of the slaves are to be counted as inhabitants along with the free whites in portioning out the Representatives in Congress and the taxes, which gives the heft of the votes and the power to the South."

The rector was about to pursue this interesting discussion when they observed the boat bearing the Bishop already coming up the harbor. Catching Jim by the sleeve, he pointed up the path a few rods across the slope to a trim cottage and told him he must come to visit with him and his family as soon as possible.

"I can offer you refreshment, Captain–milk, good cold water, and–" here he gave a sly wink and a tug on the sleeve–"something else a little stronger!"

Jim suppressed an expression of surprise.

"Milk and water are all I require in the way of liquids, Reverend. I am a strict temperance man. But I promise I will come ashore again if the wind don't favor tomorrow."

They parted. The Captain rounded up his crew and returned on board the *Alexander.*

The next day was Saturday. It stormed and rained and the wind was ahead from the east. As they were unable to go to sea, Jim sent Steve Martin on shore with the Parkman murder literature, to leave at Eaton's store for Parson Arnold. Martin rowed back with the mystifying information that the folks in the store were all talking about how the Bishop had "nulled" Parson Arnold (whatever that meant) before departing for Fox River, fifteen miles overland on the North shore of the peninsula.

Sunday came in heaven-sent, a rare midsummer gift with sky and sea of the bluest blue, the land of the greenest green and a fresh pine-scented breeze whispering off the forest to speed the mariner on his way. It was the rule of the Americans, however, not to break the Sabbath, so they remained at anchor. Captain Pattillo shaved and dressed himself in high collar, clean shirt, satin tie, vest and frock-coat and went into Gaspé early to pay his visit on Parson Arnold, instructing all hands except the cook to come on shore for services when the bell summoned from the steeple of the compact white church abreast of where the *Alexander* swung quietly at anchor.

Jim climbed the path to the parsonage, through the fields of waving grass, sweet with clover, flecked with nodding Queen Anne's lace and black-eyed Susan. The wind sighed through the woods farther up the rise, a cloud or two sailed across the sea of sky, swallows swooped and chippered overhead and altogether the big man in his Sunday suit rejoiced in the day and his heart was glad . . . until he heard the unseemly sound of sobbing as he drew near the cottage.

Strange . . . whatever could be the matter in the preacher's home on such a glorious Sabbath? He knocked and turned half round on the step to take in the sweep of view down the slope and over the trim village, away out beyond the boats and far across the rippling waters of the harbor.

A woman came to the door, a handsome woman once but now the long-suffering, bravely cheerful lady customarily taken by the Protestant clergy to wife, yet not so cheerful this morning, dabbing red eyes with the end of her broad apron. She stepped back, somewhat startled at the sight of the giant form that filled her doorway.

Good day, Marm, was the Parson in?

Her husband was off aboard one of the Yankee vessels to attend a sick man, she said, as he was skilled in physic as well as divinity, and would be back soon, surely. Was this the Captain who sent the papers to Mr. Arnold?

The same, Marm.

"Come in, Captain, come in please," invited Mrs. Arnold with a dejected shake of her head. He followed her into the sitting room. "He'll be back any minute, I'm sure. Oh dear, I don't know what to say . . . I suppose you have heard about my husband's downfall?"

"I did hear something, yes Marm. When my man Mr. Martin came back on board from the village yesterday he spoke of hearing the church had 'nulled' Parson Arnold, but we did not know the meaning of it."

"Oh Captain, they nulled him all right! We've been here over eighteen years and given our all for the flock, and now they have taken away his gown and his salary!" Unable to control herself longer, she put her head in her hands and cried out loud.

Jim had begun to suspect as much, and he thought he knew what was behind it. Long since used to dealing with hysterical females, he remained in his chair and spoke sternly:

"It was the best thing that ever happened to him, Marm, I have no doubt of it. If he drank liquor, and that was the cause, the sooner it is stopped the better."

The church bell cut short any further exchange on this dolorous subject, and its happy ding-donging through the clear air of the summer morn caused another burst of tears interrupted by the bang of the door and the entrance of Parson Arnold himself. What a transformation! A different man entirely, as sorry-looking and down at the mouth as a man could be . . . and wearing a suit of homespuns fit to be buried in. Defrocked indeed, and with a vengeance.

But when he saw the great captain in his Sunday clothes come to visit, he seemed to brighten and even forced a wry smile. Mechanically he crossed over and patted his wife on the shoulder by way of assurance that things can't be as bad as they are. He turned then to their visitor.

"Well, Captain Pattillo, a pleasure, a pleasure. Where do you come from, Captain, and what is your creed if I am not too forward?"

He hailed from Cape Ann, came the solemn reply, and if anything he supposed he was a Baptist.

This information had a profound effect on the clergyman. He took the fisherman's leathery hand in both of his and wrung it earnestly. Looking him full in the eyes, with tears welling up in his own, he declared in a sepulchral voice:

"From Cape Ann and a Baptist! Ah, Captain, you are a missionary, I say a missionary sent from God to give me consolation at this trying hour when all my flock has forsaken me. Look, Mrs. Arnold"–turning to his wife–"here is a Yankee, and a Baptist in the bargain, come to solace me in this time of my trial and tribulation!"

All the while the church bell was pealing insistently, and their visitor reminded them that it must be nigh time to commence the service.

"Oh, I will never again set foot in my little church to preach—never again!" cried the rector. "Oh my God, they have stripped me of my gown and salary!" And he, too, burst into tears.

The embarrassed visitor moved toward the door to start for the church on his own, when Parson Arnold recovered himself and begged him to remain; he would hold worship for the family and their guest right there in the house, directly.

They gathered in the parlor, the unfrocked pastor and his wife and his daughters and the great Yankee captain. The eyes of the oldest girl were red, and her cheeks wet from tears, but she sat at the little piano and struck the first chords, and her father opened the singing of an old-fashioned hymn that Jim remembered learning at his mother's knee. All took up the tune; he added his clarion baritone that shook the walls and felt it was good to be there.

But when the head of the family opened the Bible, his voice faltered and again he wept. Through his sobs he directed his youngest daughter—a pretty thing in her curls—to read the passage. When she had done, they sang another hymn. At the end Parson Arnold pulled himself together to take up the Book of Common Prayer and lead in the Litany, his loved ones following in the responses, all sobs and sniffles. The whole while Jim was thinking what a business, this shepherd pouring death and damnation down his throat when he ought to be a light to his sheep, and the quicker he is through the better I will like it.

But the next scene he liked even less. After the service the two men returned to the sitting room to wait for dinner, and three times the clergyman excused himself and went for a drink of something stronger than milk or good cold water.

It was a silent and cheerless gathering at the table. Afterwards, while the girls were helping their mother clear off and wash the dishes, the head of the house took his new friend on a tour, room by room starting in the second story, showing with pride how he had built it with his own two hands . . . and other things with less pride, bottles hid in every chamber. When they descended through the kitchen trap door into the damp dirt coolness of the cellar he struck a light and there were five whole kegs of whisky, gin, rum and brandy and fifty bottles of champagne and other wine.

The effect of this excursion on our reformed tosspot was cataclysmic. It was made the more poignant when the little girl with the curls who had read from Scripture for her Papa came skipping up to the bluff captain with a bowl of wild strawberries she had picked for him, nicely sweetened with cream and sugar. He found them very tasty indeed and thanked the child for such thoughtfulness.

And now he hoped the time had come to talk with his host on the subject of temperance, but the preacher shifted uneasily in his chair and countered with other things whenever he swung around to it. In the end he gave it up with a show of impatience and left the house for a long stroll through the village, heavy of heart and deeply disturbed by the events of this Sabbath. What *could* he do for this family?

The heat of the day hung on Gaspé, the breeze had died and the insects buzzed drowsily when the troubled captain, still in his Sunday garb, retraced his steps up the path to the parsonage. It was late in the afternoon. Hearing the sounds of pots and pans, he walked around to the back where the rector's wife was preparing supper in her summer kitchen, a cool ell away from the stove. He entered and propped a leg on a stool.

"Tell me, Marm, if I am not being too familiar with your affairs, just what the devil (excuse the word!) sort of a man is your husband, I'd like to know?"

She turned from the table and gave him a look of weariness and resignation, wiping her hands on her apron.

"Mr. Arnold is an arbitrary Scotchman, Captain. He is a good man, and he loves God and his flock, but he is not happy in some ways, and he is proud and thinks nobody knows anything but himself. All I say to him is for naught. But I will tell you this, Sir: when he came home on Friday night he said he had met up with a great Yankee captain at the store who gave him more enlightenment about the trouble in the States than he ever knew before, and he spoke more favorable of this captain than of any other man I ever heard him talk of."

They both fell silent. She resumed her work, and the tall fisherman was lost in thought. Abruptly he asked: "How would it do for me to talk temperance with him?"

She looked back at him, and her eyes said more than words.

"I think he would receive it from you better than from any other man, Captain, and I wish to God you would try it and not allow him to put you off!"

He left her and went outside under the burning July sun, still high in the west over the wilderness, and as he walked around to the front door he prayed that if the Almighty had a message for him to deliver to this poor man, he would try to do the best he could with it in the fear of God.

Parson Arnold sat slouched over the sitting room table, head cradled in his arms, bottle before him . . . a sorry picture of a man of God this Sabbath afternoon. Captain Pattillo stood over him.

"Parson, if you would like to hear a temperance story, I think I can tell you one that will interest you."

The parson roused himself and looked up. He smiled thinly.

"I will hear it now, yes . . . go on, Sir, if you please."

Jim cleared the bottle from the table and pulled up a chair. He lit his pipe and commenced to relate in the most measured yet fervent manner the story of his life from the time he started drinking when he was fourteen back in Chester up to the present. He gave all the details of what rum had reduced him to and where temperance had raised him since he took the pledge.

It was a long story. The shafts of the sun slanted lengthy through the windows, and all in the house was quiet, interrupted only when the rector's wife brought their supper to the table, casting a searching look at the captain as she left. They ate, and he talked on. The sun set and night descended and the lamp was lit. Still he continued his history, filling and refilling his pipe. His listener now was cold sober, fascinated and fearful.

Not until after midnight did the history end. There was a pause. The only sounds were the busy tick of the clock over the fireplace and the sawing of the crickets in the grass outside. The preacher had shrunk into his chair, a figure of despair, a bag of rags in the half-shadow of the low lamplight.

Suddenly fierce, Captain Pattillo swung around at him, a hulking Jeremiah cloaked in black, his eyes burning into the tortured soul. His voice crackled with foreboding intensity:

"And so this has been a commencement to tell you a little where you stand, Parson.

"Now, my friend, from what you showed me about your house and the liquor you have in your cellar, I should think you kept a tavern instead of being a minister of the gospel. This liquor has taken the gown off your back and the salary you had to live on, and the way you are pursuing, it will take you down to a drunkard's grave. It says in the word of God that no drunkard shall enter the Kingdom of Heaven.

"Parson, when you came from the vessel this morning and you found me here, you expressed gladness in seeing me. You asked me where I belonged to, and I told you Cape Ann, and what persuasion I belonged to, and I told you if anything I was a Baptist. And you said to me I was a missionary from God at the present hour, because your church and all your friends had forsaken you, and here was I all the way from Cape Ann, and a Yankee and a Baptist in the bargain, to give consolation at this trying hour.

"I asked you are you not going to church this morning, Parson? And you said you never could go there again to preach–they had taken your gown away and your salary that you had to live on and you could never go in there again. So I told you I guess I'll go to the church anyway, and you said if I will stop here you will have service in the house. So I did stop, and we withdrew into the parlor.

"You gave out with a hymn that I had learnt from my mother years ago, and your daughter presided at the piano. I joined in the singing to the best of my ability, and I felt it was good to be here. Then the next thing, you took your Bible to read a chapter, but you couldn't do it for crying, so you called your littlest daughter to you, and she had to read the chapter for you. Then you gave out with another hymn and sang it, and then you went on your knees with your prayer book and read the Litany, your family joining in the responses."

The great captain gazed searchingly at the wretched rector and then slammed the table with the broad flat of his hand.

"Now Parson, I tell you while you were on your knees I thought this is not religion, it is mockery, and the sooner we're through the better. So when you had concluded, you left my company and went for something to drink. You asked me did I see you? I said no I did not see you, but I smelt you strong as a skunk. Though you had spoken of your great regard for me and I was a missionary sent from God at this trying hour, you went three times for a drink before the dinner was put on and asked me each time if I had seen you, and I replied I had not seen you but I smelt you.

"So you see what rum has done for you, my friend. It has taken your gown from off your back and all your salary for the support of your family, and every time you feel distressed, away you go to pour this cursed stuff down your throat, and where God is you never can come.

"And now here you are with your family of your wife and your children, and I say they are worse off than any other family in the whole of lower Canada, because you never taught them to work and they are too proud to beg, and you are going down to a drunkard's grave just as fast as you can go!"

Captain Pattillo brought his hand down on the table with a crash of finality and glowered at the parson, who sat bolt upright and presented a most agitated appearance. The unhappy minister wagged his head and muttered:

"My God, I have never heard a man talk as you do! Oh my God, Captain, what shall I do?"

"Take all the liquor and stuff you have in this house!" roared Jim, making the table bounce again with a sledgehammer blow of his fist. "Take it out and knock it all in the head and do not keep it under your roof and never drink another drop of the vile stuff, and I guarantee you will be a sober and upright man again!"

"I will do it!" shouted Parson Arnold, and he jumped up from the table. Like a freed prisoner he bounded out to the kitchen where his wife and daughters had been sitting all this while, anxiously, wordlessly, and he cried out that he had been saved and was going to cast all his sin away. And the whole family ran through the house, laughing and crying through all the rooms on a hunt for the hidden evil, and they collected the jugs in a pile on the back porch. The captain and the parson lifted up the trap hatch in the kitchen floor and fished up all the kegs and bottles from down in the cellar.

When everything was brought together in a heap, they went at the lot and carried it up on the grassy knoll behind the house under the stars, the oldest daughter guiding with the lantern. Parson Arnold brought his axe from the shed.

"All right, Captain," he offered him the axe, and his voice was shaking. "The honor belongs to you. Take it and knock in the kegs and spill the wicked stuff."

Jim pushed his arm away reproachfully.

"That would be no satisfaction to me to spill your liquor, Parson, for it is not my enemy. I conquered it long ago. It is your enemy, and it is in your power to do the same and smash in the heads of the kegs."

Manfully the preacher raised the axe above his head, and there it poised for just a moment of hesitation, and in that moment his good spouse took a step toward him, and the words of the housewife tumbled out in spite of herself:

"Wait, wait! Must you smash the heads and ruin the kegs, Parson? They would do just right to put butter in!"

The bewildered drunkard slowly lowered the axe, and his saviour thought the whole evening's work was down the drain. Jim stepped up to the preacher, who was already limp from his struggle with himself, and placed a heavy hand on each of his shoulders.

"My poor friend," rumbled the captain in doomsday tones, "you have talked of our first parents when they were in the Garden of Eden. There was an Eve there, likewise a serpent that beguiled the woman and told her to eat the fruit of the tree of knowledge of good and evil. I say to you that there is an Eve here now!"

And Parson Arnold in a surge of resolve swung up his axe and crashed it down on the first keg, and then again and again in a mounting frenzy, smashing the barrels and bottles, shouting praises to the Lord and damnation to the Devil and the Demon. His wife and daughters and the great Yankee captain stood awe-struck in a circle round the madman figure and his soaking, smelling pile of broken wood and glass. The lantern held by the eldest girl cast a dancing light on the scene. The stars twinkled in the black canopy of the sky, and the stream of liquor ran down the hill toward the sea.

Captain Pattillo gravely pronounced the benediction:

"Although it be night, it is the dawn of better days for this family. The head of the monster is being crushed!"

When it was all over and he had done his work, they led the exhausted man of God down off the knoll and into his house to bed. At dawn Jim left them. He rowed back aboard the *Alexander* and shaped his course for Labrador. If he didn't catch a mackerel all season, he thought, he was well paid for his voyage to the Bay that year.

But God smiled. In a fortnight they were on their way back from Seven Islands with two hundred and twenty barrels of fat fish when a squall again struck them broad off Cap des Rosiers, and they beat into Gaspé Harbor, just as before. Parson Arnold and his beaming family were all down on the beach to meet Captain Pattillo when his dory scraped up on the sand, to take him home to tea.

Back again in the rectory, in the sitting room—their battlefield—the clergyman told his benefactor what a dreadful match he had fought with his appetite. He thought he would go out of his mind, and his wife and daughters pitied him from the very bottoms of their hearts. But he came off the conqueror and had not touched a drop and would not evermore.

As for his church . . . that very next morning the word had gone out in the village from a neighbor who saw it all through her window—how there was a great Yankee captain stopped at the Parson's house and frightened him so that he went up on the knoll in the dead of night and knocked in all his kegs and bottles until the booze ran down the hill in a stream.

In no time the news reached the ears of Bishop Mountain at Fox River, and he wrote Parson Arnold the promise that if he were true to his resolve and would not touch liquor again, he would give him fifty pounds right off to help support him, double it the next year and up to a hundred and seventy-five the third year, and his gown back, and his church.

And that was the way it came to pass, as Captain Pattillo saw with his own eyes and heart each time he returned to the North Bay in after years and the happy family took tea with him aboard of his vessel.

21

Captain Darby Meets His Match

> As a source of contention, how could we restrain our fishermen, the boldest men alive, from fishing in prohibited places?
>
> —John Adams

CAPTAIN J. W. E. Darby, the dashing and intrepid commander of Her Majesty's Provincial Revenue Cutter *Daring,* was a young man devoted to the interests of the Crown, the Province of Nova Scotia and himself, in varying orders, and he and his superiors in Halifax felt quite properly aggrieved by such comment on their efforts at enforcement as the following in *The Novascotian:*

"We cannot help thinking that the services of this fine vessel could be made vastly more available in protecting our Fisheries, if the Commissioners would but permit her very efficient commander to keep more at sea, instead of grounding on her beefbones by lying so considerable a portion of his time alongside the Queen's Wharf."

Grounding on her beefbones or at sea, it was a most frustrating assignment. An armed cutter could no more keep a constantly moving fleet of three hundred Yankee mackerel hookers outside an imaginary line along as many miles of Nova Scotian coast than it could be in three hundred different places all at once. The most Captain Darby could hope for was to catch a Cape Anner red-handed here and there and now and then, to give pause to the rest. Even this was no easy matter, because the *Daring* was as readily recognized by those whose fisheries she was supposed to be protecting as by the marauding Americans. A crop of villages, wharves, warehouses and stores had sprung up along the shores of the Gut of Canso in recent years, like the lush growth on the banks of a meadow stream, nourished by the Yankee vessels passing to and from the North Bay which purchased wood and fresh water and provisions and stored their fares for freighting back to the States while they went back to the Bay for more. No, the Revenue Officer's job was not made any easier by traders like John Maguire at Steep Creek, midway in the Gut, who instructed the captain of a vessel he owned to hoist his colors to his main truck when he was up around Margaree as a signal to the Americans if it was safe to fish inshore.

There was even a rumor that the Gloucester sharpshooters had ironed bowsprits with which their hard-bitten skippers threatened to spear any meddling Canadian vessels, like running a fork through a hot potato.

Captain Darby's only hope lay in outsmarting the Yankees; he must put his faith in guile, a quality with which he was generously endowed. Consequently, in the second week of September in this year of 1850 he snuck around Cape Canso up Chedabucto Bay to Guysborough, the county seat, left the *Daring* there in hiding and slipped out again in a little green pinkey—transformed from the handsomely caparisoned commander of Her Majesty's Cutter to the pea-jacketed master of a common coaster off on a freighting trip.

Darby wended his anonymous way up through the Gut of Canso and along the Cape Breton shore in search of illegal fishing activity, and he was not long in falling in with three American jiggers. They were plying the waters under the highlands between Margaree Island and Broad Cove, a popular watering and provisioning station. The wind had backed around stiff from the east, and these schooners were fishing in the lee.

He made note of them. One was the *Harp,* a small vessel hailing from Rockport on Cape Ann; she took in her lines (having secured a good deckload of mackerel) and kept company with him–well deceived–under reefed sails in the direction of Margaree. The second was off at some distance, but he could make her out through his glass, the schooner *Columbia* of Gloucester. The third was at anchor as he passed by, the *Alexander* of Gloucester; a wisp of smoke fled with the breeze from the galley stove smokestack called by one and all the Charley Noble, and the deck was deserted except for a boy at the quarter rail heaving chum and tending a couple of lines. Most incriminating. Doubtless the rest of the crew were below having poached mackerel for dinner. Captain Darby kept his course and his counsel and anchored under Margaree for the night.

During the evening the wind hauled around to the northward, and the next morning the Queen's Officer watched the *Alexander* weigh anchor and run down about halfway to Broad Cove under single-reefed sails. It was blowing a brisk northerly; the schooner hove to and evidently tolled up a school of mackerel almost immediately. Just as the *Harp* was about getting under way to join in the strike, Darby made his move. He put over his boat with eleven armed men, and down they rowed to the Rockporter. They boarded the little schooner, where all was bewilderment at this sudden invasion from a friendly harbormate, and their chief announced to Captain Ben Andrews:

"Skipper, I make you acquainted with Captain Darby. This vessel is a prize!"

Captain Andrews knew then that his fishing had been under observation ever since the pinkey hove into view along the coast the day before, and he knew he was caught with the goods. But it irked him that such a peace-loving fellow as he should be picked out to be made an example of, while Jim Pattillo, who was always looking for trouble and was at that moment chumming up a school practically on the beach, should go scot free. So he jerked a thumb downwind and growled at his captor, why didn't he take that vessel yonder, the *Alexander,* while he was at it . . . look at them, they're chasing the fish into the woods with pitchforks.

"Who commands her?" asked Darby.

Captain Pattillo, was the reply through a wry smile.

"Pattillo, eh? That whitewashed Yankee! Good! I'll have him too, I will–you can bet your boots on it. I've been laying for him for nine years. Oh, I'll dust him off good!"

Darby was in an ecstasy of anticipation, and didn't he wish he had the *Daring* now instead of this little pinkey! But all in good time; he would have to knock them down one by one. An hour later the *Columbia* ran down inside Margaree from the northward, and before she hove to Darby sent his captive crew below. Captain Smith stood off and spoke the *Harp:*

"Any mackerel around hereabouts?"

"Not much doing right here," Darby shouted back, making out to be the *Harp*'s master (and who could tell the difference at the distance?) "But Jimmy Pattillo over yonder in the *Alexander* appears to be in the middle of it!"

Captain Smith thanked the crafty officer, put up his helm and ran down by the *Alexander,* where he hove to and proceeded to hook several barrels.

Dusk descended, and the two Gloucestermen beat back up under Margaree and anchored for the night. At midnight Darby in the *Harp* got under way. He was sure he hadn't been recognized. His plan was to bring the *Harp* down to Guysborough and impound her there until the trial, leave the pinkey and return in the *Daring* for the *Columbia* and the *Alexander* with that great Pattillo. What a feather in his cap to take the notorious rogue! Why, they had all been waiting for him to make a wrong move ever since he escaped from Marshall and his twelve-pounder, and here he was, red-handed!

Everything went as planned, and on Saturday afternoon the *Daring* made Port Hood Harbor and prepared to put up there for the night while her commander was rowed ashore. He climbed the slope through the coal dust from the mines that besmirched the green of the hills rolling into the sea, and thumped on the door of Mr. Hiram Blanchard, the Collector of Colonial and Light Duties.

Captain Edward Watson of Gloucester was there getting permission to beach the *Orion* for scraping the growth off her bottom and caulking a few sprung seams. When this business was done, Collector Blanchard invited the two to take tea with him. Feeling affable and expansive over his prospects, Captain Darby told of taking the *Harp* and expounded confidently on his plans for seizing the *Alexander* and *Columbia* the next day.

"If I'm not back by tomorrow night," the young officer promised as he took his leave, "then you'll know I've taken my prizes." The fact is that he got no small satisfaction out of thus disclosing his intentions to the Yankee fisherman, who was certainly helpless to warn his fellow skippers, with his own vessel about to be hauled out for a bottom job.

But when the *Daring* pounced down on Margaree in the morning (it was Sunday), the waters round the island were serene and deserted. There was not a Yankee rascal to be seen.

Oh well, thought Darby, they have to pass by Canso on their way home; I'll just run back and wait for 'em.

And so he would have but for a second intervention of fate. He had put his cutter about and was reaching along offshore ten miles to the northeast of Port Hood when a black squall struck from out to sea. No time to douse sail. The water all around was feather white, and the wind hit with the force of a hurricane that whipped away both headsails and all attached to them—stays, foremast head and bowsprit. Darby found himself driven down hard on a lee shore, and it was only with the utmost seamanship that he and his crew held their crippled craft off the rocks of Mabou Head, which they cleared by the skin of their teeth. Next day *Daring* slouched through the Gut and crossed the Bay from Little Canso into Arichat for repairs.

All unaware that the green pinkey that departed during the night was Captain Darby's spy, and the *Harp* his prize, the skippers of *Alexander* and *Columbia* put out to sea in the morning to look for mackerel up around Prince Edward Island; that's where they were when the *Daring* struck, only to find her chickens flown the coop.

Monday the *Alexander* was back on the Cape Breton coast, alone. Jim was restless. Shaping his course again for Margaree, he fell in with the *Orion,* coming out of Port Hood. Her bottom was clean and her skipper was brimful of news, so when Captain Ned recognized the *Alexander* he ran up his colors for Pattillo to heave to. The two vessels head-reached to within shouting distance, and Watson called over that the tricky Darby had taken the *Hart* with a pinkey spy and was coming back in the *Daring* for the *Alexander* and the *Columbia.* These tidings were received with some surprise, and both schooners proceeded on to Margaree.

The mackerel schooled thick that afternoon, and the Gloucestermen packed off thirty barrels in each vessel before they came to anchor in the familiar lee of the island. After supper Jim rowed over to the *Orion* and Watson gave him all the details of the conversation he had heard between Darby and Collector Blanchard.

No use to tempt the devil, Jim ruminated as he stroked back to the dark outline of his schooner; he had two hundred barrels already, so why risk vessel and all for the sake of a few more? He'd raise sail and start for home as soon as he was aboard.

Which he did. But the prospect of returning to Gloucester with anything less than a full fare of fish when the mackerel were jumping all around him sat so ill with our great friend, brooding over it through the hours of early morning, that when abreast of Port Hood he suddenly ordered the helmsman to bear off for East Cape; he would just slip back and fill up the rest of his barrels over in the Bend of the Island and give Darby the slip too, he swore, or his name wasn't Pattillo!

Ten days of fishing out off Malpeque Bay topped off his fare, and Jim headed for Cape Ann. According to the information in the *Nova Scotia Almanac,* Captain Darby was due at this time of the year to be escorting the district judge around the circuit of the Province from Sydney up to Port Hood for sessions and then back down to Guysborough, so it made sense to assume that the vagabond would be otherwise engaged than in looking out for the *Alexander.* The wind was steady from the southwest, and Jim banked on its carrying him down through the Gut as far as Little Canso before daybreak.

They were halfway through the Strait at midnight and all well, so he swung the *Alexander* into Steep Creek and dropped anchor. He sent Steve Martin ashore to Maguire's to see if he had any letters directed to their store, which was the mail stop; while there he was to pay Maguire three dollars Jim owed him for a cord of wood, and find out if they knew where Darby was. Then he turned in.

Martin was back on board in an hour, down in the cabin shaking his skipper awake. The judge that Darby was supposed to be taking from place to place was right there in Maguire's, snoring away on the other side of the wall; His Honor had been obliged to ride his circuit by the mail boat because Captain Darby was too busy on more important business, namely lying in ambush for the Yankee schooners *Alexander* and *Columbia* barely six miles farther down the Gut at Sand Point. On top of it all, Martin reported dolefully, the tide was about slack and the wind was gone altogether. Should he shake the reefs out of the sails, or what?

"Do that, Steve," directed Jim with more equanimity than he felt right then, "and tumble out all hands to bend bonnet on jib and break out gaff topsail and staysail. I'll be on deck in a minute."

He turned up the lamp, washed his face and made a cup of tea. By the time he climbed on deck every sail was set, hanging limp and lifeless as clothes from a line, and the windlass gang had the anchor nearly broken out. In another couple of minutes it pulled off the bottom, and they were loose on the tide.

When they had brought the anchor home, Jim sent his crew back to sleep, except the watch, and took the helm. There was not a breath of air. A dog awoke at some distant farmhouse on shore and barked a few times. Again the night was left to its stillness . . . not even the creak of a block or the lap of a wavelet, it was so quiet.

Great! thought Jim. He lit his pipe and crooked a leg over a spoke of the wheel . . . I'd have sworn the wind would last for us to fetch Little Canso under the cover of the darkness, and here we are in a stark calm drifting right into the jaws of the monster. Man can appoint, but God can disappoint . . . so be it. Well, I won't plan anything. It will be given to me what to do at the time of action. If I have to lose my vessel, then I must—but if not, then I'll do all I can to save her, and that's that.

These and like cogitations occupied Captain Pattillo's mind for ten minutes, when he felt the stir of air on his cheek and detected the murmur of ripples against the *Alexander*'s flank. A riffle ran through the sails, the sagging sheets came to life and the deck responded with a welcome heel. In short order he had as fine a little breeze as he wanted, freshening all the time, and his vessel—though burdened with a few tons of the Queen's mackerel—plowed down through the Strait between the darkened shores under a heaven full of stars. Brisker it blew, and swifter she flew. Legs thrust apart, the great helmsman grasped the wheel in a grip of iron and urged her on, and nothing in the world could match the rapture of the master and his mistress, the ship alive, prancing through the black sea, the spray flying from her head.

In less than an hour the schooner was spanking along by Sand Point, the den of the lion. And there, just around the headland, was the silhouette of the *Daring*, riding complacently at her anchor, nothing astir, nothing suspecting.

The helmsman eased his wheel . . . two points, three points, starting to luff . . . now . . . bearing straight down on the enemy. On she rushed toward collision. And then at that split second in time he hove the helm up. His vessel careened off, the sea swimming over the lee rail. She rushed by under the *Daring*'s stern, clearing the end of the cutter's main boom by a whisker, and Jim roared across at the startled watch, running to the taffrail:

"Ahoy boys! Here comes the *Alexander*, chock full of mackerel! Now is the time for you to get your prize!"

And even as Captain Darby and his men tumbled out on deck, the Gloucester schooner disappeared into the night.

They arrived home on the twentieth of October with two hundred and fifty barrels of mackerel. Put together with the first trip to Seven Islands, this made a grand total of five hundred and eighty for the summer's work. The highliner, all agreed, was a widow's son Jim had shipped as a learner—the same boy whose idle fishing while the men were below at dinner had first attracted Captain Darby's attention to the Alexander–and it came about in this way:

While settling their first voyage of the season that resulted in the conversion of the good Parson Arnold, a difficulty arose among the crew over the amount of this youngster's share. In truth, they were chagrined that a kid still wet behind the ears had fished nearly a man's share his very first trip, for he had packed out sixteen barrels. The rule was that under these circumstances the vessel took out its half as usual, but one half of the boy's half was divided among the rest of the crew for standing his watch and grinding his bait for him, leaving him with but a quarter of what he caught.

"Well, skip, how should we settle this?" asked the men of Jim, for they didn't feel right either about leaving the kid with only four barrels out of his sixteen. "Here, you decide what's fair."

"I will," said he. "As for myself, since I'm ownership I choose to give the boy all of my half. Now you can do what you want."

Of course his crew followed suit. Taken all together, the delighted boy ended up with every last mackerel he had hooked and earned $155, more than any man on board.

After the second voyage that had left Darby standing on his quarterdeck with his mouth open, they all agreed to the same lay. But the weather being nippier, the widow's son packed out a trifle less than before, though he still made $145. So he had three hundred dollars to bring home to his mother for his first season of fishing with that great Captain Pattillo.

As for Captain Darby, after the *Alexander* gave him the slip he sailed up to Port Hood and seized the *Columbia* and took her back to Halifax to await the condemnation inquiry. Word of the predicament of Captain Smith and his vessel flew back to Gloucester. Captain Pattillo took up his pen and in a cold rage wrote a labored letter to an acquaintance in Halifax, Mr. James McNab, who happened to be the President of the Board of Admiralty which was to hear the cases of the *Columbia* and the *Harp*.

When they started inquiring, he suggested to McNab, they

Water Street, Port Hood, from the McKinley Hotel, date unknown. (Beaton Institute, Cape Breton)

might inquire of Captain Darby while they were at it how he came into possession of a number of Gloucester-marked barrels of mackerel that were stored in a certain warehouse in Halifax in his name. They did, and then the story came out.

Captain Darby had taken (or accepted) twenty-five barrels from Captain John Fletcher Wonson for letting him bring the schooner *Belle* into Port Hood to dress fish in violation of the Treaty. At about the same time and in the same harbor he had boarded the schooner *B. H. Corliss,* taken Captain Llewellyn Reed's papers in an apparent seizure, and then returned them as a consideration for twenty of the twenty-five barrels of mackerel that were standing on deck; a little green pinkey came alongside and loaded them aboard at Darby's direction.

The commander of Her Majesty's Revenue Cutter reluctantly had to own up. To add to his humiliation, his own crew refused to testify that they had seen the *Columbia* fishing inside the limit for sure, and Captain Smith's vessel was restored to him. The *Harp* of Rockport, not so lucky, was condemned and sold at auction.

"A high-handed outrage!" blustered the *Gloucester Telegraph,* in a fret of self-righteousness. "Are our fishermen to be obliged to pay tribute to the British officers for the privilege of fishing in those waters?"

Eleven months later the affair was irrevocably closed in the columns of the *Halifax Recorder:*

"A sensation of intense melancholy and sorrow was spread through the city, yesterday, by tidings of the arrival of the Revenue Schooner *Daring* from Sable Island, with the corpse of Capt. Darby on board! He expired in his berth on Tuesday night, suddenly, in a fit."

Saved

They that go down to the sea in ships, that do business in great waters; these see the works of the Lord, and his wonders in the deep. For he commandeth, and raiseth the stormy wind, which lifteth up the waves thereof. They mount up to the heaven, they go down again to the depths: their soul is melted because of trouble. They reel to and fro, and stagger like a drunken man, and are at their wits' end. Then they cry unto the Lord in their trouble, and he bringeth them out of their distresses. He maketh the storm a calm, so that the waves thereof are still. Then are they glad because they be quiet; so he bringeth them unto their desired haven.

—PSALMS 107: 23–30

THEY HAD SAILED out of Gloucester during a thaw in that bitter February of 1851. Past Ten Pound Island they looked aft at the snowdrifted town. It crowded down from the rocky pasture of old deserted Dogtown Common, a mile in back, over Beacon and Prospect hills, stuck with steeples, neat frame houses following crooked lanes. On and down the town tumbled into a jumble of sheds, right to the vessels, the water, where it collapsed in heaps of shacks over the wharves standing in the tide on thousands of spindly legs.

Too cozy a port to have to drop astern, all muffled in its puff of snow, a warm curl of smoke from every chimney.

Look ahead now. Beyond the fields of Farmer Niles, blanketed in white on Eastern Point's outer point they struck into the swells lunging along from some storm already dead and gone a thousand miles at sea. Start your sheets . . . they surged over the endlessly heaving, gray Atlantic of the winter. Two days' sail before them lay Georges Bank.

Running along east southeast from Cape Ann they made soundings at the edge of the Bank to the northeast of North Shoal. Captain Pattillo asked for shortened sail when they were over the winter ground. They baited up and jogged along the twenty-five-fathom line and fished for the cod, there to spawn, schooling thick Then the sky scowled darkly to the eastward, and at dusk they let go the anchor in thirty fathoms of whitecapped ocean twenty miles east of North Shoal. It was the twenty-sixth; they had been out a week, and dirty Georges weather was making up.

By midnight the *Alexander* was galloping and galloping and going nowhere. A full southeast gale was on them. The anchor broke out; they could feel it catch and bounce along the bottom with every rise and fall of the bow. Thirty minutes of cold toil in the dark at the windlass, drenched with spray, brought it home. Their captain hollered to jump smart and set double-reefed foresail and balance-reefed mainsail; this would furl the big canvas to a quarter of its size from throat to clew. Thus the vessel jogged, with way enough to keep her head just off the wind, the best trick of all for riding out a storm. Jim ducked below and told the watch to call him if the wind hauled.

It did, at dawn, backing into the northeast and blowing harder all the time. The watch rousted him out, and he came on deck to size things up. A heavy sea was making, and a man could not stand alone against the wind without holding on to something. Afraid they would be blown down on the rip tide, cross chop and breakers of the North Shoal, Jim told the men to try shaking the main out to three reefs; but she wouldn't carry another stitch of canvas beyond the rig she wore, and he gave it up as a bad job. They must have cleared the shoal anyway, because they shortly

A heavy sea "trips" and breaks over a Gloucester halibut schooner, which probably survives with damage. But the men on deck? (Goode's Fisheries*)*

found themselves off soundings; the leadsman couldn't get bottom with a hundred fathoms of line.

All forenoon the gale increased fearfully from out of the north. How could such tremendous seas have been raised in these few hours? They rolled under the schooner like mountains on the move. In every trough she relaxed with a groan of relief as all went slack aboard, the tempest humming harmless aloft; but then she was borne to the crest and struck pitilessly by the screaming, spuming, spitting storm, and she lay over and just let the ocean pour over the lee rail as if she were too tired to care.

All at once a great wave rose up. At that moment Jim was standing in the companionway. He gripped the hatch slide in horror and watched it coming. The schooner was wallowing in the trough when the forward slope of the wave lifted her bow, but instead of hoisting her up on its back and passing along under, it presented a sharply rising, rushing wall of water, as sheer as the side of a cliff. The *Alexander* tried to climb this cliff. Up and up the schooner hove herself, and back was she hurled, until in one split second she stood poised, incredibly, on her stern. She was on the point of toppling over backwards, upside down, when the great wave broke, and she started to fall back. A solid sheet of green water curled over from the crest of the sea, split the bowsprit seventeen inches through from pawl bitts to knightheads, severed shrouds and lifelines as if they were threads, advanced clean over the foremasthead, which was sixty feet above deck, struck the maintopmast and carried it away. Enveloping the schooner, blotting out the sky, it came down, snapped off the end of the main boom, smashed the stern davits and tore away the dory, rejoined itself . . . sea into sea . . . and was gone.

Bill Blatchford was standing by the main pump and never got wet a drop. Not a hogshead of water had it left on deck.

The oldest man on board had never seen anything the like of it in all his years at sea, and it was the conviction of the crew—each of whom had his share of narrow escapes—that they and their vessel had been participants in a supernatural event.

It did not serve to ease the troubled mind of their skipper, who was passing through another period of sore mental distress these days, obsessed with dark thoughts and foreboding, smothered by the most awful feelings of guilt, despairing of his soul's salvation . . . and yet such a practical man, a man of action quick as thought, the master, one might suppose, of his ship in every sense.

Later that spring they sailed the *Alexander* into New York, where Georges halibut was getting top price, and Jim sold the lot to Kinsley, the same dealer who bought the cargo of frozen fish, the first ever taken to the city, that he and John Fletcher Wonson freighted there in the *Forest* back in '37.

The two fell to talking in Kinsley's office, and the dealer was curious to know why Captain Pattillo hadn't gone to California when the gold fever was on in '49, along with half a dozen other Gloucester vessels that made the long voyage round the Horn.

Well, he'd had a notion to venture it, and had gone so far as to offer half of the *Alexander* to some parties for $2200 to raise money for an expedition, but they couldn't get up the cash. Kinsley knew a good thing, though; why hadn't he gone?

"Captain, I have gold enough right here," the dealer responded tranquilly.

"By thunder I wish I could say the same! Perhaps you can put me in the way of finding some!"

He could, said the merchant, and he would. He took the arm of his great rough-clad visitor and led him into his counting room. There he explained that the year past he had been persuaded to attend a series of revivals in Brooklyn with the result that he was converted . . . "and that, sir, was worth more to me than all the gold in California!"

While Kinsley was talking on in the most ardent fashion about his religious experience, the mind of his listener wandered back, so ironically, to another conversation in the very same office fourteen years earlier. Then, Captain Pattillo had been so disturbed by this man's lack of faith that he had called him an infidel to his face, and the words he had used came back to him now—"Infidelity is a bad thing to die by, but Christianity has the promise of the life that now is and of that which is to come."

And now their places were switched. Mr. Kinsley handed him a stack of religious tracts, thumped him on his broad back as they moved to the door and repeated with the most solemn emphasis that he had indeed found the true gold, worth more than all the gold in California.

His words haunted Jim night and day. He couldn't get rid of them.

A few weeks later he was traveling by train to Newburyport on business and struck up a conversation with a fellow passenger, an old gentleman wearing a beaver hat and a full beard. Each in some manner made a deep impression on the other, for when they parted this patriarch told the big mariner that though he trusted his affairs would be settled satisfactorily, he most earnestly hoped that he was a Christian man, a master of wise counsel and one who set a good example for his crew and before every other person with whom he was brought in contact.

These words, too, lodged in Jim's mind and added to its turbulence.

All that had gone before, and all that was to be, bore in on him this spring of 1851. The nettles in his soul were the fruits of his life. The pearl of great price eluded him always. He had rejected rum for the cup of cold water, swept up in the great crusade of temperance, but still he believed that he served the Evil Adversary

He strove for the peace that would not come. At last his torment beat him down. It was during a trip to the Georges at the end of May. One day he could stand it no longer, he was so wrought up, and he stumbled down into the hold of his vessel and fell amongst the fish barrels in the damp dark over the swishing bilge, his head in his hands.

"Oh God!" he moaned. "Oh God, I will not go to sea again, I swear, until I have found peace . . . if it's to be had after all my backsliding and sinning."

Saturday night they made Boston and warped into a berth with the press of vessels alongside Commercial Wharf.

In the morning the unhappy captain put on his Sunday clothes and walked up Commercial Street. The wharf was the busiest in New England, and the thoroughfare above it, lined with warehouses, was usually clogged with all the concentrated bustle of a great port. But on the Sabbath they were almost deserted, and he made quick progress over the cobbles toward a building at the corner of Lewis Street topped by a flagstaff from which a blue pennant fluttered cheerfully in the spring breeze. It was the home of the Boston Baptist Bethel Society, sometimes known as the Mariners' Church, or simply the Bethel. He was in time for the morning service and joined the crowd of seafaring men at the entrance

This seamen's mission was presided over by a magnetic young preacher from Connecticut, the Reverend Phineas Stowe, and there he was as the men sauntered in, seated behind his pulpit (he had ripped out the ship's prow his predecessor affected–"a claptrap device"), waiting serenely for the hall to fill, which it soon did to overflowing.

Brother Stowe, as he was called by one and all, was at this time thirty-nine and entering on the prime of his powers. He was of medium height, somewhat plump perhaps, with long, handsome hair, clean-shaven and soft of countenance. His most striking features were his eyes, so sad and gentle—eyes, verily, that seemed made to cry for the soul of the poor sinner . . . and so they were, for it was said that he "would take the sailor to his parlor, and talk, and pray, and weep with him there."

Equally energetic in behalf of every well-intentioned cause that came his way, Brother Stowe administered the temperance pledge and presented anti-swearing cards to thousands of sailors, whom he addressed in a respectful manner, neither as *Jack* nor *me hearty* nor in the slang of the street, for it was noted of him that "he never planted a thorn in the heart while putting bread in the mouth."

Surely, a fellow clergyman remarked of Phineas Stowe, "there never was a man of sweeter spirit. He was the most guileless, unsuspecting trustful man I ever knew. He was so good that he seemed to make everyone else good around him. You could not do or think anything wrong in his presence. Nor could any evil come nigh him. He could tread on scorpions, or take up serpents, and eat the deadliest thing, and it would not hurt him."

Brother Stowe was a powerful preacher, and this morning he took his text from the seventh chapter of John—how Christ went up and taught in the temple, and the Pharisees and the chief priests sent officers to take him prisoner, but no man could lay a hand on him, for he told them: "Ye shall seek me, and shall not find me: and where I am, thither ye cannot come."

It struck Jim that the whole sermon was meant for him, and he was mightily moved. At the end of the final hymn Brother Stowe left the pulpit and offered the closing prayer near the door so that he could give a tract and a friendly word to each man on his way out into the sun.

There was some kind of a force at work in Jim today, because after dinner on board his vessel he was drawn to return to the Bethel for the afternoon service.

Never had the preacher been more eloquent, nor his shafts closer to the guilty heart. This afternoon, he cried, a sailor had given him his text out of the first chapter of the Book of Jonah:

the Lord had ordered Jonah to rail against the wickedness of Ninevah, but Jonah fled in a ship bound for Tarshish; the Lord in his anger sent a great wind and mighty tempest in the sea; the sailors were afraid she would founder and sink, and they jettisoned the cargo to lighten her, and every man begged for mercy from his own particular god; but Jonah went below, where the captain found him asleep and shook him angrily, shouting, "What meanest thou, O sleeper? Arise, call upon thy God, if so be that God will think upon us, that we perish not!"

Every sailing man knew the rest of Brother Stowe's sermon. Jim felt better and pumped the missionary's hand as he left, but he was not yet satisfied.

In the street outside, the shadows were lengthening. He started back for Commercial Wharf, changed his mind and thought—no, he did not want to return to his vessel just now. He would find an evening service somewhere and see what it might do for him; his wife's Aunt Sarah Walker lived over in the South End—she was just the one he needed to see, for poor Anne was on his mind, too. Aunt Sally was a good old Christian lady; she kept a clean boardinghouse and allowed only God-fearing folks to take rooms. He would have supper with her, and she would tell him where to go for prayer meeting, then afterwards he'd spend the night at her place.

Having thus determined on his course for the balance of the Sabbath, he pushed up State Street, so quiet that his footsteps echoed between the granite walls of the city's financial heart. At the Old State House he rounded into Washington Street and strode along past the shops, block after block, looking neither to right nor to left, a great tall man, dark-faced and destiny-bound, such a forceful figure that the strolling couples, top-hatted and bonnetted in their Sunday best, turned to stare. On down Washington he marched to where the stores thinned out and the fine new town houses began. The road passed by the tidal flats, studded with piles of fill where more of the South End and the Back Bay was being created, and over the once-narrow strip that used to be the only connection of the town with the mainland at Roxbury, called The Neck. It was historic ground he trod, where the Lobsterbacks had set up their guns against the raw Yanks of General Washington. And so he was in the South End of Boston, just becoming the fashionable neighborhood with each new block of made land. Then up off Dover Street to Aunt Sally's.

The dear old lady wept with joy to see the great sea captain husband of her unhappy niece that was put away, and she set him down to a hearty supper.

After the usual exchange of family news, he was impatient to know if they had good meetings up her way.

They do indeed, Jim, they do over to the Harvard Street Baptist Church; it is nearly new and the Reverend Mr. Joseph Banvard the minister is a fine young man. Most of her boarders attended and would be leaving any minute.

Jim hurried to finish eating and joined them:

"There was a large congregation. I enjoyed the service very much. Before dismissal the pastor extended a cordial invitation to all those who were seriously inclined concerning their souls' salvation to stay. That was just what I wanted. I said to those in the pew with me, are you not going to stay? They said no. They asked me if I was. I said yes. So they passed out.

"I followed them till I reached the entrance of the church. I took second thought and said to myself, Mr. Devil you don't cheat me out of this, so I turned right about face and walked right to the front seat.

"I think there were about a hundred and fifty that remained for the inquiry meeting. Quite a number came and talked with me and asked how I felt. I said I was distressed about my soul's salvation.

"One man in particular came to me. His name was Thaxter; I was acquainted with him. He asked me if ever I thought I experienced religion previous to this. I told him I thought I had. He said to me, you are looking for something you will never find; you can never be born into the Kingdom the second time, and you have to go right back and take up your cross and follow Christ. He asked me if I could not say something for the Master. I told him I thought I could and was willing to try.

"So I jumped onto my feet and said, I thank God he had not

cut me off as a cumberer of the ground, that he permitted me to live. The Lord gave me enough to say. I praised God and extended for fully ten minutes. No tongue can describe my feelings at the time.

"When I went back to the house all had gone to bed but Aunt Sally. I told her what had taken place, how I could rejoice in the God of my salvation. We had a very pleasant time together. I went to my room and bid good night to her, and she gave me a Bible.

"I read and prayed and asked the Lord to show me if I was able to bear meeting him should I be called from time into eternity. Where was I standing, was my feet on the solid rock Christ Jesus. I did not want to take up anything short of a full salvation, so I committed myself to his care and keeping and got into bed.

"It was but a very little while, and it appeared to me that I was standing at the Judgment, with the Book open. All the sins and crimes that I had committed were all written there against me, and my name was right over the top.

"A man said to me, what say you to this? And when I looked at it I saw I was guilty of all. But then I said, I know in whom I believe; I do believe on the Lord Jesus Christ who died on Calvary for poor guilty sinners like me.

"At that moment it appeared to me the Saviour, where the nails had marked his hands blotted all out, and I was on end in bed, praising God and rejoicing in the rock of my salvation."

A month later, on Sunday the twentieth of July, 1851, James William Pattillo, age forty-four, was baptized by immersion following his confession, repentance and credible profession of faith, and thus admitted into membership in the First Baptist Church of Gloucester, a believing, regenerated Christian.

The Yankee Gale

It was thick all right—so almighty thick up in the Gulf of St. Lawrence at the end of September, up between the dunes of the North Cape of Prince Edward Island and the autumn-fired foliage of the New Brunswick coast, a man at the masthead couldn't see a half a mile across the water. But it wasn't fog; it was smoke . . . thick o' smoke.

The New England hookers were swarming in the North Bay this fall of 1851, perhaps five hundred sail, and the heft of them were spread out over Orphan and Bradelle banks and that way from Gaspé down by Bay Chaleur and the Island. Over hundreds of square miles of ocean where the *Alexander* and some others were fishing, the smoke lay heavy on the eastward drift of air off the New Brunswick wilderness from fires that roared through the forests around Miramichi Bay and Point Escuminac.

The smoke was pungent and smelled excitingly of distant disaster, and it veiled their world in a hot bronze haze so confusing to the senses that Captain Pattillo and crew drifted, much to their chagrin, clear out of the range of the mackerel. But they had done well enough; they stood off for the Gut of Canso and arrived in due course at Arichat, where they left three hundred and thirty barrels with a merchant who advanced *Alexander*'s master the money to fit out for a second trip.

They returned to the Bay, and to stay clear of the galling pall of smoke from the forest fires, they joined a fleet of two hundred schooners that had shifted down in pursuit of the mackerel schooling densely along the north shore of Prince Edward Island.

During the morning of Friday, the third of October, clouds hauled up over the northern horizon, and by late in the afternoon the sky was heavily overcast–nothing unusual, except that the air was warm and strangely still. Most of the fleet continued to fish, and it was not until sundown that the weather betrayed its intentions, when the northern sky glowed with a "lurid, brassy appearance"–the sure sign, according to those who had been in the West Indies, of an approaching hurricane.

The stillness continued over the sea. An hour after sunset a breeze stirred from the north, the vanguard of the rain that advanced in a rustling crescendo over the flat water; the first fat drops spattered on the deck, and then the downpour was on them. The wind increased with each gust, and the glass fell. A North Bay norther was making up.

Now there wasn't a veteran amongst the twenty-five hundred fishermen in the fleet but didn't know that the Bend of the Island was not a place to be caught in a norther. That crescent shore from North Cape to East Cape was a hundred and forty miles of virgin beach sloping out into surf-curled shoal water, pretty to admire out to sea with the green of the smooth farms rolling back from the dunes, but a deadly lee shore in a gale from the north. The principal harbors were Malpeque and Cascumpeque bays in the crook of the Bend called the Bight.

Strings of sand bars curved across the mouths of these anchorages, shoal water all around, the narrow channels between them badly marked or not at all, the very devil to search out and navigate during a gale and worse still in the night. The thing to do when caught fishing off this trap by a norther was to beat out to sea, away from the Island, and ride it out.

When the first breeze broke the ominous calm, this was what the fleet did, all moving out at once, as far as the eye carried, close-hauled and purposeful. However, the storm developed with altogether unexpected rapidity; instead of leveling off, the wind doubled and redoubled its velocity, and the seas built up at an alarming rate.

Early in the night about half the skippers in the fleet, which was at this time broad off St. Peters Bay, forty miles west of East Cape, concluded it was going to be too hard a chance to stay at sea, from the looks of things, and turned off to the westward with the intention of running for Malpeque, sixty miles away. The remainder, including *Alexander*'s, elected to keep beating out, but to the eastward, hoping to weather East Cape and duck into Cardigan Bay or Murray Harbour on the eastern shore.

In company with the *Flirt* of Gloucester and the *C & N Rogers* of New London, Connecticut, and a number of other schooners, the *Alexander* pounded out in the very teeth of the gale some seven leagues off St. Peters and anchored in twenty-seven fathoms. It was midnight, and they had been fought to a standstill. The last they saw of the *Flirt,* she was away off to the windward; the *C & N Rogers* disappeared to the eastward; one by one the others scattered. By dawn of Saturday morning Captain Pattillo and his men were alone on the wild sea, for all they knew, and the tempest continued to mount, hauling into the northeast. They lay to under two-reefed foresail, and it was all the helmsman and skipper together could do to keep her head to it.

And then the anchors broke out. The racing tide and the shift in the wind, which screamed out of the new quarter more furiously than ever, were pulling and pushing them hard down toward the Bight of the Island. They dragged their anchors thus for the better part of the day, praying for respite, for the chance to make sail, but the tempest blew on unabated. By nightfall their captain judged they were but a few leagues to the windward of Cape Kildare. They hove up the anchors and jogged.

Every man aboard the *Alexander* knew the prospects. If they drove ashore at Kildare, how could any ship or human being live through those breakers, day or night? And there wasn't a chance of clearing North Cape, fifteen miles farther up the coast, where a sand bar made out three miles, with shoal water beyond . . . it was an old saw that the mariner who valued his life didn't raise North Cape closer than ten miles in a gale of wind.

If the wind either moderated or hauled again inside of the next two hours, they would have a shadow of a chance of standing off or getting blown clear of North Cape bar. Otherwise . . . the boneyard.

The gale didn't moderate by one fiftieth of a knot–but it hauled in answer to their prayers, or curses, around to the east northeast. Judging from soundings, this would blow them clear of North Cape . . . but full onto the bar.

"Stand by with your lead!" Pattillo roared out above the shriek of the tempest. "Stand by your foresail sheets! We're going to try the bar . . . it's all we can do!"

At eleven o'clock they heard breakers off the port bow. Jim ran forward to guide the helmsman through–such as he could. The schooner lunged on, hurled closer to the bar on the crest of each huge wave. The water shoaled with every cry of the leadsman until he was drowned out by a crash of combing seas, exploding spray and boiling froth so white it shone through the blackness.

Now it was five fathoms . . . thirty feet of water, eight feet less under her keel . . . the trough of one giant wave could suck the water off the bar, drop her down and break her back on it. The breakers were all around. The sea sizzled with spume and roiled-up sand. The schooner was tossed this way and that, but she lurched doggedly on, when just at the worst of it, as it seemed that she must be thrown on her beam ends and smashed, a great sea erupted over her bow.

Jim caught it first. He had hold of a line that lashed the anchor cable to the windlass. The sea struck him square, snapped the line and knocked him off his feet. He was standing in the coil of the cable, and solid water twice his height carried him, cable and all, abaft the companionway, where the rope fetched him up short around the legs; he grabbed it while the wave passed on and left him sprawled by the pump, dazed but unhurt.

Ben Hodgkins saw it coming, leaped for the fife rail and hugged it for dear life, bracing his back against the foremast. When the water receded, he was still hanging on, gasping for breath.

The fellow standing near Ben jumped on the foreboom and

climbed half a dozen hoops up the foremast. The crest hit and tore him loose and washed him back to the mainmast. He caught it going by and saved himself; the water went down and left him dangling ten feet above the deck.

That sea swept the *Alexander* clear of everything that wasn't bolted down and left a rippled deposit of sand from the bar, scupper to scupper. Yet it was the only one that boarded them, and though they expected every breaking roller to slam them on the shoal, it was all over within less time than it takes to tell; then they were drifting in deepening water and worked ship into the lee of the lowland.

Toward noon of the next day, Sunday, the storm moderated. Against diminishing winds and great, long, easy swells they beat back around North Cape to the Bight of the Island. For ten days they inched along the coast assisting stranded vessels to get off, and the enormity of it unfolded before their eyes.

The beaches and bars were strewn with wrecks and corpses, stranded schooners, torn sails, spars, boats, barrels of mackerel, and every sort of cargo. The scene on their shores overwhelmed the Prince Edward Islanders; the first telegraphic reports to reach the United States from Charlottetown claimed a hundred and fifty vessels lost, up to four hundred dead.

Gloucester made a fast count and discovered, to the horror of her people, that she probably had a hundred and twelve jiggers fishing in the Bend of the Island. There were almost no particulars. An emergency mass meeting, helpless to do anything, hired a telegrapher to relay the latest reports from Boston and appointed a five-man finance committee of leading citizens. One of the five was Alex Pattillo, twenty-three years old and a student at Worcester Academy—a tribute to his absent and probably drowned father. At Newburyport, which had seventy vessels in the fleet, it was reported that a young mother committed suicide on hearing the news (it was false) that her husband's vessel had gone down.

Last seen by the *Alexander* standing to her windward off St. Peters Friday night, the schooner *Flirt* was found outside

Malpeque Bay, still at her anchors, dismasted, decks awash and no sign of life aboard. Apparently her crew had chopped down the mainmast trying to save her, and it carried away the foremast going down. She was towed to Margaree and beached, when five bodies were found in the cabin; the remaining eleven had been washed overboard and drowned.

The schooner *Princeton* of Gloucester, with ten men, never returned to port.

On the sands below Malpeque lay the schooner *Franklin Dexter* out of Dennis on Cape Cod. Captain James Wixon took the steamer up from Massachusetts to bring back the bodies of four of his sons who were among the ten lost; he found three of the four himself, half buried in the sands of Hog Island at the entrance to the Bay.

It was impossible to make a complete list of the dead, but it probably exceeded a hundred and fifty. No one knew how many fishermen were swept from the shrouds and booms and bowsprits or washed off the decks, because no count was kept of the toll from schooners returning during the weeks that followed, flags half-mast high.

Captain Moses Tarr traveled up as the agent for the Gloucester Mutual Fishing Insurance Company, which insured most of the town's fleet, and wired back that he had personally seen fifty-eight schooners on the beaches in the Bend of the Island, including the dismasted *Eleanor, Golden Rule, Lucy Pulcifer, Garland* and *Powhatten,* all of Gloucester and most of them later salvaged. One small vessel belonging to the Island was so utterly wrecked that her owner, who miraculously escaped, sold her remains for a half a pint of rum and walked away.

The broken fleet straggled into the North Bay ports for repairs and refit. Decks had been swept, boats lost, sails ripped to shreds, spars gone by the board, rigging snapped, thousands of barrels of mackerel carried away.

And the stories that were told . . .

It cost one skipper two suits of sails, but he drove his schooner through the surf so high and dry on the beach that he and his crew jumped off into the field. Another worked into

Charlottetown and said he had seen thirteen wrecks from his deck. Another, his own vessel at the mercy of the seas with all her canvas torn, drifted past a hooker on its beam ends; two of the crew were clinging to the mastheads, but he was helpless to save them.

Aboard of the *Mary S. Niles* the main boom slatted and broke the jaw of Captain Davis, but he remained at the wheel.

Receding from one beach, the tide left the body of a man, a dead child lashed to his back.

Saturday night, after parting from the *Alexander,* the *C & N Rogers* successfully weathered East Cape, a feat which might have been accomplished by several other vessels that went ashore had there been a light on it; her master swore she was saved only by the splitting of her foresail from foot to peak, letting the water out when a sea knocked her flat on her side.

Many were the tales of heroism. None could surpass the gallant courage of Captain Ben Small and the crew of the schooner *General Cushing* of Newburyport. The *General Cushing* was in the fleet standing off Cascumpeque Bay up in the Bight, all frantically milling back and forth in search of the narrow entrance around the sand bars. The night was at its blackest, and the storm was at the peak of fury. When the schooner *Mary,* also of Newburyport, was unable to keep up with the rest, Captain Small took her in tow until all found themselves being ruthlessly beaten down toward the bar in three fathoms of water, close on the breakers.

Leaving the others and dropping his tow, Captain Small sailed the *General Cushing* along outside the bar, discovered the entrance, shot into the harbor and found the unlighted buoy that was supposed to mark the channel. He hung a lantern on it, clawed back out again and led the rest in to a safe anchorage.

Thereafter and for good reason, the storm of the third of October, 1851–proclaimed by a lurid and brassy sky–was known as the Yankee Gale.

The Yankee fleet recovered quickly from its gale and stayed on in the North Bay until the middle of November, recouping lost fortunes with a shower of chum. The Nova Scotian shore fishermen were bitterly convinced this was wooing the mackerel away from their nets, and that the Americans were ruining them. That winter they implored their government at Halifax to protect them from the Yankees, and three thousand signed a petition demanding that the Legislature fit out a fleet of armed cutters to enforce the Convention of 1818. But they were pawns in a larger game.

When the United States six years earlier had lowered the tariff on imported fish, the Canadians found themselves for the first time able to compete in the American market. Britain eyed the returns and concluded she would gain more than she would lose by restoring to the Americans the right to fish in Provincial waters that had been secured by John Adams in 1783 and relinquished in 1818, this in exchange for free trade in fish. The United States, however, was cool toward such a proposal for Reciprocity, for much the same reasons that Britain favored it.

Opinion in the Maritime Provinces was by no means unanimously proprietory toward their inshore fisheries. For every man who felt aggrieved at the presence of the New Englanders there was at least another equally as anxious to cultivate their good will, and this was especially true of the merchants, large and small, who supplied the manifold wants of the American fleet while exporting fish to compete in American markets. The Convention, however, and the Hovering Act, were being observed so in the breach by the Gloucestermen and others that enforcement came to be a matter of Nova Scotian honor. If a crisis were to boil up in the North Bay, requiring at last a confrontation between the great powers, Reciprocity might be the only honorable way out of it for both.

In Halifax the Legislature responded to the pleas of the shore fishermen. It voted for more cutters and talked darkly of excluding foreign fishing vessels from the Gut of Canso, a threat that if carried out would force the Americans to take the difficult route around Cape Breton to get to the North Bay and lose about a third of their season; it also renewed its demands that the British government do something to enforce the Convention. In May of 1852 London finally acted; the Admiralty dispatched Her Majesty's Steam Sloops *Basilisk* and *Devastation* to the Gulf of St. Lawrence with instructions to bring violators of the Convention of 1818 to the bar of British justice.

If Sir Colin Yorke Campbell, the commander of the *Devastation,* had been given confidential orders to turn the North Bay into a hornet's nest, he could not have succeeded better. By that autumn he had stopped and boarded half the hookers in the fleet and put the Yanks all at sixes and sevens, in a fighting mood.

No one knew what to make of the temperamental Scot. One day he would be lobbing cannonballs across their bows, pursuing them with boatloads of armed sailors, boarding them and stomping up and down their decks, raging, lecturing, demanding to see their papers and generally stalking about, the equal of the veriest quarterdeck tyrant in the whole Royal Navy. The next day Captain Campbell would ignore a fleet fishing inside the limit, or if he boarded he would be so jovial and courteous as to be positively sickening; some of the fishermen thought the tide of his spirits rose and fell with their consumption.

In September Sir Colin summarily seized the Newburyport schooner *Caroline Knight.* It was the crowning blow to the national dignity; the newspapers in the New England fishing ports were beside themselves with indignation and sputtered over this rape of the rights of vessels against search and seizure on the high seas in time of peace. They demanded that the federal government take steps to protect the fishermen in the pursuit of their honest livelihood. Speeches were made in Congress, and the possibility of a clash in the North Bay and war with England was openly discussed.

At fitting-out time in July of 1853 there was bold talk along the Gloucester waterfront of what would be done if the "Devil on the Station," as someone had nicknamed Captain Campbell, continued to board the fishermen during the coming season. Several skippers stocked muskets, pistols and cutlasses, and the *Garland*—back in service after going ashore during the Yankee Gale—even installed a swivel gun. It was reported that the *Devastation* and *Basilisk* had been joined by the HMSS *Argus,* the frigate *Vestal* and seven other smaller armed vessels. President Franklin Pierce, a mild and compromising Jacksonian Democrat from New Hampshire, was forced to bring the developing crisis to the attention of his Cabinet, with the result that Secretary of the Navy Dobbin was directed to protect the American fishermen in the Gulf of St. Lawrence in their lawful pursuits (and to restrain them from starting a war). After innumerable delays, the *Fulton* and *Princeton* under the command of Commodore W. B. Shubrick steamed off to the eastward at such an agonizingly leisurely pace that the fishing season was nearly over when they arrived in the North Bay.

When returning fishermen irately claimed they had seen neither hide nor hair of the Commodore and his squadron anywhere in the Bay, it was too much for the *Newburyport Union:*

"Our vessels have been boarded and robbed as though they were pirates. Com. Shubrick–a perfect old granny, who is not worth so much as a handful of dirt from the grave of John Adams . . . spent two whole months smelling his way to the Bay, and when he got there was just as good as a Mother Carey's chicken."

On the blistering hot afternoon of the sixth of August, a scattered fleet of Gloucester hookers was lying drowsy and nearly becalmed off the Madeleine River up on the north coast of the Gaspé Peninsula. One among them was the *Star Light,* Captain Charles McDonnell, a brand new schooner on her maiden voyage, just arrived after crossing the St. Lawrence from Labrador fishing. Another was the schooner *Highland Lass,* Captain James Pattillo, a year old, eighty-five tons, and designed on the latest model as successor to the *Alexander,* which had been sold out of town at the end of '52. The perspiring crew of this lyrically named lady were engaged under the broiling sun in packing down, under the benign direction of their great master, the last of thirty barrels of mackerel hooked virtually and most unvirtuously in the mouth of the Madeleine River itself.

Someone straightened up from his work, glanced off to the eastward and yelled: "Look! There she is–the Devil on the Station!"

And so it was. A streamer of black smoke betrayed the British man-of-war churning up the coast toward them. She passed by the rest of the fleet two miles away and made for the *Star Light,* which was a mile inshore of the *Highland Lass.*

"Clear the decks, boys–clean as a whistle!" bellowed Captain Pattillo. "Get everything below! Shake a leg now, and we'll make sail and give 'em a run for their money, for they'll soon be after us!"

Ghosting along with only a catspaw of wind now and again to keep their canvas filled, the Gloucestermen watched the *Devastation* come up on the *Star Light,* put a boat over and board. There followed quite a confab, as Jim reported from watching through his glass, then an exchange of men between the two vessels.

The *Highland Lass* was three miles off and showing her heels when the warship swung off from the prize with a renewed outpouring of smoke and sparks and started in pursuit. The chase was short, because the next thing, a puff of white popped from her foredeck, and then a scream and a whistle–and a ball sailed across their bows, making a businesslike splash off to starboard.

Douse the jib, said Jim–to let Sir Colin know he was at his service–and they hove to.

Bristling with guns, her stack belching incongruous smoke through the lofty tangle of her spars and rigging, *Devastation* steamed up.

"Wha' th' divil vessel are ye?" hailed Captain Campbell through his speaking trumpet from his station on the poop.

"*Highland Lass,* Gloucester, U.S.A.!" roared back big Jim.

"*Hieland Lass,* eh? An' hoo is in command, if I may be sae boold as ta en-quire?"

"J. W. Pattillo!"

"Pattillo, eh?" There was a moment's pause.

"Weel, Captain, I shall le' ye gae aboot yer business this once. Bu' le' me tell ye, laddie, I hae just noo ta'en yonder vessel, an' I'll hae no hesi-tation to ta' ye too if I find ye inshore agin! Noo be off wi' ye!"

They put their helm down, and the Devil on the Station steamed back to his prize.

Highland Lass proceeded on her way and rounded the Gaspé into Bay Chaleur to buy stores from the Jersey merchants at Paspébiac. The British had gun barges along the coast and were attempting to shut off the entire Bay from the Americans, calling it within the three-mile limit . . . that is, it lay behind a line drawn from headland to headland–for a hundred miles behind it! So the Gloucester schooner kept sail up, peak down, at Paspébiac, and stood back out the Bay as soon as the men returned with the provisions, all laughing and decked out in the red stocking caps they'd bought.

No sooner did the *Lass* round Percé and drop her anchor in the serene waters of Malbaie for the night when in chugged the

Devastation from out at sea to do likewise. The warship had taken the *Star Light* into Charlottetown, the capital of Prince Edward Island (where the schooner was later released for lack of evidence), disembarked Captain Campbell for reassignment to England, put in to Pictou for coal and was now about to renew her hunt for Yankee poachers.

As fast as she came to anchor, one of her boats, which she had earlier left in Malbaie with eighteen men on patrol, rowed out from shore, evidently toward the *Devastation.* They changed their course, however, and came alongside *Highland Lass.* The officer demanded to see her papers.

"Papers?" said Jim, looking blank and taking a pull on his pipe. "Why, that's too bad–I threw them all away. I've nothing left aboard but maybe the Almanac." And he hollered down the companionway to his cook to pass up the Almanac if he could lay his hands on it.

This sally drew a great laugh from his crew, who were crowding the rail in their flapping red stocking caps, clenching handspikes, gaffs and whatever other implements had been handy when the Limeys came oaring up.

"Not newspapers, Captain–your ship's papers if you please!" The officer flushed and glared about him, for he thought he heard a chuckle from his own boat.

Captain Pattillo gave him a saturnine smile and went below, but when he returned on deck with the papers, after taking his time, the *Devastation*'s other boat had pulled alongside, carrying no less a personage than the young lieutenant who had taken over the command from Sir Colin. He ordered the first boat to get along to the ship.

"Well, my friend, I suppose you want to gratify your curiosity about my papers," said Jim, handing them down to him.

The lieutenant leafed through them and looked up.

"How many mackerel have you aboard, Captain Pattillo?"

"Two hundred and twenty barrels, mostly number ones."

"Indeed! Then you have double your share, because I haven't spoken a Yank yet with more than a hundred. And how many arms do you have? I heard you have arms aboard."

"Arms? Now let me see . . ." Jim muttered to himself and counted on his fingers. "Well, it comes to twenty-seven, as I calculate."

"What!" and the lieutenant burst forth with a rousing string of oaths, for at this announcement–as if on a signal–that devil-may-care Midge Procter popped up on deck, carrying an old French musket on his shoulder, his face blacked with soot, his stocking cap tossing about with every shake of his head, which was stuck through a great dickey cut from a sheet of paper that came up around his ears. He commenced strutting up and down the deck, sentry-fashion.

"My God!" cried the lieutenant (the man-of-war's men in his boat, and all the fishermen, were setting up a roar of laughter). "You mean to tell me, Captain, that's your arms?"

"Yes, yes, and good ones they are too, Admiral!" burst out Jim, hardly able to keep his countenance. "There are thirteen of us with two arms apiece, is twenty-six, and the old musket without a lock–throw that in–makes twenty-seven!"

The acting commander of the *Devastation* was nigh doubled over himself now. He handed Jim back the papers and told his laughing lads to get under way for their ship. They bent to the oars, and he called up with a grin:

"You're a lucky man, Captain Pattillo! It was only your vessel's name that saved you before. You know where Sir Colin hails from–and he said he could never take a highland lass his prisoner. Look out for yourself!"

"Have no worry about that, my friend!" roared Jim with a wave of his arm. "Give the Admiral three cheers, boys!"

And they did.

Which Touches On This and That, Concluding with a Personal Matter

"We learn," the *Gloucester Telegraph* informed its readers in early August of 1854, "that Captain James Pattillo, of the schooner *Highland Lass,* of this port, put into Halifax, on his passage to the Bay of St. Lawrence, to endeavor to obtain a British register for his vessel, he having formerly been a British subject."

Some sea lawyer assured Jim he could fish anywhere in the Bay if he converted the *Lass* into an English bottom, so he was bound to have the last laugh on the cutters before the Reciprocity Treaty between Great Britain and the United States went into effect and took half the fun out of fishing. The British had agreed in June to open the Canadian coast fisheries to Americans in exchange for a suspension of duties on their fish.

Jim had in tow a longboat with a purse seine in it, the first ever owned in Gloucester as far as he knew, though it had been tried before by several other skippers with little success. The net was a hundred and ten fathoms long and thirteen deep, held vertically in the water by corks and leads. His intention was to hunt up a school of mackerel in shoal water—and where else was the North Bay shoaler than inside of three miles, and what else could fish there legally but a British bottom?

When the mastheadsman sang out *school-ho!* the men would leap into the seine boat as if the vessel were on fire and row like mad around the school, putting out the twine until they had come back to their buoy and closed the circle. Then quick as thought they would purse it up, hauling in the purse line that made a bag of the bottom, trapping the school within. No work for boys, this. "A man who won't pull every pound he can and an ounce more is not fit to be a fisherman," was the rule of the seiners. The schooner would come alongside, and the job of bailing a few tons of thrashing mackerel aboard with the dip nets would begin. Thus might a deckload be caught in one deft maneuver without the use of a single hook; that is, if the whole school didn't dive first and escape, which was why Captain Pattillo wanted to use his net where it would drag on the bottom, as no one had yet mastered the skill of deep water seining.

The *Highland Lass* arrived in Halifax on the twenty-fifth of July, and Jim swung off the wharf up the grade of the crowded hill, through the familiar ground of the old battles, and into the Customs House, where he asked to see the boss. The Yankee captain was duly admitted and stated his errand.

"The head controller said to me," he recalled, "I would have to land what I had on board–salt, provisions and everything dutiable–on the Queen's Wharf to have it appraised, as I would have to pay duty on the same. He advised me not to have my vessel converted into an English vessel, as she would not be worth so much if she were done so as she is now. That next year there would be Reciprocity between the two countries, and I could then fish where I had a mind to. So I took his advice and did not have my vessel converted into an English vessel."

The Halifax *British North American,* on the other hand, reported a somewhat different version of the interview:

"The Comptroller of Customs refused to grant the register since the owner had no intention of pursuing the trade of the Provinces. A British subject residing in a foreign country may hold property in a British vessel; but a British subject cannot obtain a British register for a foreign vessel unless he resides in the British country where the said vessel is to be registered as

Putting their backs to it, the crew in their Gloucester seineboat row furiously to pay out the net around a school before the mackerel catch on and dive to safety.

Their circle completed, the men haul the purse line to close the bottom of the seine, trapping the mackerel within, while their schooner stands by, only the skipper left aboard.

The Gloucesterman Smuggler *has come alongside the pursed-up seine net, and the men on deck from the seineboat are bailing mackerel aboard with the assistance of a tackle from the foremasthead to the scoop. (Goode's* Fisheries*)*

British. In the case of the *Highland Lass,* Capt. Pattillo, her owner, has resided out of the country for many years, enticed away no doubt by the high bounty offered by the Americans on fish caught in American bottoms by American masters, and the same reason, we are told, induced him to become an American citizen.

"Can anything be more conclusive as to the policy and necessity of Nova Scotians neutralizing the bounty given to American fishermen by granting an equal bounty to ours? Now that the Reciprocity Treaty has received the quietus in the American Senate, we presume there will be less squeamishness in equalizing the privileges of our fishermen with those of our friends over the border."

Nothing daunted, Jim sailed five days later for the North Bay, intent on finding some secluded cove chock full of the Queen's mackerel where he could wet his twine away from prying eyes. But when they put in at Canso, he found that news of his doings had preceded him from Halifax. A late copy of *The Novascotian* was there ahead of them, and the Shipping News contained these words of greeting:

> Arr. Schr. *Highland Lass,* Patillo, from Gloucester, US, bound mkl. fishing; has put in for a British register, which, as the master and owner is a white-washed Yankee of about 10 years standing, and has no intention of employing his vessel in the trade of the Province, was, very properly, refused by the Controller of HM Customs at this port. HL sailed yesterday, and it is to be hoped that the vessels engaged in the protection of the Fisheries will keep a sharp look out for her.

Well, well–thought Jim–the seine had cost him over six hundred dollars, and what was the use to risk it after all? It had been worth the price just to stir them up.

When they passed into the North Bay, he landed the longboat with a friend in the Magdalen Islands and the seine with another at Port Hood, filled up forty fish barrels with sand for ballast (as they had come light for the seining) and went back to the old way of jigging with hook and line.

The season had been unlucky from the beginning. On the eve of their departure from Gloucester a fire broke out in a privy on Central Wharf and swept up through George Steele's sail loft. Many of the owners lost their spare canvas, including Pattillo, who ran down to the burning building that night in time to see four hundred dollars' worth of his sails go up in smoke, and without a penny of insurance on them, either.

Then followed the affair of the purse seine . . . and then the mackerel wouldn't bite, so that when they visited Cascumpeque Bay with eighty sail in the middle of September, *Highland Lass* could report only sixty barrels (the fleet average was a hundred, and that was considered poor indeed) . . . and then a good smart blow came along, and the *Lass* cracked her mainmast and lost a good anchor and length of cable.

But what started ill ended well. After they got in and out of Port Hood for repairs, they came upon a rich run of fish—all number ones—and packed three hundred and thirty-eight barrels. They arrived home a week before Thanksgiving; Jim sold his fare to Ripley Ropes in Salem for six thousand dollars, giving the men of the *Lass* more to a share than any other Gloucester vessel in the Bay that year.

Within a fortnight they sailed for Cornwallis, Nova Scotia, where he purchased two thousand bushels of potatoes at seventy cents a bushel. They coasted to New York, where he sold them at $1.05–and when the spuds were unloaded and measured, he found he had three hundred more bushels going out of the hatch than were dumped in, not counting the rotten ones. Crossing over to Brooklyn, the *Highland Lass* took on a cargo of hides for Ripley Ropes which they delivered in Salem for $150, arriving back in Gloucester on the tenth of February, 1855.

After a few days they ran down to Boston, and Jim bought twenty-four hundred bushels of Vermont potatoes from a dealer at eighty-five cents a bushel, sailed to New York and sold them for the same price as before, $1.05, except that this time the New York man turned around and resold the cargo to a buyer in

Baltimore and engaged the *Highland Lass* to freight the lot down for twelve and a half cents a bushel more, which they did without ever having to take them out of the fish hold till they reached Maryland. At Baltimore, out went the potatoes and in were dumped three thousand bushels of corn to go back to New York at the same freight.

So it went in the line of coasting that spring, and when he returned to Cape Ann at the last of April, Jim was feeling prosperous enough to turn the *Lass* over to John Fisher to take to the Georges while he relaxed.

Captain Pattillo was home in time to be on hand for the birth of his second grandchild.

Alex had been married for two years to Abby Sayward Wonson, a niece of Jim's old shipmates John Fletcher and Add and the rest of the Wonson clan over at the upper part of Eastern Point toward the head of the Harbor, that they called East Gloucester now. Many the long mile had Alex trudged on his short legs between the town and Sam Wonson's house at the bottom of Plum Street a few fathoms from high water, courting this lovely girl, the belle of Eastern Point. People said Sam's daughter might just as well marry and have a little family while she could; she had been a sickly child, not likely to live long (Abby was healthy and strong as a horse!). Alex had opened his own dry goods store on Front Street and was idyllically happy with his efficient and affectionate bride. His giant father was gruffly pleased with the whole affair. Their firstborn was named for her mother and died of dysentery after eight months. By then Abby was already carrying her second; they named her Laura May.

Along about a year later, when he was fifty, Jim took a notion that the day had arrived for him to lay smoking alongside of drinking in the grave of his vices. As a resolute Baptist and teetotaller, he knew it wasn't right to be always puffing away at the filthy weed. Being home between trips, he put pipe and tobacco aside, and that was that.

For three weeks he suffered all the agonies of the horrors, striving to replace one appetite with another so furiously at the

Alex and Abby Pattillo. (Carolyn W. Pattillo)

dinner table that he gained twenty-one pounds. It was right alarming the day he mounted the fish scales at the wharf and watched the balance slide out to two hundred and sixty-five.

"Great thunder, Captain!" exclaimed a friend on viewing these results of abnegation. "You had better go back to smoking–if this keeps up you'll be as big as Daniel Lambert!"

Calling to mind that the unfortunate Englishman weighed seven hundred and thirty-nine pounds when he died, Jim took the advice and returned to the comforts of his pipe with a groan of relief.

In the summer of 1858 Captain Moses Tarr, Deacon George Garland and the other directors of the Gloucester Mutual Fishing Insurance Company persuaded Captain Pattillo to spend the season up at Port Hood as their agent; he was to look out for the interests of the mackerel fleet, most of which they insured. The vessel owners had organized the company in the early 1840s for the practical reason that the rival Marine Insurance Company didn't look kindly on fishing risks. Equally as irksome to the fishermen was the humiliating experience of presenting themselves at the stodgy old office, which was, as Captain Sylvanus Smith remembered it, "controlled and managed by the retired captains of the square-rigged fleet, and these men carried their quarterdeck manners into business. As 'Jack' had to take off his hat when he approached the quarterdeck of the square-riggers, so they expected those coming to them for insurance, to take off their hats, and then await their pleasure."

These were the barnacled veterans of Gloucester's prosperous West Indies trade, and if they sneered at the rise of the stinking fisheries, they were willing enough to profit from the exchange of salt hake for molasses and sugar which every year attracted scores of Gloucester barks and brigs to Surinam.

This system of mutual insurance which spread the burden of losses over by far the greater part of the fleet drew yet tighter the bonds of fraternity among Gloucestermen, making the entire community party to the ancient unwritten contract of the fishermen, *share and share alike* . . . equally in the hazards of the deep and in its fruits. By means of it Gloucester could risk her fleet in the North Bay with greater equanimity (at the end of July this year she had two hundred and twelve schooners and twenty-five hundred and fifty men there). As for the Georges fishery–the hardest chance of them all, and pursued almost exclusively by Gloucestermen for generations–mutual insurance enabled the owners to send their schooners to this necropolis of the Atlantic with less apprehension than was suffered by those of any other port. For the widows and orphans there was charity.

The *Gloucester Telegraph* approved of Captain Pattillo's assignment. The company

> has upwards of half a million dollars' worth of property at risk, nearly all of which is in the Bay of St. Lawrence. The policy of maintaining an agent there is a prudent and commendable one, as hardly a year passes, that some of our shipping is not wholly lost to the company while waiting for instructions from home. Many vessels which have been driven ashore there, heretofore, and sold for a song, have been got off afterwards at little expense and made nearly as good as new. An agent on the spot will do much to prevent such sacrifice.

Jim had his hands full. A raft of schooners drove up on the beaches in the Bight of Prince Edward Island during a savage norther the night of October the second, and over the next month four Gloucester vessels were lost altogether: the *Village Belle* disappeared without a trace coming back from the Bay with sixteen aboard, including the master's wife and daughter; and three other hookers—*Three Sisters, Premium* and *Geranium*—all insured by the company, were wrecked, though their crews were saved. It was a late season; stragglers in the fleet lingered on, hoping to fill out their fares, and Jim didn't get back to Cape Ann until December.

Having sold a quarter interest in the *Highland Lass* to Captain Sam Chambers of Kittery, Maine, who was fishing her out of Gloucester for him, Jim took to hankering that winter for the feel of a deck under his boots again. With his usual energy, he hitched up and drove to Essex in the spring of 1859 to do something about it. He had been doing something about something else, too, judging from an item that appeared in the *Telegraph* on the eighteenth of June:

> Although we have seldom spoken of any particular vessel when she has appeared in our harbor, we cannot refrain from alluding to one which sailed on Thursday. We mean the *C. Campbell,* Capt. James Pattillo. This vessel was built at Essex, by Mr. Jeremiah Burnham, and in about eight weeks from the time her keel was laid, she has been completed in a superior manner, under the supervision of her sole owner, the captain, rigged by Messrs. Robert Fears and Son, fitted for sea with every improvement that has been brought into use, and started on her trip. On her stern is placed, with her name and other ornaments, a bust of a female to represent the person for whom the vessel was named. While the vessel was laying at the wharf, she was visited by large numbers, and those competent to judge of such matters pronounce her to be one of the finest specimens of naval architecture, both in regard to beauty of model and strength of construction, that has ever sailed from this port.

This notice raised some eyebrows in Gloucester among those who were acquainted with the mysterious C. Campbell, and among those who were not.

Two weeks after the *Christie Campbell* (the full name of the new schooner) sailed for the North Bay with the mackerel fleet, Anne Gorman Pattillo died. Her death was ascribed to disease of the brain. The last ten of her fifty-three years had been spent in a mental institution. The body of his wife was brought back to Gloucester for burial, but her husband did not return from the Bay in *Christie Campbell* until the end of August; so he probably didn't learn of her death until two months after the event. They were married thirty-one years.

Four months later and two days after Christmas, Captain James Pattillo and Miss Christie Campbell filed notice with the town clerk of their intention to marry. The recent widower was fifty-three. His bride-to-be was thirty-three, and she was born in Scotland, and that is all that is known of her. They were wed out of town.

Christie Campbell Pattillo.
(Carolyn W. Pattillo)

Who was this Christie, twenty years younger, who had such a hold on her man that he broke all the bonds of propriety and named his new schooner for her, even went so far overboard as to carve her bust on the stern . . . all while his poor demented wife was still alive? Was she his housekeeper—a highland lass, perhaps? They must have been waiting a long time for Anne to get on with it and go, just as Jim could not have helped but think of her as all but dead, all these years. It had been a bitter thing for a great man of hot blood to be married, but to have no wife.

For two seasons Jim took the *Christie Campbell* to the North Bay mackereling, and then he sold her in February of 1861, though she was a stout, fast schooner, one of the best he ever owned. She was the only bad luck vessel he ever commanded in all of his years at sea, and that came out of a freak accident: Jimmy McDonald, crew on the maiden voyage, died in the Bay from swallowing a match.

Maybe that bothered him about the *Christie Campbell* . . . or maybe it was some other thing.

They Sailed Away

> I think too much of my crow bait to go there. I would rather be food for crows than go there and let the fish eat me. It is a regular burying ground—a regular cemetery for Cape Ann fishermen.
>
> —Why one retired Gloucesterman quit winter-fishing on Georges Bank

AT DAWN on the twelfth of April, 1861, the misty stillness of Charleston Harbor cracked and echoed with the explosion from shore that lobbed the first Confederate shell into the federal garrison of Fort Sumter. After thirty-four hours of bombardment, the shattered Union stronghold ran up the white flag. On April fifteenth President Lincoln, six weeks to the day after his inauguration, called for seventy-five thousand volunteers. On the morning of April sixteenth, in a scene that was being repeated all over the North at that precise moment, the citizens of Gloucester poured into the narrow streets of the old fishing town to bid the boys Godspeed.

Company G of the Eighth Regiment of Massachusetts Infantry turned out in such a hurry that only thirty-nine reported on the spot; some were off fishing, and there weren't enough uniforms to go around. This vanguard nevertheless marched to the depot to the lively blasts of the Gloucester Cornet Band, accompanied by a great throng. Cheer upon cheer rent the spring air as the train

Front (now Main) Street in Gloucester, April 5, 1861, two days after a blizzard–possibly the earliest photograph of the town. (Author collection)

clanked out for Boston in a huff of cinders and a hiss of steam, bearing this first shouting, waving contingent off to swell the ranks of their regiment–for three months anyway, the term of their enlistment.

A thoroughly riled-up special Town Meeting a week later resolved in an outburst of patriotic hyperbole that the seceded states "have exhibited all their meanness and cowardice, without any of the better qualities of the REBEL, the TRAITOR, and the

PIRATE," and voted ten thousand dollars for the support of Gloucester volunteers and their families. Meanwhile a second unit was being raised, for a three-year enlistment, and on the fourth of May Company K of the Twelfth embarked on the steamer *Mystic* after an immense public demonstration during which the boys were presented Bibles by their churches and daggers by the Cape Ann Anchor Works.

The Civil War settled deeper over the land, and except for the telegraphic dispatches in the newspapers and the letters home, it meant little enough to Gloucester; her boys were a sight safer standing guard duty along the Potomac than they were at the rail of a Georgesman hauling codfish off the bottom of the shoal.

Alex Pattillo advertised wool yard goods for the ladies to make scarves for the soldiers and sailors, and his father was increasingly at home from fishing.

Having sold *Christie Campbell,* and at fifty-four being too advanced in years to begin the military or naval life, Captain Pattillo for the second season gave the *Highland Lass* to Captain Ezra Turner to go master. The two had met somewhere fishing years before, and the down-Easter was Jim's kind of man, a tough dog and hard as nails, hailing from foggy Isle au Haut off the Maine coast. Though not yet fifty, Captain Turner had fished since he was sixteen and made his first trip as skipper at eighteen, when he took the old schooner *Porpoise* from Deer Isle to the North Bay mackereling–and for another seventeen years after that.

So with no command and at loose ends (he didn't mind taking in a little slack after forty-three years at sea), Jim was induced once more to station himself at Port Hood for the mackerel season on behalf of the Gloucester Mutual Fishing Insurance Company. The assignment was not long in paying off. In August the hooker *M. C. Rowe,* only three years old, a big vessel insured for four thousand dollars, piled up at a remote place called Farther Point in the mouth of the St. Lawrence River, and Captain George Thurston called for help. Jim hitched a ride with one of the fleet that was going up that way, rolled up his sleeves, put his uncanny salvage knowledge to work and got her afloat, little damaged.

He remained at home that winter. In spite of the war, the

Christmas spirit was abroad on Cape Ann, which had not yet lost a man to the lead of Johnnie Reb. There was to be a holiday gathering in the Hancock Street house of the Pattillo clan, which was now dominated by five grandchildren. The babe in arms was Samuel, of six weeks, then Annie, Alexander Manton, Alice, and plump Abby's oldest, Laura May, going on seven years; Roscoe had died of consumption when he was eight months old, three years earlier. Jim and Christie cheerfully tramped through the snow, making the rounds of the Front Street stores, loaded down with growing packs of presents for the little ones.

Two days before Christmas baby Samuel had a sore throat; his face was hot, and he was drowsy and sick to his stomach. The doctor came and found yellow patches on his tonsils and shook his head . . . diphtheria, the killer of children. Nothing could be done except to quarantine the house. His mother watched over him helplessly for twelve days, and on the third of January, 1862, the infant died.

In three more days Annie had a sore throat. She was fifteen months. The symptoms came on, the horror unspeakable. In twelve days it was ended. Three days later, little Alice, five and a half years old, complained to her distraught mother that her throat hurt. Her breathing came harder, labored and gasping, until she too suffocated on the last day of the month.

The finger of Fate, the hand of God, the arm of Justice, or whatever agency strikes innocents to the grave skipped over Laura May and Alexander Manton, permitting Alex and Abby to thank a kind Providence that two of their five children had been spared.

At sea that January thirty-six Gloucestermen drowned and four schooners went down . . . a year's tribute paid in the first month.

February dragged out its bitter days without a loss reported.

Then at the end of the month the schooners *Peerless* and *Northern Chief* hove into the Inner Harbor, heavy and sparkling with frozen spray. They had aboard the crews of the *Borodino* and *Quickstep,* and their news gripped Gloucester.

A fearful northwest gale had burst over the Georges late in the evening of the twenty-fourth, full on the fleet of seventy sail all huddled close together at anchor. It struck with such unexpected violence that many had no time to haul anchor and get under way, a course of action that would have given them sea room and freedom to ride with the punches. The snow drove thick before a spiteful wind, mixed with frozen pellets of spindrift; it was cruelly cold, and the seas mounted by the minute. At the height of it that night *Borodino* and *Quickstep* foundered, and the crews of both were rescued in fantastic feats of seamanship by the two that brought them in.

What could the survivors say? They had passed through the worst hell of Georges and come out alive. They had seen other schooners breaking adrift, driving down past them and smashing into those still anchored, wrenching *them* adrift and the two swallowed up by the tempest, all tangled in their cables. Had they crashed into a third, and the three of them gone down? Who knew? They had no details of the fleet, no names of vessels, no idea how many were lost . . . nothing.

Each day the people of Gloucester watched for the Georgesmen straggling in around Eastern Point. The whole population was friend or relative to the six hundred men who were dead or alive. In they came, and every arrival was like a sigh of relief, for who cared if they were dismasted, stove in, decks swept, spars in splinters, rigging and sails torn to shreds, anchors, cable and boats gone, not a one that hadn't met some disaster . . . who cared as long as one more of the fleet was safe, one more schooner could be checked off the list of the missing?

In the end it came down to thirteen still not heard from, not counting the two from which the crews had been plucked. The fleet refitted, sailed off again to the Bank and again returned, and the thirteen were still unreported three weeks after the storm.

In that one night fifteen schooners had drifted under trails of bubbles to the bottom of the Atlantic, taking with them one hundred and twenty men, without leaving so much as a trace of anything that could be brought back to Gloucester, not a cap or a shoe, a fragment of a plank or a stitch of sail. In two months a hundred and fifty-six fishermen and nineteen schooners lost from Gloucester, a mass drowning that made seventy-five wives

Sloppy seas toss the Gloucester schooner Dauntless, *anchored on the shoals of Georges Bank as the crew nonchalantly handlines for codfish at the rail. A sharpshooter built at Essex in 1855, she's snug-rigged without her topmasts for the winter fishery.* Dauntless *went down with twelve men while sailing from Gloucester to the Gulf of St. Lawrence in 1870. (Goode's* Fisheries*)*

widows and left one hundred and sixty children without fathers. It was the most awful toll of death in the history of the American fisheries.

With age-old stolid resignation Gloucester bore its grief. Schooners were insured, but not fishermen, and the two hundred dollars that a highliner might bring home in a year of fishing assured only that if he were lost his family would be thrown on the town.

But this time it was too much for the usual charities. Some extraordinary effort was called for. An emergency Town Meeting gathered on the evening of March twentieth. The old Town House was packed to overflowing, and the people voted a committee to raise a relief fund. Fifteen of the leaders in the fisheries, including Captain Pattillo, were appointed by Chairman Addison Gilbert. These sorrowful men–the founders of the famous Gloucester Fishermen's and Seamen's Widows and Orphans Aid Society–straightaway set about their task with a circular appeal:

"A Great Calamity has fallen upon the Town of Gloucester, Massachusetts, in consequence of severe gales at sea, which has resulted in the loss of many vessels with their entire crews, thereby leaving in this community a large number of families who need assistance from the benevolent, in this season of their distress . . . This terrible bereavement has cast a gloom over our community, and carried sorrow and mourning to many hearts."

The epitaph was written by the *Gloucester Telegraph:*

> Had 138 men (156 by final count), nearly a full company and a half, from our town, been shot down by rebel batteries at Roanoke or at Newbern, we should have felt the disaster far more. Every pulse would have thrilled with unutterable grief; and the Flag for whose honor and defence they had so gallantly given their lives would gloriously have covered them in their death. But these now gone,–these who have gone down to the sea in ships and done business in great waters, and have found there at length their graves,–are they not, perhaps, more to be missed by us than the soldier fallen in the field?
>
> But they are no more among us. They sailed away and have cast anchor in the haven whence there is no return.

In Which Jim is Smitten with the Gold Fever, and How He is Cured

TURNING IT OVER in the back of his mind, Jim had to admit that he was smitten, as he liked to say, with the gold fever . . . not for all the gold in California that he had passed up in '49, nor for the gold that was worth more than all the gold in California–*that* he had found in abundance the night of his conversion eleven years since–but for the gold which had been discovered the previous summer in the rock of his native Nova Scotia.

The first hoarse shout of joy resounded through the Acadian hills in May of 1860 when old John Pulcifer of Musquodoboit dug rough particles of gold from the white quartz in boulders near the beach at Tangier, forty-five miles to the eastward of Halifax. The word sped along the coast; a few weeks later Joe Smith discovered it while prospecting along the wild southwest shore of Indian Harbor, another fifty miles toward Cape Canso.

Come spring of 1861, and the south shore of the Province from Lunenburg to Wine Harbor was in the grip of the fever and rang to the sound of pick and shovel. There was much toil and little reward that second summer of the strike, and of course it attracted a few of those nomadic old Forty-niners from

California, always on the prowl for the end of the rainbow; they tried out the rock and pronounced it "mighty hard diggin' fer sech pore pickin's." This was the opinion of Her Majesty's Surveyors, too; they puttered through the various diggings, assayed the quartz which the prospectors called "white flint," proclaimed it to be auriferous indeed where the pay streaks shot through the beds of slate, but most difficult to extract, and sent their reports back to Halifax. The government soberly advised would-be miners to stay put unless they were well supplied with capital and energy, for the ore could only be made profitable through large-scale operations.

Always the whitewashed Yankee, that great Pattillo was willing to put back, boat and bank account into any venture that held a chance of increasing his own assets at the expense of the Queen's–besides which, the price of mackerel was the lowest since he'd arrived at Gloucester twenty-eight years ago, so what was the use of fishing for the present, war or no war?

Ezra Turner was all for the idea, too; he ran down to Isle au Haut in the *Highland Lass* and was back at Cape Ann on the seventh of April, 1862, with a slew of Turners–young Ezra, Bill, Haskell and Jim–all raring to go. Resuming the command of his vessel, Jim filled out this crew with six more hearties, not forgetting good loyal old "Uncle John" Parsons, and signed on ten additional young fellows as passengers, all to form a mining company under his direction. They agreed to strike out for the diggings on about the same lay as if they were fishing; that is, the captain and owner of the vessel would stake the expedition, fitting out the schooner, providing all the tools, stock, materials and food for a summer of prospecting (even the lumber for a barracks), and buying the necessary claims, for all of which he would receive one half of the profits. Just as he would never have set a course for the North Bay without taking a few articles for trading, Jim stowed aboard on his own account about a thousand dollars' worth of boots and shoes, oil clothes, flour, tea, tobacco and sundry notions.

It took only ten days of commotion under his bellowing management to get the *Lass* ready for sea after Turner brought her into Gloucester from down East. On the fine mild morning of Thursday the seventeenth of April, to the shouts and waves of a goodly crowd on the wharf, the schooner with her deckload of argonauts stood out the Harbor under a full press of canvas, off for the diggings at Lunenburg.

Good luck to them, wished the *Cape Ann Weekly Advertiser.* "They are mostly young and able-bodied men of industrious habits, and if there is any gold there, we predict that they will get their share of it. May success attend them, and we hope to chronicle their return in the fall, with pockets full of the yellow stuff."

Somebody climbing around the bluffs at a peculiar place called The Ovens, on a point of land at the southern side of the entrance to Lunenburg Harbor, had stumbled on a vein of gold-specked quartz, three-quarters of an inch thick, angling across the cliff. These Ovens were deep caverns in the bluff, some as high as eighteen feet, and after a storm the surf struck into them with the noise of a cannonade. Legend had it that an Indian of yore ventured with his canoe into the largest cave, came to an underground river and emerged in his own good time, blinking from the unaccustomed glare of day, at Annapolis Royal, seventy miles across the Province as the crow flies, or the Micmac paddles. When the first lead at The Ovens was followed by Her Majesty's Surveyor's discovery of free gold in the sand of the beach under the bluffs, a small rush started, and over the course of a year or so some thousand ounces of the stuff for which men die were recovered from the strand.

This modest deposit was giving up about an ounce a month a miner, as the men of the *Highland Lass* learned to their disappointment on arriving at Lunenburg. No better than fishing. So they hove up anchor and skipped across the western reach of Mahone Bay–how many hundreds of times had Jim made this passage?–past tree-studded old Oak Island where Captain Kidd's treasure still kept its secret from adventurous boys, and up to the mouth of Gold River, a mere three miles west of Chester.

There was a glint of gold at Gold River when the sun caught it in the rock or sand, and a gang of prospectors was toiling away, trying to sweat the stuff out of its hiding places. They earned every ounce they got, ten times over; nor was this what the Gloucestermen had bargained for, and all their leader mined in the few days they tarried there were nuggets from the vault of his nostalgia. Only a week from Cape Ann and discouraged already, four of the company quit and headed home aboard the schooner *Wild Wave.*

To the eastward past Halifax they sailed, a day's sail with a fair wind around Cape Jeddore and five miles up that long harbor to Salmon River. The story was the same: gold to be had by the parties that could finance the crushing and washing of mountains of quartz, the only way to make it pay. They poked around the boulders and the river bed for a day or two, held a confab and agreed with Captain Pattillo that they should make one more stab at it, at least, so as to be able to give a good plausible account of their failure when they got back to Gloucester empty-handed. The word all along had been that if a man stood a chance any place it would be around Sherbrooke on the St. Mary's River or at Wine Harbor, up that way in the woods where the diggings were said to be the richest and the busiest on the coast.

So Sherbrooke, here we come!

Another day's sail to the eastward and *Highland Lass* was off the entrance to St. Marys River. With a light southwest breeze on his beam, Jim took the helm and they reached with caution up the middle of the stream, the leadsman rhythmically heaving his line and singing out the soundings. The mouth of the St. Marys was half a mile wide at places, and it penetrated with hardly a bend through the wilderness that climbed back from the banks in a dense green darkness of spruce and hemlock, brightened by the verdant splotches of the budding birch and maple.

Once or twice as the *Lass* glided upstream, almost silently save for the shiver of her sails and the regular cry of the leadsman, the wind carried the distant honking that heralded the approach of a high-flying flock of geese even before the eye could make them out; and then the gracefully undulating V was overhead on whispering wings, purposeful, crying its way northward . . . and was gone. Or over there would be mother bear and cubs, lumping out of the forest for a lesson in fish-catching–or a deer, poised and nervous, staring at them, ready to dive back into the protecting thicket. Or a-way high over the masthead, old osprey circling on motionless wings, watching and waiting.

The sole unnatural sound to break the serenity of such a sweet spring day was the irregular mutter of thunder across the hills. These grumblings might have struck the uninitiated as remarkable utterances from a cloudless sky; but they quickened the pulses of all aboard, who recognized them as the reverberations of blasting. The men were using plenty of powder up this way . . . that meant business!

When the schooner had drifted into the head of the inlet, luffed up, slowed and dropped anchor, Jim and his company hurried ashore and trekked the couple of miles to the diggings at Goldenville, the newly named camp outside of the village of Sherbrooke, only to hear the same old story: the rich are getting richer in this line of work, and the poor poorer.

For the fourth time, the fishermen turned away dejectedly, swallowing their disappointment and about ready to cash in their chips.

All right boys, said Jim, one more try and we'll call it a day.

So they sailed down the St. Marys and around the cape three miles more to the eastward for a look at Wine Harbor.

It was May fifteenth–four weeks to the day since they'd dropped Cape Ann–when Jim and his impatient goldseekers put into Wine Harbor, and the sight that was spread before them as they rounded into the lee raised all spirits. Several vessels swung at anchor, and some rough-hewn wharves stood out from the shore. Back from the water the slope had been cleared of forest and presented a scene of exciting activity. Acres of the hillside were quilled with stumps, interspersed with several score of shacks, log cabins and some larger structures going up, most of them strung out beside the ruts of the main drag. The blue smoke from a couple of dozen stovepipes lazed down toward the anchorage, mingling the woodsy smell of burning spruce with whiffs of hot coffee.

Pattillo was anxious to get moving. Once ashore, he strode about making inquiries, and with the size of him and his usual bluff way of getting to the heart of things, he had no trouble obtaining all the information he wanted.

Joe Smith, who had found the gold there the previous summer, was still the big man in Wine Harbor, and the lead named after him was still the fattest. The place was a bedlam of comings and goings, several hundred men already in camp and more arriving all the time as word spread far and wide that the diggings there were the richest in the Province. It was a real live little mining town, no question of that. All around were growing piles of slate shale. The air crackled with the scrape of pick and shovel, the ring of the axe, the warning yell, the sudden eruption of rock and dirt and then the *crump* of the blast and the shake of the ground, the shouts of the men and the clatter and squeal of the quartz-laden wagons rumbling down behind the slow oxen to the wharves for loading on lighters and the trip to the stamp mill.

The main thing holding up operations, Jim learned, was the distance to the nearest crushing mill (about ten miles), its limited capacity and the expense of taking the ore there. However, two mills were being built right now at Wine Harbor and might be working by the fall of the year; just last week a quartz miner from California turned up with a scheme for putting up a mill but found others had beaten him to it.

So far there were seven leads, and some of the parties were sinking shafts as deep as forty feet to get at the best of the pay streaks. The lodes had been found to consist of laminated veins of a bluish, oily sort of quartz that was embedded deep in the slate; the gold was finer in this ore than in the white flint, but there was more of it. The hitch was in getting it out, as usual; the most practical method was to crush it in the heavy machinery of the stamp mill, then wash off the gravel and hope the gold would stay put.

The Smith lead was yielding six ounces a ton at a depth of thirty feet, though some of the chaps over on the Hattie lead were able to grind out eight thousand dollars' worth by hand mortar, one particular batch of five tons of quartz producing a hundred and twenty-five ounces of gold.

What they called the Major Norton lead was about all taken, and Jim was advised to buy in, which he did immediately, picking up an old claim of five acres for sixty dollars.

Landing picks, shovels, crowbars, axes, drills, powder and the rest of their mining equipment, the men from Gloucester tramped off to their claim with hopes high. Clearing the trees as they went along, they commenced to dig a trench around the outside boundary of the plot, purposing to intercept a lead this way. Their claim was in the south portion of the Major Norton, and they started at their north boundary and sweated their way around several hundred yards toward the southern border, with no luck, when one morning there was a whoop and a holler and all dropped their tools and ran to the spot.

The diggers up front had struck a vein.

"Follow it along!" roared Jim, grabbing a pick. "Follow it along! Bring up your drills and your powder! Look alive there, boys, this is what we've come for!"

More frantic digging to the southward, then fanning to the interior of the claim . . . and after one trench had been worked in from the line some two rods, a little hell broke loose when they encountered four more veins within a space of eight feet.

The hand drill was hustled over and put to work, a slow job of boring through the slate and quartz, down fourteen inches–then a charge of black powder in the hole, fused and touched off . . . heads down, fingers in ears, a satisfying *harrump,* the ground heaves, rocks rain round and the breeze carries away the little cloud of acrid smoke.

Fourteen and a half pounds of quartz were picked up by the men of the *Highland Lass.* They pounded it, ground it, washed it, and there in the bottom of the pan gleamed a half an ounce of gold, nine dollars and fifty cents worth.

Well, a person would have thought they were on their way to their first million, with all that jumping up and down, yelling like wild men and pounding each other on the back. The news of the strike spread around Wine Harbor as if on wings, and in short order a speculator sidled over and offered them a thousand dollars for their claim; they turned him down, and then another rushed up and wanted to give them five thousand.

They had a confab. Jim was of the opinion that they should sell out while they could, but the rest swore that if the claim was worth five thousand to the speculator it was worth it to them, so they voted to keep on and sink a shaft.

Digging and sweating, sweating and digging, drilling, blasting and piling up the ore, they labored on, with little time or energy left to sample the life of Wine Harbor, which was the opposite of the mining town of the roaring American West, anyway, because there were neither saloons nor desperadoes, gun fights nor naughty women, and the whole population turned out for divine services every Sabbath.

When the shaft was two fathoms down they had mined two tons of quartz. Captain Pattillo bossed the carting of this to the wharf, where they shoveled their fortune into two small hired boats and sailed it to the crushing mill.

But after it was all over, and the glistering dust had been taken to the office, it was just enough to cover the crushing and the hire of the wagons and boats, with five dollars left over.

They took their profit, returned on board of the *Highland Lass* and had a meeting.

What a collection of long faces!

Now, said Jim, according to calculations that mess of ore should have been worth something over twenty-five hundred dollars, so the heft of the gold must have gone off with the washing. If the men wanted to stick with it, he was game until the fall. He would build them their bunkhouse on shore with the lumber on board, and he would go through with it and stake them to a regular mining operation as planned.

But when it came right down to it, nary a one of them was possessed and taken hold of by that wild-eyed, compulsive drive that marks the life-long gold hunter; they hemmed and hawed and debated their prospects, rubbed their blisters and aching muscles and decided, at last, to quit. Not without regrets, they packed up their gear, raised sail and arrived back in Gloucester, sadder and possibly wiser, on the twentieth of June, having been gone on their quest for the yellow stuff but two months.

Later, Captain Pattillo was interviewed by the *Cape Ann Advertiser* and allowed as how he might return after the mackerel season to resume work on his claim with a new and smaller company. True enough, the Nova Scotia diggings require considerable capital and hard work; he would have to blast out a shaft to a depth of thirty-five feet at least, at a cost of fifteen dollars a foot, just to reach the level where the old gaffers claimed the pay streak was. And once down there, who knew what you'd hit? Of course, some of the neighboring claims were producing as much as a hundred dollars a day.

"But there are more blanks than prizes, as a general thing," Jim mused, and any young feller who was getting a living some other way would be well advised to stay where he was and steer clear of the diggings.

Had it not been for the cargo of trading notions he had taken along, almost out of force of habit, Jim would have lost his shirt on his venture. As it was, he sold the lot before they returned, and after paying the duty and toting up a balance on the whole affair, he concluded wryly that his spell of gold fever had set him back four hundred dollars.

So he gave the *Highland Lass* to Ezra Turner to finish out the summer mackereling up to the North Bay, and it was the good old gold of the sea that recouped his fortunes. She cleared a thousand dollars for him, and Jim wound up that year 1862 six hundred to the good—not counting the five acres of Wine Harbor rock and rill, which he never quite got around to getting back to.

Fire

WHILE GRANT stubbornly stormed Vicksburg and Lee marched toward Gettysburg and defeat, a less epic episode of the Civil War was about to unfold, far from the sound of battle—on Georges Bank in the North Atlantic, to be exact, where the crews of several Gloucester schooners were placidly plying their lines early in the morning of June the twenty-second, 1863.

Had they delayed their departure from Cape Ann a few days, they would have been fishing with less complacency, keeping a nervous watch on the southern horizon for a black-hulled bark, tautly rigged, with light spars and carrying a boat on her starboard quarter. For they would have read in the newspapers all about the capture of the bark *Tacony,* 375 tons burthen, bound home for Philadelphia from Port Royal in ballast, by the tender of the marauding Confederate Steam Sloop *Florida,* broad off the Delaware Capes. This tender was the brig *Clarence,* an earlier prize of the *Florida,* and they transferred gun, ammunition and supplies to the *Tacony* after her capture, and then burned the brig, just to keep the Union cruisers guessing. Lieutenant Reed, United States Naval Academy Class of 1860, was put in command of the *Tacony* and was understood on the highest authority to have made specific inquiries concerning the precise whereabouts of the Gloucester fishing fleet.

All this the Georgesmen would have read in their papers, if they had cleared Gloucester but a few days later, along with the pointed suggestion that a dozen fast fishermen could easily overpower and capture the Confederate pirate if they were prepared for her, as she carried only one gun.

But they hadn't, and the black bark that was standing toward them a league or so to the southeast this morning, flying all canvas, was merely a friendly merchantman, and the Gloucestermen paid her no mind. Each concentrated on his hundred and fifty fathoms of steam-tarred cotton line trailing an eight-pound lead and double-hooked sling ding, tending bottom with the run of the tide (it took half an hour to haul in a pair of codfish), and the War of the Rebellion was the farthest thing from his thoughts.

When the *Tacony* bore southwest from the fleet she wore ship; a thick fog chose that moment to roll in, and she was lost from sight. And then, all of a sudden, the bark loomed out of the soup like an apparition, a cable's length from the schooner *Marengo.* She put over her boat, as if for an innocent gam; ten men jumped to the oars, and before they fairly knew what was up the Gloucestermen had been boarded on the high seas and informed by a pistol-waving officer that they were prisoners of the Confederacy. They had ten minutes, he declared, to collect their gear, get their dory over and head for the *Tacony* before their vessel was set afire and sunk.

This announcement had the desired effect on all but one of the crew, who evidently had a big codfish on the hook, for he continued to haul away at his line, cool as could be. Somewhat nonplussed, the officer told him to leave off and get moving.

"Oho!" cried the fisherman, turning to his captor. "I've got a fine fellow on–let's pull him in!"

The Southerner strode over to the rail in some exasperation, drew his cutlass and severed the tugging line with a whack.

Under the cover of the thick, drifting fog the privateer laid about her with all the relish of a fox loose in a chicken-coop. Although there was precedent for regarding fishermen as noncombatants to be generally unmolested during war, the raiders put the torch to the *Marengo;* then, in the same fashion, they materialized out of the fog and fired the *Ripple, Elizabeth Ann, Rufus Choate, Ada* and *Wanderer.* Whilst the pirate was licking her predatory chops by the light of her flaming victims, her commander was below in his cabin, entertaining their skippers with traditional southern hospitality and offering them commissions in the Confederate Navy. These overtures were declined, as one report described it, because "the patriotism of the New England fishermen was as firm as the rocks which form their rugged coast, and true to country were the hearts which beat in their manly bosoms."

Insulated in sight and sound from these events by the fog, the crew of the *Cadet* were busily tending their lines when it momentarily lifted and disclosed the sinister bark in the midst of her fiery depravations, still some distance off. As one man they jumped for the windlass and hove up anchor. There was no wind, but the fog mercifully shut in again, and thus shrouded they took to their dory and warped their schooner into a patch of air, where it breezed up and the *Cadet* escaped, sailing into Gloucester two days later with the news that the Rebel privateer *Tacony* had burned the defenseless fleet to the waterline and even now might be on the way to wreak havoc in the port itself.

Gloucester was pitched into a state of agitation just short of hysterical. The leaders of the fishing industry came together in emergency meeting, posted off delegations to the Governor and the Commodore of the Charlestown Naval Shipyard in Boston and a wire to Secretary of the Navy Gideon Welles demanding the protection of a cruiser. No warship was available, but the Navy did agree to commission and arm the fast schooners *Thomas Woodward, J. G. Curtis* and *William S. Baker* with thirty-two-pounders and fighting crews to cruise in search of the privateers. And the Army, in response to immense public pressure, began to dig an earthwork fort for the protection of the Harbor on the high land of the curmudgeon of Eastern Point, Farmer Thomas Niles.

These piratical outrages against the fleet aroused Jim's old fighting dander.

Having several years since abandoned the rigors of the Georges winter fishery to younger men, he remained at home after his bout with the gold fever and in January purchased a half interest in the ancient little Essex pinkey *Echo,* still sound as a dollar after thirty-seven years of hard working. That April he sold *Highland Lass,* his bread and butter for eleven years, and sentiment tugged at him as he watched her clear the Harbor for her new berth down East to Swan's Island. It was always hard to part with a good vessel that had served him faithfully, but a good offer was a good offer. Within a fortnight, however, he was the half-owner (four others sharing the other half) of the hundred-ton schooner *Rose Skerritt,* only five years old and a big hooker he had seen in action many a time and much admired. He bought her from Ripley Ropes of Salem, and was fitting her out for the North Bay when the *Tacony* struck.

Bolt a swivel gun to your deck and show your crew how to use it, the *Cape Ann Advertiser* advised Gloucester skippers: "The time has come for action and every vessel which sails under the Stars and Stripes should be able to show fight in case it is necessary."

Here was a clarion call. Jim sallied forth to the Charlestown Navy Yard and inveigled from the brass a license to fit out the *Rose Skerritt* as a letter of marque. Back in Gloucester he hired a six-pounder brass cannon and a copper powder magazine from Captain John Day which he insured for four hundred dollars, handing the policy to the owner to hold in case he should engage a Confederate privateer and come out on the losing side. He installed the gun, stowed aboard twenty-four rounds each of ball and grape, powder enough to blow all to kingdom come, issued cutlass and pistol to each of his crew and set sail with the fleet in July for the Bay St. Lawrence.

"I fitted out against anyone who should trouble me anyhow," he was accustomed to growl, "and I was determined, if necessary, to fight my way. If that bark had come across me, I would have done my best to take her. The fact is, I was all cut and dried for her!"

How he prayed for an encounter! How he paced his deck for days on end, straining his eyes at the horizon, yearning for the sight of an enemy sail!

Alas, no one troubled Captain Pattillo, as they had been wont to do in his palmier days. The crew of the *Tacony,* after freeing their burden of captured Gloucester fishermen, ran afoul of the peaceful people of Portland, Maine, while stealing one of their steamers, and were captured themselves. The tides of war carried the Confederate privateers to other waters, and Jim had to settle for seven hundred and fifty barrels of mackerel, taken with the greatest equanimity during two trips to the undisturbed expanses of the North Bay.

When he returned to Cape Ann, restless as ever, he sold the *Rose Skerritt* down to Provincetown and bought out the interest of his partner, Captain Jimmy McPhail, in their old pinkey *Echo.* Then, as a patriotic gesture, he agreed to serve on a committee of august citizens organized to recruit sailors for the United States Frigate *Niagara,* stationed temporarily in the Harbor for the purpose of filling out her complement from amongst the young hearties of the fishing fleet.

Ironically, the Navy was having particular trouble enlisting men at Gloucester. For generations the halls of Congress had rung with the oratory of the delegation from New England, swearing up and down that the bounty to the fishermen must be kept on, for were not the fisheries the "nursery of our seamen" and the "cradle of the Navy"? Yet the *Niagara* and all the blandishments of her officers had such a miserable time of it trying to arouse the patriotism of the Gloucestermen–who apparently preferred to take their chances in a wood ship on the Georges than on an ironclad at New Orleans–that they finally begged the people of the town to come to their aid. The citizens subscribed thirty thousand dollars for bounties to enlistees, each of whom was promised at least a hundred and fifty for his oath alone. In the end, by these combined efforts, sixty good men and true were induced to sign with the *Niagara* . . . and it was like pulling hen's teeth, everyone agreed.

Fall withered into winter, and the War dragged along in the bottom of its third year. The fishermen were out fighting their own first peculiar battles of the season on the Georges. A northwest gale moaned through the empty streets of Gloucester, hustled the dead dry leaves in a scurry around the corners, rattled the windows and whistled down the flues. It was knifing cold in the early morning of the eighteenth of February, 1864. The temperature was six below zero, and sensible gentry, including the Pattillos young and old, were in bed and asleep under a double layer of quilts.

At quarter to four Mrs. Harmon awoke to the smell of smoke. She got up and crossed to the window. From the rear of Andrew Elwell's tailor shop on the Harbor side of Front Street, the town's main road running east and west, she saw a spurt of flame. She swirled a shawl over her nightgown and dashed into the street, screaming. Two men leaning up the lane from Porter's Wharf against the wind called out—"What's the matter, woman?"

"Look!" Mrs. Harmon cried. "Fire! Fire! Elwell's—it's all in a blaze!"

By now it was.

"Fire!" the men took up the shout on the run—"Fire!" they yelled above the gale—"Fire! Fire! Fire in the Sawyer Block!"

Someone saw the leaping light reflected in a window and ran off to toll the alarm bell in the Town House. *Fire*—the cry was picked up and hurled through the streets from comer to corner and window to window. The bell clamored and clanged in the wind. The call firemen jumped from beds into clothes and sprinted to the engine houses, seized the tow ropes of their rattly-wheeled old pumpers and hose carriages and hook-and-ladders and hauled away over the cobbles and ice toward the red glow that could now be seen by all.

Quick as they were, they were too late. When Mechanic Number 1 reached the Sawyer Block the spark from the tailor shop had been bellowed by the gale into a furnace that entirely enveloped the wooden complex and reached through the roofs toward the structures to the east.

Scarcely more than a block to the leeward of the flames—though to the north side, on Hancock Street—the Pattillo families were out of bed and throwing on their clothes helter-skelter, as were hundreds of others in the neighborhood. Jim's house was up one from the corner of Front Street, vulnerable only if the fire should jump across the street against the wind. He and Christie hustled next door up the hill to Alex's home on the other side of their lot. Abby was bundling Laura May and Alexander in warm clothing, ready to move all to safety if they were told to evacuate, and taking mental inventory of her valuables.

A general alarm was sounded. Chief Engineer Pettingell perceived as soon as he arrived at the scene that his job was to save half the town from destruction in this gale, which by the grace of God was blowing toward the Harbor; he sent men clattering off on horseback over the frozen pre-dawn roads to summon help from all the rest of Cape Ann, and a telegraphed SOS to Salem where the nearest steam pumper was, a Portland.

Mechanic Number 1 pulled up short on Porter's Wharf. The men dropped the suction line into the Harbor, reeled the leading hose off the carriage and ran it up the lane toward the fire. Then they jumped to their positions at the brakes, ten at either end, seesawing up and down in a back-bending rhythm of sixty strokes a minute. When the first shift was breathless and beat, twenty more sprang to take their places, and on it went, round and round through the sixty men of the company. Mechanic contained the fire from spreading to the west but was helpless to stay its eastward rush through the waterfront and the southside stores on Front Street. Torrent Number 5 tried to hold it below Middle Street, that ran parallel to Front and above, while Hydraulion Number 4 was raced down to Steele's Wharf for water.

Valiant old Hydraulion! She was Gloucester's first suction pumper acquired after the big fire of 1830; her bully boys once braked a vertical stream six feet over the ball on the flagpole in front of her engine house, and that was a hundred and nineteen feet high. She gave it her all tonight, but the flames licked closer, blistering her fancy paint and trim; her loyal crew stuck to their brakes to the last and took to their heels only when she burned and plunged into the Harbor.

The same blast of heat drove a young mother and her child down onto a nearby wharf and trapped them there at the water's edge. The girl spied a tied-up dory, dropped into it with her little one and rowed across Harbor Cove to safety.

The cold biting their faces and watering their eyes, the whole night sky lit up before them, the firemen jogged at the tow ropes. (There was not a horse-drawn pumper on Cape Ann.) They came out from East Gloucester dragging Gloucester Number 6, from Lanesville with Lanesville Number 7, from Annisquam with Deluge Number 8, Votary Number 2 from Rockport and Pigeon Hill Engine from Pigeon Cove, six hard miles across the Cape. One by one they came in, cheered on by the gathering crowds, and bravely did they begin squirting their puny trickles into the laughing flames. And imagine it!–even two old hand tubs that had been collecting dust in retirement were awakened and creaked into battle–Cataract Number 2 and Extinguisher Number 3 (going on half a century)–and they had to be filled by a bucket brigade from the wells and cisterns along Middle Street.

Such a wicked cold it was that it froze the water in the pumps, which slowed and finally stopped the pistons. The desperate firemen commandeered barrels of rum, gin, whisky, wine, beer–any source of alcohol that came to hand–and dumped it into their machines most intemperately, most of it; but far from quenching the flames, this drenching with spirits made them lick ever closer, grinning and greedy.

Housewives stoked the stomachs of the exhausted fire-fighters with coffee and vittles, and there was "one good woman filled her oven with pies, to warm for the hardy firemen; if she had waited half an hour the fire king would have warmed them, and no thanks to the stove. As it was, she was obliged to leave them in the oven, and her house was soon in ruins."

Dawn crept up. Nobody noticed it. Sheets of flame flickered and crackled overhead. Roof after roof collapsed; floors crashed down and walls fell in with explosions of snapping timber from which blossomed incandescent showers of sparks and embers that were swept aloft by the gale. Mingled with the dark clouds of choking smoke, these hordes of arson drifted down, sizzled in the Harbor, set a thousand little fires in the sails and tarred rigging of the schooners, on the wharves and away across at East Gloucester Square, on the shingled roofs there and in the frozen fields.

The whole downtown was ablaze, out of control, like the end

of the world. Every street and structure in the path of the monster was a wild and eerie scene by the dancing hellfire that daubed buildings red as blood and made every window look aflame. Families in all states of dress ran in and out, carrying from their threatened or burning homes whatever came to mind. Over the din of it all rose hoarse shouts, curses, calling orders, screams, yells, the sobbing of children and the wail of infants, barking dogs, the whinny of the horse. Wagons loaded down with every foolish thing that could be thrown on them stood in the streets, and when horses couldn't be found, were pulled away by men and boys.

Alex Pattillo's dry goods store on Front Street, only a few doors to the east of the ashes of the Sawyer Block, went up in smoke. The fire surged across to the north side of the town's main thoroughfare in the very teeth of the gale, which had been feared the most, and burned its way along, picking up strength. It jumped Centre Street and attacked the bookstore and presses of the Procter Brothers, printers of the *Cape Ann Advertiser.* It was now a block–no more–to the windward of Hancock Street and coming with a roar. The Pattillos had cleared their families from their homes. Along with everything else, the street in front of their adjacent houses was barricaded on the one side by kegs of rum salvaged by someone not a Pattillo, and in grim opposition on the other by a breastwork of caskets rescued from Ben Ellery's Furniture and Coffin Store.

In a wild gamble to cheat the fire, Chief Pettingell ordered buildings in its path blown up. High explosives were stashed against the foundations of the Babson Block on the north side of Front Street. It crumpled, and the fire swept through the rubble, faster than ever. Across the street to the east they blew up the home of Captain Parsons with the same results.

On it crackled to the lower west side of Hancock Street, where the flames rose higher and higher, gathering strength to make the leap. And when everything there was furiously afire, they reached across the street on the back of the wind and caught the roof and siding of Captain Pattillo's house. The family stared, unseeing, fascinated, helpless, resigned, while everything was

The great Gloucester fire of February 18, 1864, leveled Front Street, as photographed three years earlier (page 283). The Pattillo houses were at the top of the street. (Frank Leslie's Illustrated Newspaper, *March 5, 1864)*

destroyed. Long before the still-flaming skeleton had toppled into the grave of its cellar the fire was gone, blazing through the next block. The south wall of Alex's house was scorched by the heat from his father's, but his slate roof and a dousing from a hand tub saved it

The great fire was still out of control when the first train from Boston, brakes screaming, jolted to a stop at the depot a few minutes after nine. Up on a flatcar, her buxom metalwork gleaming, resplendently painted, an amazon about to conquer, was Salem's Steam Pumper Number 2. Her company poured out of the coach, a ramp of planks was made and down she rolled, rumbling off into the choking cloud of smoke and ash. The sight of her, as her attendants stoked and got steam up, brought croaking cheers from the dog-tired fire-fighters of Cape Ann. Within minutes she was throwing a heroic stream into battle, her firebox glowing, smoke and sparks belching from her stack, her governor twirling and tooting, pistons clattering, puffing white in the frosty morning air.

She saved the day, did Salem Steamer Number 2, hurling such grand quantities of water into the inferno that she sucked the cistern dry; whereupon a hand tub was assigned to refill it for her from an artificial pond in a resident's back yard.

The tide was turning. They blew up Dr. Garland's house on Pleasant Street, and that stopped the fire from spreading to the north. Salem's Fire Queen soaked the brick Customs House, and the flames could go no farther to the east on the upper side of Front Street. They reached Vincent's Cove and drowned in the Harbor to the south.

Now, only on the lower side of Front Street did the fire still sweep onward to the east. So they brought up gunpowder and touched off Captain Low's elegant mansion in its path. The house was too tough for the first blast, and they placed another charge; this knocked it to the ground, bruising a fireman who didn't quite get out in time–the sole casualty of the fire. Beyond the shattered remains of Captain Low's pride and joy was a garden, and then the Mansfield house.

There in the garden the Salem Steamer and Votary Number 2 poured it on. Their streams coated the fruit trees and the Mansfield place with ice, while a bucket brigade of artillerymen from the fort at Eastern Point handed water up the stairs and out to soak the roof. There in the garden, at eleven o'clock that morning, the fire sank back and died.

28

For Fifty Years I Ploughed the Sea

> Good-bye, brothers! You were a good crowd. As good a crowd as ever fisted with wild cries the beating canvas of a heavy foresail, or tossing aloft, invisible in the night, gave back yell for yell to a westerly gale.
>
> —JOSEPH CONRAD, *THE NIGGER OF THE NARCISSUS*

DEPENDING ON THE vantage point, sundry explanations were advanced to account for the ruin which had blackened fifteen acres of the choicest real estate and destroyed a hundred and three buildings in the heart of old Gloucester.

Returning Georgesmen were abruptly confronted round Eastern Point by a smouldering and chimney-studded rubble where their hearts were accustomed to leap at the sight of the warmly beckoning home from the sea. They sailed fearfully up the Harbor under the misapprehension that while they were away fishing the town had been shelled by Confederate cruisers.

From the perspective of his pulpit the following Sunday, on the other hand, the Congregational minister, Mr. Thacher, gave his studied opinion that God visited the catastrophe on Gloucester "to rebuke us for our worldliness and impiety."

Mr. Skinner disagreed. Speaking in the church where American Universalism took root, he inclined to attribute the fire less to a heavenly judgment than to the wretched human habit of jamming wooden buildings together. Invest in more insurance and a couple of steam pumpers, he advised.

It was the Unitarian pastor, Mr. Rogers, who struck the brightest note of the day, calling his flock to rejoice with him that Gloucester "has not so many sinks of iniquity in it as it had a week ago."

The backward leap from effect to cause was not so very great for that respectable, church-going, money-making, temperate class of landowners who had been the largest losers by the conflagration, and in short order speculation that *rum did it* was rampant in the town (though no culprit worse than a faulty stove in Elwell's tailor shop was ever found). Angry Gloucester folks poking through the ruins of their homes and stores wanted a more vulnerable whipping boy than God Almighty. For nine years there had been a law on the books totally prohibiting the sale of liquor in Massachusetts, and for nine years the dries on Cape Ann and elsewhere had been trying to push their police to enforce it, with a total lack of success.

Now, while iron, ashes and tempers were hot, was the time to strike, and strike they did–the temperance forces–as reported on March the second in the *Gloucester Telegraph,* which, as every reader knew, was "Devoted to Patriotism, Sound Morals, Temperance, Literature and News," though not necessarily in that order:

> A petition has been in circulation and received quite a number of signatures asking for the appointment of a special police to enforce the prohibitory liquor laws. The Selectmen have appointed Messrs. James W. Pattillo, Curtis C. Cressy, Richard W. Ricker and Cyrus Haskell, as special police in accordance with the prayer of the petitioners. These gentlemen are to give their entire attention to this matter, and the petitioners hold themselves responsible for the expense if the town refuses to endorse the doings of the Selectmen. They were to commence operations yester-

day by notifying dealers in liquor that the law would be enforced. Owners of buildings are also to be notified that they must eject tenants in the rum business, or they will be indicted.

Cressy was a blacksmith and Ricker a laborer and both were already constables. Haskell was a temperance enthusiast. That great Pattillo, who had missed being elected a constable by sixteen votes a month earlier, appears to have been the chief of this burly troop, which he led into battle against the bootleggers with his accustomed energy and directness. They were heartily endorsed by the Town Meeting, and their pay was set at fifty dollars a month. After driving the more blatant of the liquor sellers into at least an apparent suspension of business, they made the rounds of the apothecaries with the warning that they, too, must "discontinue the sale of ardent spirits on their premises."

Within a fortnight the *Telegraph* could state emphatically that the rum shops had been closed. Strange, though, that the number of drunks in the streets remained undiminished . . . Captain Pattillo and his stalwarts were enjoined that they must be vigilant in their duties indeed, particularly against midnight carousels in certain private homes where rum was undoubtedly being dispensed.

If they were ever overvigilant, it was never clearly established. They hailed one John Shaw into Police Court and charged him with keeping a liquor nuisance. He was found guilty. In due course he sued the four of them for a thousand dollars, alleging that they broke down the door of his house during the night, beat him up and dragged him off to the lockup for twenty-four hours. When the suit came up for trial in Salem, however, Shaw withdrew it.

March and April went along this way. The rumfighters snooped and sniffed, stole through the streets and stalked the walks of the waterfront. At most sessions of the Police Court they produced for Justice Davis some culprit or other to be fined and perhaps sentenced to a brief purgative stint in the House of Correction. It was noteworthy that not a few of the defendants were represented by the lawyer for the big out-of-town liquor dealers' lobby, who appealed their cases to the Superior Court which would be sitting up to Newburyport in May.

Gloucester awoke to the balmy breezes of spring. The buds burst, the birds billed, the bushes blossomed, the bees buzzed, the belles bloomed, the beer bocked and bungs banged as barrelled booze broke all bounds. Putting down rum, to the frustration of the temperance police, was like bailing out the Harbor with a dip net. Jim was disgusted with the whole business and hankered to get back to sea. The fact is that he was quarter owner of a new schooner building on the stocks of Cyrus Burnham at Salisbury Point, above and across from Newburyport on the Merrimack River. This handsome clipper of a hundred and five tons was shaping up, Jim had the spring fever, and his enthusiasm for law enforcement diminished with every crack of the caulking beetles that echoed deliciously through the mew of the gulls across Gloucester Harbor.

Pattillo, Haskell and sailmaker Sam Colby were elected constables at Town Meeting on the sixth of May. In a fortnight they traveled to Newburyport to testify against sixteen of the rum sellers who had appealed to the Superior Court. Jim could scarcely wait to get it over and done with. He took Colby and Tom Hardy, another crony, over to Cy Burnham's before the trial, and they brought the new schooner, launched, sparred and rigged but unnamed, down river to Captain Charley Lunt's wharf at Newburyport, where they tied up.

Next day they took the stand and gave their solemn testimony about the rum doings in Gloucester. Some of the defendants were convicted and fined, others were acquitted, and then all dispersed. Pattillo, Colby and Hardy booked their names at a waterfront hotel for the night, intending to take the schooner to Cape Ann in the morning.

After a good supper, Colby and Hardy strolled off for a look at the town, and Jim walked out on the piazza, settled into a rocking chair and hauled out his pipe to have a smoke and take in the air of a May evening before the sun went down. He had lit up and was surveying his surroundings when a rough-appearing fellow ambled out from the lobby and inquired if he was one of the special policemen from Gloucester.

Jim slowly withdrew his pipe from his mouth and stared up at this intrusion.

"I am," said he–"instead of a better."

"Hmmm," replied the fellow, looking at him curiously from behind his whiskers. A pause–"And how many men like you d'ye spose it would take to put down rum drinking in Gloucester?"

Constable Pattillo squinted, and his long face creased into a whimsical smile. He rocked back in his chair.

"How many? Why, twelve thousand I'd say, because that's the number of the inhabitants. But if they were all like me there'd be no rum drinking in Gloucester, I'll warrant you that!"

Three waterfront characters sauntering up the street with their hands in their pockets had stopped in front of the hotel and were listening casually to this exchange. Jim's piazza mate winked at them, a signal the great captain did not fail to mark, then leaned over toward him and sneered through his dirty brush:

"Well, mister, you've been spotted, I'll tell you, and I wouldn't make no plans for a long life!"

The object of this warning calmly continued to rock back and forth in his chair, somewhat obscured behind a cloud of pipe smoke. For a few moments the only sound to break the early evening quiet was the regular squeak of the rocker over a loose board in the porch floor. Then he rumbled:

"Oh, I don't know about that, Jack. I reckon I'll live as long as Tantra Bogus, and he lived till he died, and I expect to do about the same."

By this time more ruffians had made their appearance by twos and threes from various quarters, and they joined the bunch in the street. Waxing bolder, the bearded spotter took a step back, threw out his chest and declared loudly that he knew of little men weighing only a hundred and fifty pounds who could flog the big cop from Gloucester all to pieces.

Jim brought the rocker up short and stared again at Mr. Whiskers. In a voice for all to hear, he boomed:

"You're a great talker, friend, and I don't doubt but what there are such men around, because I'm not a fighting man just at the present time. But I can manage if there is any necessity for it. Now you can talk as much as you've a mind to–I know your game–only don't put a hand on me. . . . If you do, you'll rue the day."

Wordlessly the gang in the street were peeling off their jackets, as if they had a matter of everyday business to attend to. Jim counted eighteen of them; no doubt they had been hired by the rum party to give the temperance police from Gloucester a thrashing, and with Colby and Hardy off somewheres, it made their job all the easier . . . ah well. He rose from his rocking chair, knocked the ashes out of his pipe and stuck it in his pocket. He took off his coat, tossed it in the seat and strode to the edge of the piazza, rolling up his shirtsleeves. With shoulders the breadth of a mackerel barrel and arms as big around as a leg o' mutton, he was a figure to make a person think twice. Grasping the railing with his huge hands, he leaned over it and addressed the gathering as follows:

"All right, you vagabonds! You can pull off your jackets, and you can put 'em back on again, and it'll be a sorry day for any one of you lays a hand on me!"

They hesitated . . . and that was when Captain Charley Lunt, who had heard what was going on, came running up from his wharf where Jim had the schooner. Lunt was a big man in Newburyport, and everybody knew him.

"For God's sake, what are you men doing?" he yelled, coming between them and their intended victim up on the porch. "Put your coats on and go about your business and have nothing to do with this man. If you knew Jim Pattillo a particle as well as I do, you'd steer clear of him. He is the strongest man I've ever seen or heard of, and if you tangle with him, I tell you he will knock in the whole lot of you, piece by piece or all at once. Go on, go on–break it up!"

Captain Charley had always been one person to take at his word, as the men knew–and not to be crossed, either. They picked up their jackets and walked off.

The next morning Officer Pattillo and his cohorts sailed out the Merrimack, by the dunes of Plum Island and skirted Cape

Ann into Gloucester Harbor. And when he got home, Jim resigned from the constabulary, informing the town that he had better things to do than putting down rum selling, for it couldn't be done; and besides, all they wanted was the money from the fines anyhow. His new vessel he named *Oliver Cromwell* in keeping with his late burst of militant puritanism, although this must have caused his Scottish ancestors to rotate in their graves.

Jim fitted out his newest command as a letter of marque, arming her with the weapons from the *Rose Skerritt,* and departed for the Gulf of St. Lawrence at his usual time. The week after the Fourth he stopped at Halifax for salt, and while it was being loaded quite a crowd of Haligonians drifted down to the wharf to inspect the six-pounder. The way Jim liked to tell it, the folks there tipped off the Rebel cruisers when they came into Halifax not long afterwards that the Cape Ann fishermen were all fitted out for them and bristling with arms, and if the Confederates attempted to chase them and tackled one, it would be like going into a hornet's nest. So nary an enemy warship entered the North Bay the whole time they were there, and he enjoyed thinking it was all because the *Oliver Cromwell* had put in for salt and showed off her brass six-pounder, the only one in the fleet.

It was a good season, that summer in the Bay, the best he had ever seen fishing. The *Cromwell* made only one trip but shipped home twice. Jim carried a big crew of sixteen, mostly young fellows hoping to escape the draft, though they needn't have worried because the volunteers filled Gloucester's quota that year after all. Nevertheless, to avoid the chance of losing his crew in mid-season, he landed three hundred and thirty barrels of mackerel at Maguire's in the Gut of Canso, to be freighted back to Gloucester by a Novie coaster. Then they sailed back into St. George's Bay and hooked two hundred and thirty more in the waters around Antigonish, landed that load and returned once again and caught three hundred and eighty which they took back with them to Cape Ann. Close on to a thousand barrels that made, at thirty dollars for number ones, which was the top price for mackerel in thirty-four years. The Gloucester inspection was the biggest in the records of the fishery—a hundred and fifty-five thousand barrels—and that didn't include many more thousand that were sold out of pickle for packing at other ports. There was a great demand for fish on both sides of the War; prices leaped, and many a barrel of Gloucester mackerel ran the Union blockade into the Confederacy. The fishermen prospered . . . to the extent that fishermen ever do.

Jim and his co-owners sold the *Oliver Cromwell* down to Nantucket in March. The end of the Civil War now was certain, the outcome sure, only a matter of time and place. Grant took Richmond, breaking the back of the Confederacy, and on April ninth of 1865 accepted Lee's surrender at Appomattox Court House. During those four endless years of the War, Gloucester had lost thirty-six of her soldiers killed in battle, but she had sacrificed two hundred and fifty-eight of her fishermen to the enemy she could never come to terms with.

Two more days, and President Lincoln lay dead of the assassin's bullet.

April nineteenth was for mourning. The town was funereal. Every store along rebuilding Front Street was closed and draped in black. As if presciently, Alex Pattillo had received a stock of mourning goods the week before the assassination and had been selling crepe by the fathom from his new establishment. Every home in Gloucester was curtained with the cloth of death. Most folks kept pretty much to their houses, preparing themselves for the noon funeral service in the Methodist Church. It was no shame for hard men of the sea to join the women in crying out loud this day. Old Abe, who had brought the country through the darkness and into light again, was gone forever.

Every flag was supposed to be at half-mast high, on every staff and every vessel, at the order of the Selectmen. At sunrise, however, it was observed that several *coppery* citizens had failed to conform to this directive. Their political views had been the cause of some muttering among the home front warriors, and only the greatest restraint the previous day had averted the application of a coat of tar and feathers to a returned Georgesman rumored to have expressed the wish that thirty more like the martyred President might be shot. "The time had arrived," as one observer phrased it, "when forbearance with these men ceased to be a virtue."

A dawn gathering of patriots determined to right matters. Word of their intentions flew through the town, and in no time eight hundred mourners in search of an emotional outlet had assembled. First they visited George Steele, Jr., at his home^yelling, whistling, catcalling and cursing–and took him down to his wharf to raise the flags on his vessels with his own hands. They moved on to the wharf of Epes Porter, where they caught hold of him, wrapped him in a flag from head to foot and forced him to kiss its folds. Thomas Hall, forewarned by this time, was on the roof of his net and twine loft, hoisting away, and at the direction of the throng he saluted the colors vigorously, as did the merchants next called on.

But when the home of John Wheeler was reached up on Washington Street, this aged resident, who had two sons in the War, refused to perform any such nonsense, whereupon the angry crowd seized and trundled the feeble old man on a rail through the streets to the Customs House.

It was midday now, and the church bells were tolling for the murdered President in Gloucester and in ten thousand towns. The crowd had become an inflamed mob, and the mob had lost its head to a gang of half-drunk toughs. What had started out as a popular demonstration against a few scapegoats was turning into a riot. Much alarmed, Addison Gilbert, the Chairman of the Selectmen, mounted the steps of the Customs House and implored his fellow citizens to do nothing further to shame the town on this of all days. His cool head prevailed, and they broke up.

When he disposed of his share in the *Oliver Cromwell* Jim at the same time sold a half interest in his old pinkey *Echo* and made plans to build another new schooner, this time electing to try out the shipwrights of George Christenson in Kennebunkport, Maine. Planked, planed, caulked and painted, she plowed into the Kennebunk River on the high course tide of the eighth of July.

Jim gave the carpenters good business this year, because at the very same time they were framing in the house he was erecting over the charred celler hole on Hancock Street.

Scotland he named this vessel. She was a quarter his, following his recent habit of dividing his eggs among several baskets, and the heft of the wharfside opinion in Gloucester pronounced her a fine, modern, able-looking hooker in the Pattillo tradition. By the end of July he was off to the North Bay in her; and by the first of November he was back home and glad enough to hole in for the winter by the hearth in his new house.

Far from the spitting gale and pitching deck of the North Atlantic himself that frost-bitten January of 1866, Jim sent the *Scotland* under Captain Blair off with the herring fleet to Newfoundland, and poor work they made of it, back in March with thin fares. It was a month of sour news for all of Gloucester, in fact. First the United States terminated the Reciprocity Treaty with England; restoration of the old shore fishing rights on the Provincial coasts had been more than offset by the loss of duty on Canadian imports . . . besides which, it was a chance to rap Canada for her friendliness to the South during the War. Although the British allowed American vessels to continue fishing inside of three miles if they bought a license, they raised the fees so high that few would take them out. Then, in July, the Congress finally repealed the old bounty on codfish.

An old-timer could see the writing on the wall. Every season another skipper or two succumbed to the purse seine, and there was no doubt that within a few years this way of capturing a school of mackerel in one set of the net would make jigging a thing of the past. There were those who shook their heads over the prospect. Seining was a hard man's work; where would the youngsters find sites to learn the business, as they did now on board of the hookers, starting at ten or twelve years old? The handline fishery on Georges was the same as ever, but the old bankers had gone by the board, and now there was a great fleet lighting out from Gloucester for the banks—for Brown's, Le Have, Green, Banquereau, Western, St. Peter's and the Grand Bank and all up that way—with nests of dories and tubs of trawls on deck,

Probably the earliest photograph of Gloucester Harbor, credited to William Elwell in 1876, not long after Captain Pattillo's retirement from the sea. It looks across Harbor Cove from the Belmont House hotel on what has been renamed Main from the gutted Front Street, and over the Fort section to Ten Pound Island beyond and Eastern Point in the distance. (Cape Ann Historical Association)

setting miles of line and thousands of hooks for the codfish and halibut, where one man before took a half hour to haul a big one aboard. Seining and dory trawling were the way of the future, and the future was passing into the hands of the younger men.

Jim made two trips mackereling to the North Bay that summer and fall, and in the course of the second one he turned sixty. In the spring of 1867 he sold out his half interest in the *Echo.* Instead of taking the *Scotland* to the Bay St. Lawrence come July, he went fresh halibutting in her on the new-found grounds up on Western, or what some called Sable Island Bank, off to the eastward of Novie, and St. Peter's Bank south of St. Pierre and Miquelon, the French islands. All was peaceful now.

After this, he stayed ashore for the space of a year, giving the *Scotland* to Captain Bartlett to fish for him. He was wearying of the sea.

Fifty years back to the month from this summer of 1868 Jimmy Pattillo, all of eleven years old and an overgrown colt of a kid, went off on his first trip coasting to Halifax with brother Tom. He had been at it ever since, without ever the loss of a man or a vessel at sea. The anniversary would not pass unnoticed.

On that grand early autumn morning of 1868, Captain Pattillo took the helm of the *Scotland*, and while she slammed out around Ten Pound Island in the fresh west-southwest breeze off the land, full and by, he sent them forward and aloft to break out flying jib and gaff topsails. Between the rusty ledges and the tucked-in beaches of the greatest fishing port in the world he held her, steering by the wind, bracing his legs on the canted deck. He could see the spray off the lee bow and hear the wake gurgle by her quarters, and he watched for the wind to head round more into the southwest when they worked out between Muscle Point and Round Rock Shoal with the buoy on it.

Clear of the end of Dog Bar, he sang out to slack off sheets and eased her helm. The sails spread off to port, and she stood more upright running before it, keeping up with the wind so that it was all still and warm in the sun on deck, past Eastern Point and its guardian light.

Stand by to jibe! And the men jumped again to the sheets. *Haul aft on your foresheet and jibe the foresail!* Two of the crew brought the sheet taut with a half turn, and he put up the wheel a spoke. As the schooner swung off ever so slightly, the wind caught the big sail aback, the boom flipped over, and it filled away to the starboard while the men slacked off the sheet to trim. *Unhook your boom tackle and gather aft on your mainsheet!* The great sail inch by inch came inboard, tug on tug, blocks screeching as the sheet rove through, and when it was in to his satisfaction, he bawled out, *Take a turn with your main sheet!* and they belayed to the bitt with a round turn and held on. He put up his helm some more . . . easy . . . and held it, and she wore around. The vast stretch of the mainsail for a moment hung slack; then the air caught the peak and swung the gaff, and the rest followed and bellied out to starboard with the wind kicking full across from the opposite quarter. The great figure at the wheel boomed out in quick succession: *Slack off your mainsheet! Hook on the boom tackle! Draw away your jibs!*

And the *Scotland* went pounding along off the back shore of the Point by Brace's Cove and Bass Rocks to take her departure for the eastward from the twin lights of Thacher's Island. How many times had he dropped Cape Ann astern this way since he came there that fugitive day so long ago?

They hooked four hundred and fifty barrels of mackerel up between Prince Edward Island and the Magdalens, and when the Arctic winds came off the Labrador coast, scuffing up the whitecaps and making the men break out their monkey jackets and mufflers, the *Scotland* joined the fleet bound home.

It was Friday the thirteenth of November, 1868—that was the day Jim brought his schooner back round Eastern Point and down the long reach of Gloucester Harbor to rest at her berth.

Another winter was setting in. Fifty years was a good round number . . . and it was long enough. He sold the *Scotland* before Christmas and retired from the sea.

And Now I Plough the Land

SOMETHING IN GLOUCESTER was forever catching fire. Eighteen months after they dedicated the new brick and red granite Town Hall with a speech by General Ben Butler and a fancy dress ball put on by the Steam Fire Association, it burned.

Somebody had tossed a match in a spittoon full of sawdust. It smouldered all night and burst into flame at sunrise on the sixteenth of May, 1869. The members of the Association had another ball trying to put it out, but they were too late on the scene. Within an hour the roof fell in. As thousands watched, the flames reached up and caught the wooden steeple on the tower. North, south, east and west in turn, the grand dials of the magnificent Howard clock given the town by Samuel Sawyer fell in, all blazing, followed finally by the ponderous works when the clock deck gave way, crashing down through the inside of the tower, sending up a farewell puff of black smoke and sparks.

It was a most exciting conflagration. The town's only irreparable loss was the pair of panoramic views of the Harbor painted by her recently deceased native son, Fitz Hugh Lane, already regarded as one of America's great marine artists.

Rebuild at once–that was the unanimous wish of the citizens–and while the Building Committee pondered plans for an even finer edifice to rise from the ashes on Dale Avenue, a de facto sidewalk committee of bystanders, oldsters, loungers, passersby, neighborhood folks and fishermen retired or between trips came to order promptly every morning to urge on the workmen, criticize their wrecking methods and sometimes even to help. The unofficial chairman, oracle, technical adviser and sage of this group was the recently retired Captain Pattillo, who resided but a block away and now had unlimited time on his hands for such civic responsibilities.

So conscientiously did this corps of sidewalk superintendents muster on the fringes of the job every morning during those warm days of early June that the de jure Building Committee was advised by the *Cape Ann Advertiser* to erect seats, provide an awning and some umbrellas, and a stand from which to dispense cool temperance drinks to the parched observers.

While the charred walls crumbled under the picks and sledges of the workmen, the tower's brick bastion remained untouched. Each day this eighty-foot challenge gained prominence and lost stability as the rest fell away, until the temptation exceeded all bounds. It was on a Friday—the eleventh of June to be exact—that the sidewalk committee succumbed at last. By jingo, they would pull it down themselves after the regular men went home for the day!

Chairman Pattillo had all organized and knew just how he was going about it. One lieutenant was sent off for fifty fathoms of three-inch Manila, another to fetch a codline and a two-pound lead sinker. Jim bent one end of the line to the sinker, the other to the rope, and off with his jacket.

"Stand clear!" he roared out. "Give me the room to swing a cat here, and we'll see what we can do!"

Of course the word had gone out, and a goodly crowd was on the grounds, for most Gloucester people had heard tales of Captain Pattillo's giant strength, and legends of his prowess, but had never seen him in action. Still and all . . . the old dog *was* sixty-two . . . been away from the sea a while . . . the tower up there *was* eighty feet high . . . a two-pound weight . . . hmmm. Frankly, not a soul believed the Captain or any other man alive could do it.

Jim cocked an eye at the ragged ramparts away above him, hiked up his breeches, grasped his line and swung it round and round, faster and faster till the lead was a whistling, whirling circular blur at the end of it, and with a final grunting heave, let go. Up, up, up it soared, the twine trailing off behind, all heads tilting back, tonsils on display. Clear over the top of the tower it flew, to an *ahhh* and an *ohhh* from the crowd on the ground, and then a burst of applause and cheers galore as the weight thumped out of sight over the other side, and all came to a realization of what they had seen.

Some almost doubted their senses, reported the *Advertiser*—"We don't believe there is another man in town who can do it."

What followed then was described by the man from the *Telegraph.* They hauled the rope over the tower with the fishline and knotted it around, and now came the turn of the members of the sidewalk committee to be the "recipients of some extra compensation not put down in the contract . . . Some twenty or thirty of the committee took hold of the rope to see which was the strongest. The tower, supposed to be the weakest, proved the strongest, and wouldn't budge. The sidewalk committee wouldn't give it up so, and gave another pull all together; consequently something must give way, and it proved to be the rope. The tower remained standing, but the committee didn't, and there the laugh came in. The extra compensation was the dust carried away on the backs of the committee."

Chairman Pattillo was not a man to be put down so easily, however. He brushed himself off and confabbed with his bunch, and they concluded to bide their time until the base of their objective had been a trifle further weakened.

Ten days passed, and they were ready to strike again, as chronicled by the *Telegraph:*

> After a full consultation the committee adjourned to meet upon the grounds at 7 P.M. The chairman of the subcommittee on heaving the lead was promptly on hand, and a line was thrown over the top of the tower. The chairman of the rallying committee was soon on the ground, and a large and enthusiastic body of citizens were ready and anxious to man the ropes. It appeared almost certain that if no

The ruins of Gloucester's town hall–and its tower, brought down by the mighty Jim Pattillo's final fling. (Cape Ann Historical Association)

> mechanical obstacle was interposed, the tower would come down. . . . Fortunately however for those who dislike this rapid and summary method of doing work, an injunction was served upon the committee, and thus the tower continued standing.

In due course the workmen took it down, and no thanks to Chairman Pattillo, whose feat of twice heaving a two-pound lead over an eighty-foot tower was the talk, if not of the town, of all those who admired such performances.

Came and went a year, and in the spring of 1870, having sold his new house on Hancock Street to Captain Procter, Jim moved lock, stock and barrel, bag and baggage, down to a nine-acre farm he had bought in the somnolent inland village of North

Stoughton. The place was bucolically located fifteen miles due south of Boston on the old Taunton Turnpike.

Whatever possessed him to make this shift–forsaking the sea-smashed shores of Cape Ann, home and haven for thirty-six years, all the places he knew like the back of his hand? For what did he leave the houseful of Pattillos next door, and the wharves, the ups and downs of the tides and the comings and goings of the vessels, the endless talk of where the fish were and where they weren't? And where would he share a mind's eye view of the old days with the cronies, puffing away on the pipe in the sun, spitting in the dock . . . "Now Jack, d'ye mind that time on the Georges in the spring o' forty-two . . . ?"

It was said that he left Gloucester for his wife's health–for Christie's sake (though the salt breezes that waft across Cape Ann are the world's most bracing tonic). Maybe at sixty-four he wanted more from the rest of his life than to finish it out puffing on his pipe in the sun, expectorating in the Harbor. He had notions of becoming a gentleman farmer.

And he had other notions, too. He took his Bible literally, and nothing in it more to heart than the cheerless counsel of Moses that the days of our years are threescore years and ten. It was intended that he should die when he reached seventy, he believed with all his heart and soul, and so he divided his savings into equal parts, one for each year that remained to him, the idea being to leave the slate (and apparently poor Christie, who was twenty years younger) clean when he went. How better to live frugally than in North Stoughton, where there was nothing to spend his money on anyway?

The custom of the folks there of voting dry every year was perhaps another attraction to the totally abstinent Captain Pattillo, and though rum-selling persisted in a diffident sort of way, it was as nothing compared to the fierce grogging that went on in Gloucester, where the drunks had staggered up and down in front of his house most every evening of the week, making the walls ring with their revelries and reminding the old rascal in him too keenly of the days and nights of his youth.

Life in the rustic New England countryside of North

Stoughton had compensations for a former seafaring man whose stormy years were in back of him and who sought only to occupy the balance of his allotted span in earthy pursuits, far removed from Georges Bank. In short, as one of his neighbors mused, "North Stoughton may be a little one horse place, but it is bound to grow. We are entirely free from all kinds of nuisances, except it be from half a hundred stray dogs, more or less. We have two good general stores, church, post office, manufacturing shop, school, public hall, barber shop, livery and sale stable, no doctor, lawyer, millionaire or other loafers, not that we wish to insinuate for a moment that all doctors and lawyers are loafers, but they would be while here from sheer necessity. We have in fact nearly all the advantages of city life, and none of its disadvantages."

Unfortunately there was not a Baptist church in Stoughton, and the Pattillos faithfully maintained their connections with their old Gloucester parish. Yet other places of worship in nearby towns were happy to welcome an upright, retired fishing captain who had turned to the mother soil, if only in a modest way, and Jim took sufficient pleasure in prefacing his testimonials at prayer meeting with the gruff introduction: "For fifty years I ploughed the sea, and now I plough the land. . . ."

So neither ice, snow, gales of wind, wild horses nor the incontrovertible fact that the days of his years were six months past threescore and ten could have kept Captain Pattillo away from Boston when the world-famous evangelist team of Moody and Sankey launched into a mission there that was to last thirteen weeks and set all of staid old New England on its ear. The Tabernacle seating six thousand, had been built especially for this campaign; it sprawled splendiferously on the extension of Tremont Street between Berkeley and Clarendon, and ninety churches cooperated to keep it filled. There was some concern over how Boston would react to these embarrassingly effective savers of souls, but every anxiety of the sponsors vanished on that frosty twenty-eighth of January, the year of our Lord 1877 and the day of the opening.

Not once but time and time again did Jim catch the train into Boston to join the immense throngs in the Tabernacle. He was mightily moved by the magic of the powerful Dwight L. Moody, his prophet's beard quivering with fervor, piercing to the middle of a man's soul with his earthy message of salvation or be damned And it was a hard heart that failed to melt under the spell of Ira D. Sankey, truly senatorial in his mutton-chop whiskers, ringing out the old hymns in the spirit-rending baritone that had brought half the world to its knees.

"A man asked me," cried Moody one night, "if I could quote Scripture against the use of tobacco! I replied, no, I can give you no verses in the Bible against the habit of smoking, but I can give you a verse in favor of it–'He that is filthy, let him be filthy still!'"

And at the after meeting for inquirers, up thumped John MacDonald to the front to tell of his experience–a man Jim knew personally to have been a hard drinker and heavy smoker like himself. The Lord had taken away his appetite for rum and tobacco! shouted John MacDonald before the multitude, and he had no more desire for either! Praise the Lord!

So the Lord can do the same for me, thought Jim.

Home again, he filled his pipe and placed it on the mantel over the fireplace where he could see it every time he passed through the parlor. He dropped down on one knee and prayed God to take away his appetite for smoking after fifty years of it. From that day on, his pipe never left its place.

Two years after Captain Pattillo made his final trip in the *Scotland,* the United States and Great Britain were at it again over that old fishbone of contention between them: the Canadian three-mile limit. After Uncle Sam abrogated the Reciprocity Treaty in 1866, John Bull allowed the Yankee hookers to continue fishing inside the limit by license, a privilege they increasingly evaded as the fees mounted until 1870, when England, exasperated, stopped licensing and started seizing. In 1871 the two countries were back at the bargaining table. This time the result was the Treaty of Washington, to be effective in 1873, covering among other matters the fisheries question and restoring, in essence, the mutual inshore fishing rights and free trade in fish that prevailed under Reciprocity. It was further agreed that a joint commission should be appointed to convene in Halifax for the purpose of fixing how much, if any, compensation should be paid Britain by the United States for the right to fish inshore during the twelve-year term of the Treaty, over and above the value to England of American markets for Canadian-caught fish.

The crux of the issue was the value to the Yanks of the inshore mackerel fishery in the Gulf of St. Lawrence. England asked upwards of fifteen million dollars; America claimed free admission of Provincial fish alone offset the privilege of taking mackerel in Canadian territorial waters. Hundreds of witnesses, most of them fishermen, were primed and trundled up to Halifax by both sides, and hundreds more affidavits were taken by traveling investigators, as the hearings in the Legislative Council Chamber wore on through the summer of 1877. The President of the Commission was its neutral member, His Excellency Monsieur Maurice Delfosse, Envoy Extraordinary and Minister Plenipotentiary of His Majesty the King of the Belgians at Washington. The case for the United States was in the hands of Judge Dwight B. Foster, with the assistance of W. H. Trescott and that eminent lawyer and author of *Two Years Before the Mast,* Richard Henry Dana, Jr.

Among the boatloads of fishermen from down East, Cape Cod and Cape Ann who made the trip to Halifax at their government's expense–all prepared to vouch for the worthlessness of the North Bay inshore mackerel fishery–was Captain James William Pattillo, retired mariner, just turned seventy-one, of North Stoughton, Massachusetts. His turn came on the seventeenth of October. He took his place and was sworn to tell the truth before the august body that he faced.

Jim harked back over his thirty years as a mackerel hooker and poured forth a torrent of dates, places, names, numbers of barrels and where caught, prices, natural history, wit, wisdom, fishing methodology and rousing accounts of his encounters with Provincial officials–all of which brought him back to testify the next day, to the fascination of his hearers. It occupied nineteen of the liveliest pages of an interminable transcript and caused Her

Majesty's Counsel from New Brunswick, Mr. S. R. Thomson, to doubt out loud the absolute accuracy of the witness's admittedly "exceedingly retentive" memory in the light of his statement that every last one of his records of a lifetime had burned with his house in Gloucester's Great Fire of 1864.

This caustic insinuation by the lawyer for the opposition nettled the Yankee captain, and he shot back with some heat that he could remember what happened forty or fifty years ago better than yesterday, and furthermore (thundering out with the old fire) "I have tried to overhaul my memory the best I could, and I have done the best I could! If anybody could do it any better, I would like to have him try it! I have done the best I could, and if I have done wrong, I have not intended it! I would not lie for the Commission, whether they give fifteen millions or not!"

He had hooked no more than ten per cent of his fares over the years inside the limit, Jim supposed, and as for the advantage of fishing within three miles of the Canadian shore–"I would only go inshore to make harbors and dress fish. I would not give a snap of my fingers for the inshore fisheries. When licenses cost fifty cents a ton I would not pay it. I would rather fish in my own waters, because I could do better there."

Then why did the witness go back to the Bay year after year?

"Well, there was just one principle on which we used mostly to go to the Bay. The fact is that when we shipped a crew at Cape Cod, after we had been off for a fortnight or three weeks on our shore, men would leave the vessel. But when we got a crew and came to North Bay, they had to stay on board. There was then no back door to crawl out of. This was one of the chief reasons for coming to the Bay, as we then had no trouble in the shipping of hands, good, bad or indifferent. But when we were down on our shore, men would go off, and we would have to secure new hands. Men would think they might do better, and they would go where the highliner was, and we were then under the necessity of supplying their places. Another thing was that by going to the Bay we got clear of the fog. On our coast there is a great deal of fog, but when we reach North Bay we get clear of it."

Mr. Thomson in his cross-examination indicated that he, for

one, remained unconvinced that these were Captain Pattillo's only reasons for visiting the Gulf of St. Lawrence so perennially.

The broad-shouldered old captain was at last released from the stand and departed Halifax for his adopted country, having done his duty by her as he saw it. Before they were through, however, the American lawyers wished they had never heard of him, although in truth it must be allowed that his testimony probably did not affect the outcome of the hearings in the least.

In the course of his long closing argument for the United States two weeks later, Mr. Dana alluded to the Provincial cutters of the old days "and that whole tribe of harpies that line the coast, like so many wreckmen, ready to seize upon any vessel and take it into port and divide the plunder"—a reference to the late Captain Darby much resented by Mr. Thomson. But then the author in the lawyer burst all bounds:

"We did not suffer so much from the regular navy. But the Provincial officers, wearing for the first time in their lives shoulderstraps and put in command of a vessel, 'dressed in a little brief authority, played such fantastic tricks before heaven' as might at any moment, but that it was averted by good fortune, have plunged the two countries into war.

"Why, that conflict between Pattillo and Bigelow amused us at the time, but I think Your Honors were struck with the fact that as Pattillo escaped, was pursued, and the shots fired by his pursuers passed through his sail and tore away part of his mast and entered the hull—if they had shed a drop of American blood it might 'the multitudinous seas incarnadine' in war.

"Why, people do not go to war solely for interest, but for honor, and everyone felt relieved, drew a freer breath, when he learned that no such fatal result followed."

This was just the kind of rhetoric Mr. Thomson was waiting for, and he pounced on it gleefully during his final argument in behalf of Her Britannic Majesty:

"We have very strong language used in reference to Mr. Pattillo, and it has been said that if a portion of his blood had been shed the seas would probably have been 'incarnadined.' But what is Pattillo's own statement?

"A curious subject was Mr. Pattillo to go to war about. What kind of a character he was when young I know not. But some person told me that he had experienced religion before he came into this court. I thought that if he had, the Old Man was not entirely crucified in him when he gave his evidence there.

"What did he tell you? That he was a Nova Scotian by birth, that he went to the United States–as he had a right to do–and that he took the oath of allegiance there–as he had a right to do. And when I put him the question as to whether, when he had taken this oath of allegiance, he had not taken an oath of abjuration against Queen Victoria and everything British, he admitted that he had.

"Now, in this there was nothing criminal. He had a perfect right to take the oath of allegiance there. And certainly nobody cared to have him remain in Nova Scotia.

"But what did he do? After becoming an American citizen–and a citizen more American than they are themselves–he takes his vessel in to the Gulf and systematically trespasses on our fisheries.

"It is not attempted to say that when it suited his convenience he did not go in and trespass on our fishing rights. He had no scruples, when it suited him to do so, about fishing inside the limits–and so far did he carry this matter that he absolutely sailed up into the territorial waters of Newfoundland and got into the ice close up to the shore, and when some officers came there he armed his crew and set them all at defiance. He said that he drove away 'the whole calabash' of the officers. At all events, he kept them off and stayed there the whole winter, cutting holes in the ice, fishing, taking herring up and walking off with them.

"This man did not appear to understand that there are national rights which he could at all infringe. Was a man like that a man to go to war about?"

There followed an exchange between Judge Foster and Mr. Thomson, the American arguing that Collector Bigelow tried to seize the *Abigail* because Captain Pattillo had the charity to take a young lady home from the States. The Canadian countered that the Customs man had merely attempted to collect the light dues from this whitewashed Yankee, and "to suppose that any officer of any English or Dominion cutter would undertake to fire shots after him, because he landed a lady to whom he had charitably given passage to some place in the Gut of Canso, is simply too ridiculous a supposition to be tolerated for a moment."

> FOSTER (testily): The whole of that recital is something which you introduced in your cross-examination.
>
> THOMSON (triumphantly): I certainly introduced it in my cross-examination. There can be no doubt about that at all. There were a good many disagreeable things which I introduced into my cross-examination of American witnesses. I was probably here for that purpose. It was hard to get at all that this gentleman had done. But I wanted to discover it, and there is the story as told by himself.

Presently the Halifax Commission awarded $5,500,000 in gold to Great Britain, which the United States grumpily paid.

As for Captain Pattillo, one must assume he remained totally unaware that there was anything at all controversial about his testimony.

Had a First-Rate Time

> The days of our years are threescore years and ten; and if by reason of strength they be fourscore years, yet is their strength labour and sorrow; for it is soon cut off, and we fly away.
>
> —PSALMS 90:10

THE LORD DECLINED to summon Jim before the Throne of Grace on schedule but extended his corporality to threescore years and eleven, twelve and so on. It was an inconvenience, if not an embarrassment. However Christie managed to keep this unexpectedly reprieved body and soul together after the last of the frugally husbanded annuities had been spent, she did—all two hundred and forty pounds of them^and in a most cheerful state of good health.

Jim's faith remained absolute and unshakable. It gave him tranquility and humility, but spared him the dreary complacence that so commonly breeds in Protestant fundamentalism. The last of his succession of pastors in Gloucester said of him that "he had great physical strength, a giant's frame, and he went abroad among us as an impersonation of power. But his living, loving knowledge of God was more than all. He had once spoken of his power to lift, with a natural pride, but there was a happy glow in his features as he afterwards spoke of the grace of God which had reached down and lifted him up from this world and given him a faith in the life to come."

He took high pleasure from his periodic trips back to Gloucester with Christie, putting up for the few days with his bushily bearded, trimly tailored merchant son and matronly daughter-in-law and the four of his ten grandchildren to survive childhood (Maude, the eighth, had died at the age of four in 1868; Guy and Caroline had been added to the household on Hancock Street after the Civil War). As bald now as could be, he solaced his vanity and covered his massive head with a dark brown wig that curled at the ends around the ears. He looked quite terrifying indeed until the heavy, beefy, battered face of age cracked into the whimsical smile of old, and the blue eyes twinkled under the beetling brows, thinking perchance of a good joke or wry observation to rumble out in his usual uproarious style. And how Grandpa discomfitted his granddaughters, setting off with them for church in his canary-colored britches!

With his bluff seafaring ways and a cargo of yarns for every occasion, Jim was partial to quaint puzzles and conundrums with a mathematical twist he enjoyed fishing from his memory to stump folks with, such as the one concerning the old lady who went to market with a basket of eggs:

> A rude man came across her and knocked over her basket and broke all her eggs, so the old lady was crying, and the fellow went off. He said to himself, after having gone a little way, "I have treated the old lady shabbily," so he went back and said, "Old lady, tell me how many eggs you had in your basket, and I will pay you for them."
>
> She said, "When I put in two at a time I had one left, and when I put in three at a time I had one left, and when I put in four at a time I had one left, and when I put in five at a time I had none left." How many eggs did the old lady have in her basket?

There was no getting around him, as on the day when Abby set out a plate of her extra-special fruitcake on the dinner table within the fathom-long reach of her father-in-law. Jim latched onto this morsel with such an appetite, while the soup was still on, that she hastened to save at least a scrap for the others by drawing his attention to the rolls, which she pushed toward him invitingly.

"Oh no, Abby, no thanks–this brown bread here is good enough for me!" was the hearty rejoinder as he reached for the last of the family dessert.

Ah, the eggs. Twenty-five.

During one of these returns to Cape Ann ("he must have a look at the harbor, and a snuff of the sea-breeze, enjoy a cruise around the wharves, and a talk with his old companions"), Jim was interviewed by his friend George Procter, editor of the *Cape Ann Advertiser,* who wrote a short account of his confrontations with those foes of long ago, Bigelow and Gaden, for the remarkable volume of Gloucester miscellany he published in 1873, *The Fishermen's Memorial and Record Book.*

Doubtless it was this salty tale that inspired some anonymous writer to dash off a brace of articles on the same adventures for the *Youth's Companion.* They were penned with gusto ("Pattillo came off to them in nothing but a pair of duck drawers and slippers; a veritable athlete, tall, and sinewy, his white skin gleaming in the sun"), and illustrated in the Victorian mode, the artist modestly clothing the author's half-naked hero from head to toe in a suit of long winter underwear. The issues reached the hands of young America in November of 1883.

Out of homage to its local celebrity, the *Stoughton Sentinel* reprinted the first of the two, remarking that although Captain Pattillo is seen round about occasionally, "it is evident that age is getting the master of him now, and home is the pleasantest place. . . . The publishing of these stories is of no little pleasure to him."

The next January Jim and Christie traveled to Gloucester for the wedding of their eldest grandson, Alexander Manton Pattillo (the middle name, that he went by, after one of the family's former ministers). The Captain was "looking as happy as ever," the *Advertiser* noted.

In October they returned for the annual sojourn. The patriarch was seventy-eight, and the son was fifty-five, and with these realities in mind evidently, Alex wrote his father asking him to recollect for the family record the kinfolk of the auld Scot who had landed in the Chester wilderness a century and one year before. Jim replied (his information about the dates, in this case, was incorrect) as follows:

> North Stoughtn oct 20 84
>
> Dear Alex i receivd your letter And i will anser your questiens the bes i can mi farther Name Alexander Pattillo & he had one sister i dont no her name but she wose mard to a Man hise name Robert harey And they had one child nansey farther had two brothers i no James Pattillo William i wose Namd after 2 of them i thinck That farther had a brother robert i am pretey shure farther berth place carn hils near eddinburer farther wose 42 years when he came to the provincis and he wose 94 years lacking 14 days hise berth day wose the 14 of jenawarey and he died new years eve in 1832 so he lacked 14 days 94
>
> brother Thomas had all farthers papers so all i got is by memrey & so far is corect to the best of mi memrey farther sister name wose nancey I thinck but not shure i thinck i have givin the best i no or can thinck of at Preasint Mrs P joines with mee in kind love to you & abbey and All the childrin i will close and sill remain your afftenitt farther
>
> JAMES W. PATTILLO
>
> i had a furst raite time down with you i hope you will gett the histrey i shuld lick to see it

It had been fifteen years since Captain Pattillo and his lady moved into Stoughton. Newcomers were not accepted lightly by the small towns of New England, not until after a long period of probation stretching sometimes into the grave. Consequently, his fellow Stoughtonians paid the old gentleman some considerable tribute at the Town Meeting in March of 1885 when they elected him one of the eight Field Drivers for the ensuing year.

Now this was a mark of esteem, especially for a man of his years, and Jim huffed and puffed through meadow and glen, across gardens, between orchards, over fences and under clotheslines, waving his hat and hallooing at wayward cows, colts, pigs, chickens and surely some of those half a hundred stray dogs that made a nuisance of themselves in North Stoughton, for such were the duties of the Field Driver–to police the animal population of the community.

That summer, when he was not stamping around the countryside after somebody's porker on the loose, the old Captain was pulled up in his favorite easy chair (the one bequeathed him by the late Reverend Lamson of Gloucester) in his pleasant parlor, calling to mind the days of his years for the benefit of a guest.

This visitor was Mr. W. J. Rakey, an evangelist preacher who boarded in the Pattillo house for several weeks while laboring in the spiritual vineyards of North Stoughton. Unlike the general run of his brethren, Mr. Rakey was a good listener and an accurate chronicler, and he sat patiently, indeed enthusiastically, writing it all down in longhand with a purple pencil, while Jim spun off his recollections of the long voyage–the bad with the good–from the beginning to his retirement from the sea, reaching back, as he liked to say, into the stackhouse of his memory with a power of almost total recall.

When Jim had ended his narrative and made a few corrections in the manuscript, Pastor Rakey looked around for an "experienced manipulator" to make a book of it, as he wrote an acquaintance: "My hero before conversion was a coarse, vulgar, profane man, a hard drinker, and when under the influence of ardent spirits, he was ungovernable, and like a young bear did not know his own strength. If what is objectionable could be expunged and the mighty miracle of this man's conversion conserved, when his feet were taken out 'of the horrible pit and the miry clay' and planted upon the 'solid rock Christ Jesus,' He who is mighty to save, I believe under God, it could be made a powerful agency for good among seamen and people of that class."

The hero was willing, but before he would sanction the publication of memoirs which might cause some squirming amongst

Still giant of frame at eighty, Jim sits for the camera in 1886, a few months before his death, with son Alex, grandson Manton, and Carl, his first great-grandchild, who lived but two years. (Carolyn W. Pattillo)

his descendants, he told his Boswell that their release would have to be cleared with his son. That strait-laced little man, learning probably for the first time of his sire's early exploits, closed the matter with a resounding NO. Alex locked away this family skeleton–and with it, so far as the old Captain ever knew, his chances for immortality, in this world at least.

The day was a roaster in the middle of September of the next year, 1886, and what Jim called a smoky sou'wester breathed hot across the fields of North Stoughton. The first tongues of autumn flame flicked from the higher tips of the maples. Goldenrod piled up along the dusty roadside, and the woodbine curled crimson over the stone walls around the Pattillo place.

His summer chores were most done. In a fortnight, the days of his years would be fourscore years, by reason of his strength . . . would that strength be soon cut off, and he fly away? The thought was never far from his mind now.

He was leading the horse, when something startled it. The animal bolted, knocking him to the ground. But he held on to the reins and was dragged for some distance before he was able to pull himself to his feet and subdue the frightened creature. He hobbled back, the horse now following obediently behind. He stabled it and hauled himself into the house, much hurt.

Jim's eightieth birthday came and went with no fuss, as he wanted it, and a month after the accident he felt enough recovered to make the annual October visit back to Gloucester. The Treaty of Washington had terminated, and once again Yankee schooners were being boarded and seized by Canadian cruisers. In a great stew about it, Jim limped over to the offices of the *Cape Ann Advertiser* to get things off his chest with his old friend George Procter:

> Captain James W. Pattillo, the veteran Gloucester skipper, is in town for a brief visit. He is in his 81st year and still in good vigor except a lameness caused by a fall about a month ago. He says he is on the down hill road but thinks he could still do effective work with his flippers if driven into a corner.
>
> He is naturally indignant at the recent outrages upon our fishermen and the insults to the old flag, and says that when he thinks of the course of the Administration he is almost ashamed that he is a Democrat, and sighs for one hour of General Jackson.
>
> He is old fogy enough to believe in retaliation, and says if their waters are too good for our fishermen to visit, they should be shut out from our waters. His reminiscences of the fishing troubles of the forties are full of interest.

Back at North Stoughton, winter came on and with it a return of the troubles from his tussle with the horse. A few days before

Christmas Jim took to his bed. His suffering increased. His great body weakened. His spirit sank (was it so that old fishermen ebbed with the tide?), and he longed to be taken.

His mind stayed clear, and as the New Year dawned he gave his final commands. He was to be lugged back to Gloucester where he belonged and buried from the good old Baptist Church. He selected three hymns to be sung by the male quartet, one of them that he remembered from the funeral of his mother. He wished to have a wreath of ivy and a sheaf of grain on his casket, and for folks to have a last look at him before it was shut up. And then they should take him and plant him in Oak Grove Cemetery.

He died during the evening of Monday, the third of January, 1887.

They said the old man could have saved himself just by letting go of the reins. But he was bound not to admit that his horse was stronger than he, and it wasn't.

Afterthoughts

A COUPLE OF YEARS after the publication of *That Great Pattillo* in 1966, I stumbled on a vigorous reminiscence by George Wonson, a retired East Gloucester fisherman of about eighty, in a 1908 *Gloucester Times.* He vividly recalled signing on a fishing trip in the small pinkey schooner *Fair American* as a boy, Captain Pattillo a member of the crew. He thought 1839, but it must have been earlier, for *Fair American* was lost on Georges in 1837. Here is his account, some seventy years later:

> We sailed on the Maine coast, entering Northeast Harbor, Mount Desert, where we found a number of vessels at anchor. An elderly gentleman by the name of Roberts kept a store there, and among his stock was a large box of sugar weighing fully 500 pounds.
>
> When the men went ashore they visited Mr. Roberts's store, and the proprietor slung the box to see if any of them could lift it. Several were unsuccessful, and among the rest, Captain Pattillo tried his luck.
>
> Imagine their astonishment when he took hold of one of the straps and lifted the great box with comparative ease, and his fame for strength was ever afterwards remembered.
>
> The old man sold rum to the sailors, and when he thought they had enough he would lock up the store and go home. The crew having in his opinion had enough, the

doors of the place were closed. The proprietor was crippled, and Captain Pattillo, who did not drink [?!], acted as a sort of police when the men had taken too much aboard. But the crew wanted liquor, and when they found they could have no more they commenced to get wild.

Finally one of them went off the vessel and procured a gun barrel and an auger, bored a hole through the side of the store into a barrel of rum and drew off a bucketful. Some of them got good and drunk and began to fight, which did not please Captain Pattillo. Grasping two of them by the collar, he led them to their boat and said to me, "George, scull those men aboard the vessel and come back again."

I was very much frightened to be in the boat with them but did as I was told. Coming back ashore, he picked up two more and put them in the boat and told me where to carry them.

While I was ashore I picked up a mackerel gaff and was proud with my find and resolved to present it Captain Pattillo, but a man came along and took it away from me and carried it on board a vessel that was anchored near shore. When Captain Pattillo came down I told him what the man had done.

"By Jerry," said he, "scull alongside of that vessel," pointing to the craft where the man had gone. I said that I could, and pointed to the fellow on the deck. Without a formal invitation he went aboard but could not find the man, who disappeared as soon as he saw that trouble was ahead.

Coming on deck, Captain Pattillo inquired for the gaff the man took from the boy, but all apparently knew nothing of the transaction. Being unable to get any information, he hove off the main hatch and threw twenty empty barrels up on deck, and descending into the hold, made a diligent search but was unable to locate the man or gaff.

He remarked there would have been trouble if the man had the gaff on board, and I guess all were pretty frightened. Then we left the vessel, leaving the barrels on deck.

Another time while laying in Northeast Harbor, Captain Pattillo suggested that I accompany him on a trip up the mountain as he wanted to select a handle for an eel spear.

It looked gloomy up there, the fallen trees and underbrush bringing a sensation of loneliness, and I knew there were a great many bears on the mountain as several sheep had been victims of their preying.

We procured a fine pole and started for home, and after having descended quite a distance Captain Pattillo wanted to know if I had seen anything.

I told him no, to which he replied that he was glad that I did not, for there was a large bear in a path near which we had passed, and he was afraid I would have screamed had I seen it, and this would have aroused the animal, and he would have had hard work to handle it, although he had an ax.

Sources

THE ORIGINAL MANUSCRIPT of the memoirs dictated by James Pattillo to Pastor Rakey is freely quoted from with the permission of Carolyn Wonson Pattillo of Boston, the captain's great-granddaughter, who gave me access to other family records and photographs.

I first knew of this astounding document through the Cape Ann Historical Association, which had guarded for some years a copy typed by Gilbert Sayward Pattillo of Boston (1890–1955), a great-grandson of my subject and a cousin of Miss Pattillo—together with fragments of family reminiscences he had assembled, a few documents, Rakey's letter looking for an "experienced manipulator" and the only existing letter, to my knowledge, written by Captain Pattillo, which is reproduced in the text.

In his introduction to the copy of the memoir he began typing in 1938 Gilbert Pattillo wrote:

> When I was a boy, my Father used to tell me about my Great Grandfather. He told me tales of his great physical strength and of his smartness as a Gloucester skipper. Father's eyes always shone with pleasure and admiration when he spoke of him. 'He was very powerful,' Father said, 'and very big. Why, his hand would make three of mine. His arms were as big round as my legs. His eyes were small, and

he shut them up tightly when he laughed. He died before you were born.'

Some of my Great Grandfather's adventures at sea had been written by Gloucester newspaper reporters, and I was given yellowed clippings to read. Some of them had been published in *The Youth's Companion*. . . .

Mr. Rakey wanted to use the autobiography as a religious tract, as he vividly explains. I think my Great Grandfather hesitated over this purpose, torn between love of recounting his adventures and rather sharp qualms about what my Grandfather would think of having such a tale published. So he compromised by making the stipulation that the autobiography should not be published unless his son gave his consent.

Had he been living at Gloucester, he would have talked the matter over with my Grandfather and received a prompt refusal. In that case there would have been no manuscript. But at the safe distance of North Stoughton, he dictated to his heart's content.

My Father thought my Grandfather was ashamed of many of the things my Great Grandfather told. Perhaps he was. But I like to think he chuckled over them in private. Anyway, so far as publication was concerned, he said NO emphatically and kept the manuscript in seclusion.

Yet in the spring of 1915, when I finally persuaded my Father to ask my Grandfather to let me read it, much to my surprise I was given permission. While I had the original manuscript in my possession I made a typewritten copy of it. But at best it was a flimsy thing.

When I found out about two years ago that part of the original longhand manuscript had been lost, I began to type this present copy, keeping at it at odd intervals since December 1938, and finishing it on December 30, 1940. I did not attempt to do any editing when I made the copy of 1915, and I have done none in making this copy. This is exactly like the original longhand of Mr. Rakey, with the exception no doubt of some minor typographical errors,

> and of those I think there are none that would lead to any misunderstanding.
>
> To me, this Autobiography of my Great Grandfather's, ever since I first heard of it, and even more since I first read it, has been a treasure. I suppose it has no real importance and perhaps no great interest except to a few. Yet some day I think it should belong to the Cape Ann Scientific, Literary and Historical Association of Gloucester. In his time my Great Grandfather was a figure in the seafaring life of Gloucester. The Gloucester picture of those days is not complete without him.

I am further indebted to Gilbert's sister, Mrs. Alice Pattillo Cobb of Menlo Park, California, and Arthur S. Pattillo of Toronto for additional family background of value.

A motor tour of the Nova Scotia and Cape Breton coasts was just what the mind's eye needed, topped off with several days of feasting on a banquet of source materials at the Public Archives of Nova Scotia in Halifax, served up by assistant archivist Phyllis R. Blakeley, who was responsible for numerous authentic details of the Bear's life and high times in the Provinces.

Judge Des Brisay's old history of Lunenberg County is salted with nuggets about Chester and up that way, and *he* is the one who recorded the testimony of the man who witnessed Jim's little trick with the barrels of mackerel on George Mitchell's wharf. I am triply indebted to Judge Haliburton for his early history of the Province, for giving Sam Slick to the world as the first genu-ine literary humorist on the Continent . . . and for not salting Jimmy Pattillo too hard that day in Lunenberg.

Of course, it would be as unthinkable to launch an old literary schooner into the waters of time around Cape Ann without Howard I. Chapelle's loftsmanship as it would be to sail it without Samuel Eliot Morison as the pilot, without Babson's *History* as his Bible, or to picture it without falling under the spell of Fitz Hugh Lane's evocative scenes of the Harbor.

But here is the heaviest debt: the unfathomable and so very complex drama of the great Gloucester fishery in its prime has been frozen in time, as it were, by three unknown men, long in their graves and forgotten. They are John S. E. Rogers, for two generations the editor of the *Gloucester Telegraph* and a most wonderful chronicler of his times; George H. Procter, for equally as long—but later—editor of the *Cape Ann Advertiser,* author, publisher, intensely devoted to Gloucester and her fishermen and one of the truly superb newspapermen of his or any day; and finally Captain Joseph W. Collins, master mariner, naval architect, biologist, innovator, explorer, adventurer, career man with the United States Commission of Fish and Fisheries and principal author of the Gloucester section of Goode's monumental work, editor, self-taught authority on the fisheries of the era covered herein, whose vivid and prolific writings are masterpieces of sea narrative and exposition.

In conclusion, I acknowledge my dependence on the resources of the Cape Ann Historical Association and the Sawyer Free Library of Gloucester and give thanks for the assistance of Alice E. Babson, Thomas E. Babson, Mary Ann Ball, Marion Gagnon, Kimball R. Garland, Leola M. Lee (registrar of Deeds, Chester, N.S.), Mrs. Sydney Pattillo of Bridgewater, N.S., Dana A. Story, and Captain Tom Morse.

Bibliography

(The following bibliography and institutional directory are intended to impress the reader with the author's scholarly attributes; he will not be so easily cozened, we fear.)

ADAMS, JOHN *The Works of John Adams.* Boston: Charles C. Little and James Brown, 1851.

ANGAS, W. MACK *Rivalry on the Atlantic.* New York: Lee Furman, 1939.

BABCOCK, F. LAWRENCE *Spanning the Atlantic.* New York: Knopf, 1931.

BABSON, JOHN J. *History of the Town of Gloucester, Cape Ann.* Gloucester: Procter Brothers, 1860.

Belcher's Farmer's Almanac, Halifax.

BIGELOW, HENRY B., and SCHROEDER, WILLIAM C. *Fishes of the Gulf of Maine.* Washington: Fishery Bulletin No. 74 of the United States Fish and Wildlive Service, Volume 53, 1953.

BLUNT, EDWARD M. *The American Coast Pilot.* 11th ed. New York: E. and G. W. Blunt, 1827.

BRADFORD, GAMALIEL *D. L. Moody–A Worker in Souls.* New York: George H. Doran, 1927.

BREBNER, J. BARTLET *Canada–A Modern History.* Ann Arbor: University of Michigan Press, 1960.

BUTTS, I. R. *Laws of the Sea, The Rights of Seamen, Coaster's and Fisherman's Guide, and Master's and Mate's Manual.* Boston, 1854.

The Century Dictionary and Cyclopedia. New York: The Century Company, 1902.

CHAPELLE, HOWARD I. *The National Watercraft Collection.* Washington: United States National Museum Bulletin 219, 1960.

Chester, Nova Scotia, Township Records (Public Archives of Nova Scotia).

COLLINS, JOSEPH W. "Evolution of the American Fishing Schooner." *New England Magazine,* May 1898.

CONRAD, JOSEPH *The Nigger of the Narcissus.* New York: Doubleday, Page, 1924.

COPELAND, MELVIN T. and ROGERS, ELLIOTT C. *The Saga of Cape Ann.* Freeport: Bond Wheelwright, 1960.

CROCKETT, ASA J. Wine Harbor Library. *Collections of the Nova Scotia Historical Society,* XXVII, 1947.

DAVIES, BLODWEN *Gaspé: Land of History and Romance.* New York: Greenberg, 1949.

DEMPEWOLFF, RICHARD, *Famous Old New England Murders.* Brattleboro: Stephen Daye, 1942.

DES BRISAY, MATHER BYLES *History of the County of Lunenburg.* Toronto: William Briggs, 1895.

Diary of Simeon Perkins 1780-1789. D. C. Harvey and C. Bruce Fergusson, editors. Toronto: The Champlain Society, 1958.

——1790-1796. C. Bruce Fergusson, ed. Toronto: The Champlain Society, 1961.

DICKENS, CHARLES *American Notes and Pictures from Italy.* New York: Macmillan, 1893.

Documents and Proceedings of the Halifax Commission, 1877, under the Treaty of Washington of May 8, 1871. Washington, 1878.

EVANS, GEORGE R. *Gold Mining in Nova Scotia during the Nineteenth Century.* Master of Arts Thesis. (Public Archives of Nova Scotia.)

Family History: Stairs-Morrow. Halifax: McAlpine, 1906.

Genealogical and Personal Memoirs–Relating to the Families of Boston and Eastern Massachusetts. W. R. Cutter, ed. New York: Lewis, 1908.

Gloucester Ship Enrollments (Peabody Museum).

GOODE, G. BROWN et al. *The Fisheries and Fishery Industries of the United States.* Washington: United States Commission of Fish and Fisheries, 1887.

HALIBURTON, THOMAS C. *An Historical and Statistical Account of Nova Scotia.* Halifax: Joseph Howe, 1829.

HART, HARRIETT C. *History of the County of Guysborough, N.S.* Windorr, 1877.

History of Halifax City. Collections of the Nova Scotia Historical Society, VIII, 1895.

LAWSON, MRS. WILLIAM *History of the Townships of Dartmouth, Preston and Lawrencetown.* Halifax: Morton, 1893.

LOMAS, ALTON A. *The Industrial Development of Nova Scotia 1830-1854.* Master of Arts Thesis, Dalhousie University, Halifax, 1950 (Public Archives of Nova Scotia).

A Maritime History of New York. Writers Program of the Works Project Administration for the City of New York. New York: Doubleday, Doran, 1941.

MARTIN, JOHN P. *The Story of Dartmouth.* Dartmouth, N.S., 1957.

MCFARLAND, RAYMOND *A History of the New England Fisheries.* New York: University of Pennsylvania, 1911.

MOCKRIDGE, CHARLES H. *Bishops of the Church of England in Canada and Newfoundland.* Toronto, 1896.

MOORE, JOSEPH *Navigation Improved, with a Number of Requisite Tables to Ascertain the Latitude and Longitude at Sea: together with Proper Rules and Examples for Illustrating the Same.* Salem: Thomas C. Cushing, 1815.

MORISON, SAMUEL ELIOT *The Maritime History of Massachusetts 1783-1860.* Boston: Houghton Mifflin, 1921.

MORRIS, LLLOYD *Incredible New York.* New York: Random House, 1951.

The National Temperance Offering. S. F. Cary, ed. New York: Vandien, 1850.

Newfoundland Almanac for 1854. St. Johns: Joseph Woods, 1853.

PATTILLO, JAMES WILLIAM *Memoirs.* Dictated to Rev. W. J. Rakey, probably in 1885. (Manuscript courtesy of Carolyn Wonson Pattillo.)

Phineas Stowe, and Bethel Work. Henry A. Cooke, ed. Boston: James H. Earle, 1874.

POLLOCK, J. C. *Moody.* New York: Macmillan, 1963.

PRINGLE, JAMES R. *History of the Town and City of Gloucester, Cape Ann, Massachusetts.* Gloucester, 1892.

PROCTER, GEORGE H. *The Fishermen's Memorial and Record Book.* Gloucester: Procter Brothers, 1873.

——*The Fishermen's Own Book.* Gloucester: Procter Brothers, 1882.

Quebec Almanac, 1833.

Ship Registers of the District of Gloucester, Massachusetts, 1789-1875. Salem: Essex Institute, 1944.

SMITH, SYLVANUS *Fisheries of Cape Ann.* Gloucester: Gloucester Times Press, 1915.

Tales of Old Ships and Sailors (Series). *Youth's Companion,* November 1 and 15, 1883.

WALLACE, MARGARITA *Notes on the Pattillo Family* (Public Archives of Nova Scotia).

NEWSPAPERS

Acadian Recorder (Halifax); *British North American* (Halifax); *Cape Ann Advertiser; Cape Ann Bulletin; Gloucester Democrat, Gloucester News, Gloucester Telegraph; Gloucester Times, Halifax Morning Chronicle, Newburyport Herald; Newburyport Union; Stoughton Sentinel; The Novascotian; The Prince Edward Islander.*

INSTITUTIONS AND PUBLIC OFFICIALS

Boston City Clerk; Boston Public Library; Cape Ann Scientific, Literary and Historical Association, Gloucester; Essex County Probate Court, Registry of Deeds and Superior Court, Salem; Essex Institute, Salem; First Baptist Church, Gloucester; Gloucester City Clerk; Halifax Public Library; Lunenburg County Registry of Deeds, Bridgewater, N.S.; Norfolk County Probate Court and Registry of Deeds, Dedham, Peabody Museum, Salem; Public Archives of Nova Scotia, Halifax; Sawyer Free Library, Gloucester; Stoughton Public Library; Stoughton Town Clerk.

Joseph E. Garland is a leading chronicler of the golden age of the North Atlantic fishery. His books include: *Lone Voyager,* the biography of Howard Blackburn, a Gloucesterman who lost his fingers in a blizzard off Newfoundland and went on to be a legendary sailor; and *Down to the Sea,* a celebration of the schooner age and the men who made it great. *Bear of the Sea,* his biography of Nova Scotia native and Gloucester fishing captain James William Pattillo, was originally published in 1966 as *That Great Pattillo.* Garland lives in Gloucester, Massachusetts, with his wife Helen.

ALSO BY JOSEPH E. GARLAND:

The North Shore: A Social History of Summers Among the Noteworthy, Fashionable, Rich, Eccentric and Ordinary on Boston's Gold Coast, 1823–1929

Eastern Point: A Nautical, Rustical and More or Less Sociable Chronicle of Gloucester's Outer Shield and Inner Sanctum, 1606–1990

The Gloucester Guide: A Stroll Through Place and Time

Adventure: Queen of the Windjammers

Gloucester on the Wind: A Photographic History of America's Greatest Fishing Port in the Days of Sail: 1870 to 1938

Down to the Sea: The Fishing Schooners of Gloucester

Lone Voyager: The Life of Howard Blackburn